In Diasporic Lands

In Diasporic Lands

Tibetan Refugees and their Transformation since the Exodus

SUDEEP BASU

with a Foreword by
Samir Kumar Das

Orient BlackSwan

IN DIASPORIC LANDS: TIBETAN REFUGEES AND THEIR TRANSFORMATION SINCE THE EXODUS

ORIENT BLACKSWAN PRIVATE LIMITED

Registered Office
3-6-752 Himayatnagar, Hyderabad 500 029, Telangana, India
e-mail: centraloffice@orientblackswan.com

Other Offices
Bengaluru, Bhopal, Chennai, Guwahati, Hyderabad, Jaipur, Kolkata, Lucknow, Mumbai, New Delhi, Noida, Patna, Vijayawada

ISBN 978-93-52870-85-1

026149
17102017

Typeset in
Centaur MT Std 11/13
by Manmohan Kumar, Delhi

Printed in India at
Glorious Printers, Delhi

Published by
Orient Blackswan Private Limited
3-6-752, Himayatnagar Hyderabad 500 029
e-mail: info@orientblackswan.com

In memory of my grandparents, Chinta Haran Bose and Swarnalata Bose

So we are necessarily strangers to ourselves, we do not comprehend ourselves, we *have* to misunderstand ourselves, for us the law 'Each is furthest from himself' applies to all eternity—we are not 'men of knowledge' with respect to ourselves.

—Friedrich Nietszche, *On the Genealogy of Morals*, trans. W. Kaufmann and R. J. Hollingdale (New York: Random House, 1969), section 1, p. 15.

Contents

Images

Tables

Foreword

Never before in its history has forced migration studies in India faced such an acute crisis as it does now. The discipline seems to have reached a plateau and unless we are able to make some radical breakthrough sooner rather than later, the future of the discipline, by all means, looks extremely bleak. For one thing, the nature and context of migration have changed in a way that it no longer becomes possible to understand the phenomenon with the help of the same tools and concepts that one would have used and deployed in the post-War era. The circularity of forced migration in which one migrates by being displaced from one's home and reaches a destination and then finds (or does not find) a way to return home is being seriously challenged now. For another, forced migration studies today is caught as it were in a quandary and is perched rather uneasily between the twin extremes of positivistic analysis supplemented more often than not by hard facts and figures on the one hand and cultural studies with deeper understanding of texts and field narratives on the other—without any communication whatsoever being established between them. Basu's book, in that sense, offers a welcome relief insofar as it seeks to explore the possibilities of dialogue between these two extremes without falling prey to either.

Most importantly, he views homelessness as part of the lived experience. As one lives in a protracted state of homelessness, one is too often assumed to be what Said would have called 'out of place' and one yearns for returning to home. Forced migration studies of this genre continuously shuttles between protracted homelessness and the yearning for home, in short the loss and recovery of home. In general, migration studies is thus informed by—as Laclau puts it albeit in a different context—'a sense of lack' that pushes the political subjects to replenish and compensate it in order that the refugees might return home—'returning to where one flees from is the same as going home'. Basu's book interrogates this commonplace assumption of circularity by developing the argument that as one lives, so one *makes* home wherever one migrates.

Migration studies has so far viewed home as a static object that is lost and recovered like inanimate property without being made. Basu's contribution lies in redefining home as practice that requires the mediation of refugee agency. The imperative of living in a protracted state of homelessness impels the Tibetans to turn the 'outside' into a 'home'. It is through the exercise of the agency that the apparent binary between home and outside falls through, thereby exposing their extremely contingent nature. This book is not so much about the loss and recovery of home as much as about the social and cultural practice of reconstructing home in ever-so-alien and hitherto unfamiliar contexts, about making exile one's home through everyday social practices, about making place in an otherwise irredeemable state of displacement. The book shows how its reconstruction is not monochromatic, but is reflective of the differences in locales in which the process is under way. In other words, what is called 'Tibetanness' is not one, but many insofar as it gets refracted through and is configured in an irreducible variety of context-specific practices.

Tansen Sen's recent study on the Chinese of Kolkata, for instance, points out how the diaspora experience is mediated not only by the local context, but by the place they come from and the route they took while migrating to the city several generations back. Basu has effectively deconstructed the concept of home by bringing forth its fragmented and sectoral nature. Tibetans were/are never one, for there are Muslims and communist-atheists amongst them, besides the followers of other minority sects. Issues of home and homeland do not give unto them only one history, but many histories precariously folded into one another, contesting and intersecting each other in a variety of ways. The book tells us why the timing of migration is also important in the reconstruction of home and homeland. Human agency plays out in this conventional story of loss and recovery—in effect their proportionality—in a particular way. While loss is involuntary, recovery as a means of replenishing and compensating for the loss calls for an exercise in agency on the part of the refugees. So, what is lost is also recovered with or without humanitarian assistance. Basu's analysis destabilises the commonplace binary between the loss and recovery by emphasising the multi-valued nature of agency. The exercise of refugee agency does not necessarily express itself through the process of recovery, that is to say, by recovering exactly in proportion to what is lost. I think this understanding of agency encourages us to redefine the concept beyond the well-known binary between loss and recovery that dominates much of the literature on the political sociology of protest and resistance.

Basu argues that the stories of binary are far from being benign and politically neutral and the way they are told also privileges a particular power relation and cultural authority. Thus to continue with the same argument, the singularity of the Dharamsala (the headquarters of the Dalai Lama-led government in exile)-based discourse is steeped in its preservationist bias that never stops insisting on the need for preserving the essential 'Tibetanness' in its most pure and unadulterated form against all the threats from the surroundings, invests itself with an authority that allows it to speak for *all* the Tibetans regardless of their internal divisions. It is this act of self-arrogation that threatens to homogenise the Tibetans and tie them into a unity by levelling off their local differences.

Basu's historico-ethnographic method drives him to diligently dig deep underneath the dominant Dharamsala-based discourse and discover a multiplicity of narratives on 'Tibetanness' that interestingly do not necessarily throw up a challenge to the Dharamsala-based authority, but silently negotiate its own Tibetanness in a way only specific to itself, yet over-determined by the universal Tibetan discourse. In a sense, the singularity and multiplicity exist at the same time—the former over-determining the latter and the latter negotiating with the former without undermining it. To my mind, this offers a new understanding of power in which its exercise is not necessarily defined in zero-sum terms. The book does not pit this multiplicity against the singularity and thus avoids the temptation of falling prey to their dichotomy. Being a sociologist, Basu finds no difficulty in their co-presence compelling us to revisit our very conventional understanding of power and authority.

Many Tibetans, as the book copiously records, celebrate their identity as Indian, but not in an exclusionary manner. Their Indian identity is played out and enacted rather seamlessly within the framework of Tibetan identity and most importantly vice versa. For, the same Indian as a Tibetan takes part in the protests and demonstrations, adheres to the symbolism of His Holiness and generously contributes to the Patriotic Fund and can easily 'convert to' being Tibetan when Tibet becomes free. I quote from the reflection of one of the author's respondents, a Tibetan refugee himself: 'We have a dream of a free Tibet. In everyday life, the dream sometimes vanishes. But it is in there. It cannot be erased or something. It is in there. Anytime it can come up. Even if it does not come up, it is in there'. Tibet figures in Tibetan public memory as an abiding theme within which all other identities surface as variations.

One of the key contributions of the book is to implicitly link the evolution of migration studies as a discipline with the imperatives of administrative rationality. The story of loss and recovery, as we have noted, feeds into the growth of an entire body of humanitarian establishment in which relief and rehabilitation extended to the Tibetan refugees are designed also to benefit the host population and ensure their integration into the local societies. The Tibetan refugee is unlike a hapless Rohingya from Myanmar who is currently being detected and hounded out from India or Bangladesh or whose life is relentlessly massacred in the high seas of the Andamans on their way to Indonesia or other Southeast Asian destinations. For them, place-making is nearly impossible. The Rohingya is the archetypal 'homo sacer' whose life is 'lost without being sacrificed'. A comparison with other refugee experiences in South Asia thus gives us a glimpse of how humanitarian regimes are evolved in a highly discriminatory manner. Interestingly, the present book tells us how the Tibetans have remained relatively outside any 'serious administrative control' in India.

There is not one Tibetan homeland as much as there is no one Tibet-in-exile. As Basu puts it: 'a unified, homogeneous Tibet-in-exile identity is more of a rhetorical device and imaginary construct than some verifiable reality'. The Dharamsala-based discourse's claim to cultural authority also constructs Tibetanness as not only one, but pure and authentic—purer and more authentic than even the Tibetans of Tibet whose culture is believed to have been adulterated and rendered impure by the Chinese authorities.

The Tibetans are not global nomads. A nomad remains in a state of perpetual homelessness, while Tibetan refugees of Darjeeling or elsewhere are at home in Darjeeling. Theirs is not a celebration of homelessness, but rather the celebration of making the outside their home. But to the extent they develop relationships with multiple homes, the singularity of home back in Tibet disappears, making room for movement across many homes. One is struck by the apparent distinction between one's home in Tibet and one's many homes that one makes in India where they are in exile. The homes that are made are neither single nor permanent. They are not temporary either. I think the book can claim to have made an important contribution to the sociology of home and movement.

I am sure the book will be widely read amongst various sections of students, scholars, policymakers, lawyers, human rights activists and so forth.

Samir Kumar Das

Acknowledgements

The beginnings of my interest in the Tibetan refugee community can be traced back to my graduate days in the late 1990s, when as a Sociology student at the Delhi School of Economics, I used to make occasional visits to the Tibetan refugee settlement in Old Delhi. The pre-reflective impressions of Tibetan exile life back then served as a marker for later research enquiries into refugee life and diasporas. This book emerges from my Ph.D. work, which I completed from the Department of Sociology, Jadavpur University, Kolkata. Following my Ph.D., forays into the broader field of forced migration and diaspora studies led me to reconsider some of my approaches to and concerns within refugee studies in general. Having seen this work through now, I feel a great debt of gratitude to all those who made it possible. My doctoral supervisors, Ruby Sain, Professor at the Department of Sociology at Jadavpur University and Pradip Bose, Former Professor of Sociology at the Centre for Studies in Social Sciences, Calcutta provided the necessary critical advice and guidance. I particularly owe a lot to Pradip Bose who initiated me into forced migration studies through his own work and discussions.

Along the way, I was fortunate to meet Tibetan exiles and a few members of the Bhutia community in Darjeeling, Kolkata, Delhi and Dharamsala, who, as my interlocutors, effectively gave substance and form to this book. I respect their wishes for anonymity. I would like to mention a few persons in Darjeeling without whose unstinting support, I would not have been able to progress an inch with my fieldwork. I am deeply indebted to K. T. Bhutia, who was like a window to the Tibetan world and who first introduced me to Darjeeling town and to the life of Tibetan refugees living there, beginning 2004. I can never forget the help and hospitality of Dawa Tshering Amdo who facilitated entry into the Tibetan Refugee Self Help Centre (TRSHC) in Darjeeling town. I express my gratitude to Dawa for sparing time for me. I am particularly thankful to Narpati Sharma and his family, and Sonam Bhutia for sharing their house with me. They made me feel at home in Darjeeling. I benefited greatly from discussions with the late Ngawang Jinpa, a Tibetan scholar who was living in Darjeeling at the time.

I owe thanks to the Indian Council for Social Science Research for funding my research study during the initial phase of my doctoral work from 2004–05. Subsequently, I benefitted immensely during my stint as a lecturer at the Institute of Development Studies Kolkata (IDSK), while I was pursuing my doctoral work. It was an ideal setting for serious academic work. My gratitude to Amiya Kumar Bagchi, Professor and former Director of the Institute of Development Studies Kolkata for his support and encouragement when I needed it most. I embarked upon writing this book after entering the Central University of Gujarat (CUG), Gandhinagar, where I am presently working. CUG provided a congenial academic environment for an intensive venture of this kind. My interactions with fellow colleagues, Sony Kunjappan, Litty Denis, Roja Lakshmi and Ranjana Singh and students at the Centre for Studies in Social Management, CUG, have enriched me in many ways. I owe my thanks to them.

The critical feedback that I received from the participants in the International Cultural Studies Workshop on Political Cultures held in Hyderabad from 28 January to 2 February 2007 made this research work richer. I benefited greatly from the valuable comments and suggestions offered by participants on the papers that I presented in two more workshops and conferences over the years: one, at the 14th International Association for the Study of Forced Migration (IASFM) conference at Kolkata during 6–9 January 2013 and two, at the International Seminar on 'Migrations, Heimat and Homelands', held on 11–12 February 2016 at the Centre for Regional Studies, Department of Sociology and Centre for Women's Studies, University of Hyderabad.

The interactions and stimulating discussions with friends, academics and former colleagues over the years have allowed many of my ideas to grow spontaneously and some of these have found expression in the book. I owe a lot to Ranabir Samaddar, Professor and former Director of Mahanirban Calcutta Research Group (MCRG) for providing an intellectual leadership and inspiration in the field of forced migration studies. Samir Kumar Das, Professor of Political Science at Calcutta University and a member of MCRG has always been generous with his time and his valuable suggestions have always been of help; my sincere thanks to him for agreeing to write the foreword to the book. I have benefitted a lot from conversations with other MCRG members, among them Paula Banerjee, Nasreen Chowdhory, Sabyasachi Basu Roychowdhury, Sibaji Pratim Basu, K. M. Parivelan, Atig Ghosh, to name a few. My engagement with MCRG in its various activities has immensely helped in shaping my academic outlook over the years. Thanks are due to Bidhan Kanti Das, Subrata Mukherjee, Satendra Kumar, Sarasij Majumdar, Mrutuyanjaya Sahu and Kshamanidhi Adabar for providing great company. The lively discussions with them have only brought out the best in me.

I would like to express my gratitude to Roopa Sharma of Orient BlackSwan for seeing a potential in my manuscript. She thoughtfully clarified many aspects that go into the making of a book. Thanks are due to Parvati Mohan of Orient BlackSwan for her excellent editorial assistance and her meticulous reading of the manuscript. I also owe thanks to an anonymous reviewer of my manuscript.

This book would not have been possible without the love and support of my family. Anurima, my wife, has always been there, providing constant encouragement. I saw my son, Samik, grow during the course of making this book. His playfulness took away the trying moments from my work. My parents and my brother were the deepest sources of inspiration and strength.

1

Tibetans as 'Refugee Diasporas'*

Most refugee situations involve cultures and people in violent confrontation. According to Harrell-Bond and Voutira (1992: 7), 'refugees are people who have undergone a violent rite of separation and unless or until they are "incorporated" as citizens into their host state (or returned to their state of origin) find themselves in "transition," or in a state of liminality." This "betwixt and between" (see Turner 1969) status may not only be legal and psychological, but social and economic as well'. The elementary understanding that refugees are humans bereft of culture and history underpins contemporary discourses on refugees. Here Malkki (1992) draws attention to the fact that if territorially uprooted people are so easily seen as 'torn loose from their culture', this is only because culture is itself a profoundly territorialised concept in so many settings. Anthropology, sociology and forced migration studies are increasingly taking into cognisance the need to rethink roots not only metaphorically, but also materially, in terms of concrete links between people and the places they inhabit. As Malkki states, 'There has emerged a new awareness of the global social fact that, now more than perhaps ever before, people are chronically mobile and routinely displaced and invent homes and homelands in the absence of territorial, national bases – not in situ but through memories of and claims on places that they can or will no longer corporeally inhabit' (1992: 24).

Even so we find, as Appadurai (1990), Said (1979, 1986), Clifford (1998) and Rosaldo (1988) have suggested, how notions of nativity, autochthony, cultures, places and belonging become even more complex and paradoxical with respect to people like the Tibetans discussed in this book, who while identifying themselves as refugees to begin with,

* Previously published as Sudeep Basu, 'Of Camps and Communities-in-exile', *International Journal of Migration and Border Studies*, vol. 2, no. 2, pp. 176–86, 2016. This article has been modified by the author for the current volume.

find themselves becoming increasingly diasporic (dispersed across geographical spaces) and categorisable in reference to deterritorialised homelands, hostlands, origins and return. Being a refugee is not a simple identity construct that emerges from one or several experiences of violence, war and displacement from the homeland. It is rather, in Malkki's words, 'process of becoming...a gradual transformation, not an automatic result of the crossing of a national border' (1995a: 114). For analytical purposes, the use of the term 'refugee diasporas' for Tibetans would be based on a conceptualisation of 'refugeeness' and 'diasporicness' that is rooted not only in the flight and rehabilitation of particular individuals and groups, but also in the making and unmaking of diasporic identities through the daily practices of living in one or several host societies.

For long, Tibet has served as a distinctive and an all-embracing mental and affective map for Tibetans in exile, referring to a lost world not yet retrieved. Tibetan identity in the present is therefore founded upon the fact that the Tibetans are refugees to start with, once they have crossed the border into India. This context therefore provides a framework for the formation of Tibetan identity in the diaspora and much of the reflexive discourse in the diaspora is concerned with how this context should be defined and interpreted. Taking an Indian town like Darjeeling as the site where Tibetan refugee identity gets refracted through diasporic modes of cognition and affectivity, the ensuing work shows how places and spatialised identities get redefined and transformed through practices of 'place-making', implying an increased awareness among Tibetan refugees of the interconnectedness of places and negotiation of belonging over time. This field enquiry aims to show how Tibetans in exile, in an urban setting like Darjeeling, have devised strategies and tactics, both material and symbolic, to undertake 'place-making', as prospects of an immediate return to their homeland diminishes with time.

The concept of diaspora is a vexed one. We should be wary of any attempt at conflating the term with that of a refugee community for it can lead to ambiguities in our enquiries into the processes of change as well as strategy, practices, and the social structure of displaced

Tibetan community since 1959. This work seeks to discuss the usage of the term 'diaspora' (having a semantic domain that recognises hybridity, transformation, dispersal and return) in understanding the dilemma of Tibetan refugee identity. The ethnographic study of the refugees of Darjeeling town is meant to understand how the place (Darjeeling town) produces series of negotiations, as Tibetans while formulating and reformulating their refugee identities take advantage of the opportunities available to citizens while contending with the extraordinary pressure to assimilate into the host society. This ethnography of the displaced seeks to explore how the refugee–host dynamic in a 'place' and the individual accounts of Tibetan/refugee identity that emerge from there both reinforce the static rendition[1] of diaspora and the model of a unified Tibetan subjectivity. On the other hand, those articulations that angle away from the stereotyped ways that Tibetans are read and suggest alternative currents that produce plural or hyphenated identities. The study also seeks to look at how the diasporic condition in turn frames Tibetan refugee identities that are contested and 'rooted' in and 'routed' (Clifford 1997) through several places. This study in forced migration takes seriously David Turton's (1996) assertion, 'The academic study of human displacement is less likely to be relevant to policy, the more closely it follows policy related categories and concepts in defining its subject matter and setting its research priorities.' It grapples with one of the principal assumptions governing policymaking on refugees and displaced populations, which is the link between identity and place.

The broader aim of the book is to understand what it means to be displaced. This study of the Tibetan diasporic community endeavours to show that the experience of displacement is not only about the loss of place and the pain and bereavement this entails. It is also about the struggle to make a place in the world, a place which according to Xenos (1993), 'makes action meaningful through shared understandings and a shared interpretation of action'. It seeks to know how Tibetans as refugees experience place (Darjeeling) and how it becomes 'inextricably bound up' with their identity. The study however does not seek to limit itself to a theorisation of place. It also attempts to understand how the experience of movement (typical of refugees and diasporics) to and from a place reconstitutes the idea that people have of their relation to a specific place in the diaspora; of how this sense of place in the diaspora gives meaning and purpose to Tibetans-in-exile.

Outline of the Research Problem

Akhil Gupta and James Ferguson, in their article *Beyond Culture,* remark (1992: 6), 'Representations of space in the social sciences are remarkably depended on images of break, rupture and disjunction. The distinctiveness of societies, nations and cultures is based upon a seemingly unproblematic division of space, on the fact that they occupy "naturally" discontinuous spaces'. The assumed isomorphism of space, place and culture, they stress, results in some significant problems:

> [O]ne is the disjunction between place and culture. Second, is the implicit mapping of cultures onto places in order to account for cultural differences within a locality.[2] Conventional accounts of ethnicity even when used to describe cultural differences in settings where people from different regions live side by side, rely on an unproblematic link between identity and place. Although such concepts are suggestive because they endeavour to stretch the naturalized association of culture with place, they fail to further interrogate this assumption (Gupta and Ferguson 1992: 7).

The idea of diaspora enables a move away from the supposedly stable connections between identity forms and place. Admittedly, we do find how diaspora groups indeed have multiple links not only in terms of time (dwelling in the here and there) but also being deterritorialised and rooted at once (Carter 2005). As Clifford puts it, 'the empowering paradox of diaspora is that dwelling here assumes a solidarity and connection there. But there is not necessarily a single place or exclusivist nation' (1997: 269). Paradoxically, we do find how diasporas can also have essentialising tendencies in the practice of place-making and identity formations. In his summary of current approaches to diaspora, Cohen suggests that 'diasporas are positioned somewhere between nation-states and traveling cultures in that they involve dwelling in a nation-state in a physical sense, but traveling in an astral or spiritual sense that falls outside the nation-states space/time zone' (Cohen 1997: 135–36). With the changing configurations of socio-political relations, it is well-nigh impossible, theoretically, to restrict the usage of the concept of diaspora to the condition of the Jews. Rather it is increasingly used to include a range of historical, ethnic and national communities. Also as Carter (2005: 55) states elsewhere, 'Diaspora is now conceived together with a range of other concepts (hybridity, nomadism and creolization) that seeks to celebrate the progressive potential of such positions, to overcome the fixed and essentialized assumptions regarding both identity and territory'.

Clifford's most explicit treatment of the notion of diaspora can be found in a number of essays in his 1997 book, *Routes: Travel and Translation in the late Twentieth Century*. Within these essays, Clifford develops a discourse on the relationship between diaspora and territory, not least through his discussion of what counts as diasporic. Clifford offers a diacritical definition; what does diaspora define itself against? Primarily, Clifford suggests that diasporas are defined against nation-states. This is not a clear, simple opposition (one of 'absolute othering') but rather a process of 'entangled tension' (Clifford 1997). According to Clifford, 'diaspora discourse articulates or bends tighter both roots and routes to construct...alternate public spheres, forms of community consciousness and solidarity that maintain identifications outside the national time/space in order to live inside, with a difference' (Clifford 1997: 251). That the diaspora consciousness (which talks about 'displaced dwelling' in Clifford's terms) has the possibility of destabilising the nation-state, both notionally and in geographical terms, is now commonly understood. Clifford points to the inherent tendencies of the diaspora of maintaining connections with multiple places and its emphasis on non-absolutist practices. At the same time, he is well aware of the growth of nationalism, xenophobia and chauvinism, espousing violence, that is also emergent from within diasporas.

What is assumed in diaspora theorising is a centre from where dispersion occurs and returns. It is in this that Clifford sees the possibility of authoritarianism making its way back in. In empirical terms, this may not be the case at all times. Diasporas indeed do celebrate heterogeneity, difference and identity. In the literature on diaspora, it is the rise of absolutism emanating from diaspora, which is relatively neglected.

Sean Carter's article, *The Geopolitics of Diaspora,* is relevant here for he emphasises that 'the recent literature on diaspora is of considerable interest to geographers, as the spatial, if largely only used in a metaphorical sense, is never very far from the centre of much of this work. There is a tendency within diaspora studies, however, to utilize these spatial metaphors whilst simultaneously denying the significance of geography. In many of these accounts borders are traversed, boundaries are dissolved and space is something that is invoked but often left un-interrogated.' (2005: 55) The ensuing ethnographic study of the Tibetan refugees in Darjeeling town would take cognisance of this shortcoming within diaspora studies which tends to discount the re-territorialising elements of diasporic practices. New conjunctures of theoretical enquiry in social sciences and forced migration studies are making it possible and necessary to rethink the question of roots in relation to identity and to the forms of its territorialisation.[3]

Rationale for the Study

According to P. Christiaan Klieger, 'One inescapable characteristic of a refugee experience, in comparison with many types of voluntary emigration, is the desire to hold on to one's identity and place in the world even as, in time and space, that homeland drifts away from practical reality into a state of the ideal. These behaviours inevitably leave a record through the artistic expressions of material culture' (1995: 59). What the Tibetan exodus produced in its wake was that the institutions, habits and culture that the Tibetans had taken for granted were suddenly given prominence. The will to survive and to preserve the cultural identity in exile was a sentiment echoed by the Dalai Lama and lay Tibetans.

Melvyn Goldstein, while writing about the development of ethnic boundaries operative within and outside of the Tibetan community, remarked that the 'two critical aspects of the Government of India's

(GoI) policy towards the Tibetan refugees have been 1) the liberal "non-assimilative" framework as reflected in the separate settlements and 2) the broad "delegated" authority of the Tibetan leadership headed by the Dalai Lama over the Tibetan settlements in India' (Goldstein 1978: 398). From the beginning, the Tibetan government-in-exile interceded with the GoI on behalf of the Tibetan refugees. They immediately set themselves up as spokesmen for the mass of disparate refugees and even maintained offices in the transit camps. The GoI refused to resettle all Tibetans in one area in north India as the Dalai Lama and his government had suggested. It also did not want to scatter them in small family units (as, for example, the Canadian government is doing with their Tibetans). According to Goldstein (1978: 398), 'The proposed settlements were a kind of compromise because their envisioned size of three to four thousand was large enough to sustain Tibetan language and other institutions easily. The GOI further facilitated this cultural preservation effort by allowing Tibetans considerable autonomy and in particular by permitting the Dharmasala administration to exercise administrative control over the settlements'.[4]

The highlight of the rehabilitation strategy was the creation of a series of permanent agricultural settlements throughout India (these settlements have been discussed in detail in chapter 5). The idea was to resettle Tibetans living in transit camps or working on road repair and to provide them with assistance and resources so that within a period of five years they could become economically self-sufficient. What characterised Tibetan and host interactions was one where the latter, the host government, ensured that the former could retain their cultural identity and autonomy, as in south and north India. This had a marked effect on the way the Tibetans have interacted with sections of the host population. The domain of interaction is seen to be limited to market transactions, as observed by Palakshappa and Goldstein, who reported instances of how Tibetans have provided job opportunities to the hosts by way of employing them as labour to till the soil or sow the seeds, among others. Palakshappa notes that 'such job opportunities have smoothed the relations between the Tibetans and the Indians. Although local Indians might resent that their land had been given to some outsiders, they feel satisfied that they have benefited by the establishment of the Tibetan settlement. At least, it provides the Indians with jobs continuously throughout the year, which many of them did not have before' (1978: 99). The presence of the Tibetans has had beneficial outcomes for host communities. Yet the remoteness of some Tibetan settlements has been the reason for their relative neglect by way of development funding emanating from New Delhi or Dharamsala (Norbu 1994).[5] Tibetan schools and hospitals established in those areas remain open to the host population. Most settlements have linkages with international donors, that is with NGOs as well as with individual sponsors, who support children in the SOS (Save Our Souls) Tibetan Children's Villages or individual monks in the monasteries. Indirectly, the local people too profit from the inflow of foreign exchange (Norbu 2004: 206). This scenario or arrangement seemed understandable in the decades of the 1960s and 1970s but it has come under scrutiny in recent times. As Dawa Norbu points out, 'this criticism centres around the argument that Tibetans in India should no longer maintain their social and cultural boundaries from the host society; it implies that Tibetans should integrate with the Indians' (2004: 204). The Tibetan refugee settlements designed as self-contained cultural units proved more than sufficient for the first generation of refugees. During their lifetime in exile, they have creatively deviated from the planned agricultural economy to the sweater-selling business, which they find more lucrative and less time consuming, though more intensive. Dawa Norbu writes, 'As it stands now, the new generation of exiles born and brought up in India or Nepal appears to face a dilemma in both their education and economy. They have reached the limits of educational levels and economic choices offered in the settlements. Where to go from here?' (2004: 209).

Subba (1990), Palakshappa (1978) and Saklani (1984) unequivocally agree that Tibetans have been extremely successful in retaining their ancestral way of life in the face of acculturation and have constituted a model of good integration with their host populations. These early anthropological studies emphasised notions of adaptation, acculturation and change as the key processes through which a history of Tibetans in exile might be charted. These studies assumed the continuity between the past and the present, of identifying how the past actually was and then looking for traces of the past in the present, of how well the past has been preserved. It is for this reason that anthropologists following the continuity thematic had, as their research focus, the objective to assess the adaptation of Tibetans to their host conditions and their acculturation. In consequence, there has been a tendency to portray Tibetan self-settled refugees as an emasculated version of an earlier, pre-exilic Tibetan society.[6] Furthermore, the refugee social formation that emerges in exile is thought of in intellectual and lay circles as 'inauthentic' or 'less Tibetan'. The over emphasis on acculturation and adaptation has had the effect that the varied strategies and tactics adopted by Tibetans in their attempt to make sense of their place in the diaspora has not been given due scholarly attention. Here, the focus of fieldwork turned away from the subjective notions in relation to the exile present. It is as if when one conducts fieldwork among Tibetans in host lands—like in Darjeeling one works with the impression that refugee societies in host contexts—like Darjeeling, home to Tibetan exiles since 1959, is a tainted or contaminated field of enquiry. As Audrey Prost notes, 'For all the local talk about the importance of cultural preservation and faith in the eventual return, the "uprooted", as many described them had grown roots' (2006: 236). As the Tibetan exiles' recollection of their 'homeland' past becomes grounded in their experience of an 'exile' present, it takes on new meanings and inspiration from Dharamsala as a contemporary nexus of identity (Nowak 1984). The Dharamsala-centric presentation of exilic Tibetan culture has had the effect of portraying the tale of exile in reified terms, one that is produced and sustained and justified by Tibetan lamas, intellectuals and administrators. They are the ones who set the tone and tenor of the debates surrounding the 'building and preservation of Tibetan culture in exile' in complicity with the tastes and preferences of Western audiences. The rationale for engaging in the study of Tibetan refugees in Darjeeling has been to critique, along Toni Huber's lines[7], this primarily Dharamsala-centred construction of Tibetan exile culture. Without making any definitive claims about the prevalence of a distinctly 'Darjeeling Tibetan exile culture', the focus of the research study would be on bringing out the refugees' multiple incarnations of exile subjectivity associated with the place.

Plan of the Book

This book comprises seven chapters. The first chapter sets the tone for the ensuing discussions, by recognising that the reflexive notions of Tibetan refugee identity and culture have to be understood as part of a diasporic world within which Tibetan exiles are increasingly representing themselves and being represented by others. Notwithstanding its exotic traits, real or imagined, scholars on exile and diaspora belonging to the social sciences and the humanities have not given their due attention to Tibet, past and present, and Tibetans in exile. While work has been undertaken on Tibetans in exile, little attempt has been made to understand the refugee–host dynamic and the emerging Tibetan exilic culture within specifically urban host settings, of settings that are mixed, heterogeneous, where there is greater scope for play of identities. This study attempts to bridge this gap in Tibetan and refugee studies.

The second chapter, 'Methodology and Imperatives in Refugee Research', begins with a consideration of the analytical usages and dimensions of the concept of 'refugee' and then 'diaspora'. Both concepts are highly contested and an indiscriminate use or conflation of the terms can obfuscate our understanding of change and continuity with respect to strategy, daily practices, agency and social structure of a dispersed group. For analytical purposes, the terms 'refugee' and 'diaspora' will be taken separately and any attempt to bring the two together for analytical purposes will be in relation to an interpretive context. The fieldwork site would be introduced by giving a brief historical and geographical account of the Darjeeling town/district followed by an elucidation of the fieldwork challenges and the need to choose between the different methods depending on the contingencies in the field. The methodological issues would centre on the problem of accessibility, representation, trust and sampling strategy typically in the study of urban refugees.

The recent works related to Tibet and the Tibetan refugees that draw upon new ideas culled from various social and cultural studies are discussed in the third chapter, titled 'The Tibetan Paradigm of Exile'. That there is no single dominant orientation to life in exile is emphasised through texts and in accounting for the life of Tibetan refugees. It is also imperative to relate the Tibetan data comparatively to the experiences of other refugee communities, since, as Clifford writes, 'diasporic forms of longing, memory and (dis) identification are shared by a broad spectrum of minority and migrant populations' (1994: 304). Until the last two decades of the twentieth century, Tibetan studies laid overwhelming emphasis on Buddhism and pre-1950s Tibetan history. This stemmed partly from the predominance of an exoticised or 'Shangri-La' (Bishop 1989) imagery of Tibet propagated by the Western world for over a century, and partly from Chinese representations of Tibet and several Tibetan youth who are not as religiously-oriented as their elders. This is revealed in the several works on Tibet, discussed in chapter four, titled 'Tibetan Question: A Reappraisal', where one encounters a set of claims about Tibetan identity and the character of pre-exilic Tibetan society and culture. A few important episodes in Tibetan history are critically examined, particularly those that are closely connected with the question of who the Tibetans are as a people, nature of their claims to the land of Tibet and those that are consequential to Tibetan refugees.

Chapter five, titled 'Organising for Exile!', begins with a description of Tibetan settlements in India with a view to providing a comparative assessment of the ways by which Tibetans have organised their lives in Dharmasala-administered centres and in spontaneously settled in refugee settlements in India. Darjeeling as the primary field site where Tibetan refugee identity gets refracted through diasporic modes of identification and affectivity is appropriately placed in comparative framework.

Chapter six, 'Preservation, Integration and Pragmatics of Diasporic Identity', focuses on the lived meanings that displacement and exile can have for specific people, in this case the Tibetan refugees in Darjeeling town. It would draw attention to the local differences in the construction of categorical identities like refugeeness and Tibetanness, and their ties with specific settings in the town, such as the Tibetan Refugee Self Help

Centre (TRSHC) and the neighbourhoods where Tibetans work and reside. The combination of lived and remembered experiences, and the official cultural preservation efforts in exile have helped coalesce and promote a certain body of knowledge that is widely shared and valued. As I have stated (Basu 2013) elsewhere, 'With a potential to unpack the notion of Tibetanness as an ensemble of varied, contested and complex practices and imaginaries, the conception of diaspora and diasporic subjectivity questions the degree to which it is realistic or even in the refugee's long-term interest to attempt to create and maintain a spatially bounded notion of Tibetan culture, wherein the acts of preservation signify political acts have unifying effects'. The sixth chapter opens up a debate on what constitutes Tibetanness, refugeeness, and the nature of diasporic identity and its association with place.

Notes

1. The static rendition of diaspora has the following dominant features: a history of dispersal, myths/memories of the homeland, alienation in the host country, desire for eventual return, ongoing support of the homeland and a collective identity defined by this relationship (Clifford 1994: 305).

2. In this context, it would be prudent to introduce the concept of 'multiculturalism', which is a feeble acknowledgement of the fact that cultures have lost their moorings in definite places and looks beyond the attempts to subsume this plurality of cultures within the framework of a national identity. The other concept is the idea of 'subcultures', which attempts to preserve the idea of distinct cultures while acknowledging the relation of different cultures to a dominant culture within the same geographical and territorial space (Gupta and Ferguson 1992: 7).

3. Territoriality as a concept would be used in the specific sense as 'the attempt by an individual or group to affect, influence or control actions and interactions of people, things and relationships by asserting and attempting to enforce control over a geographic area' (Sack 1983: 55) in the ensuing study of Tibetan refugees in Darjeeling town.

4. This did not mean that the GOI abdicated its authority over the Tibetans. Rather it means that the GOI (and the state government) had no objection to giving the Dharamsala administration de facto internal administrative control of the camps and to working with the individual refugees, so long as the latter did not object (Goldstein 1978: 398).

5. For more on the development projects both ongoing and envisaged, see 'Tibetan Refugee Community: Integrated Development Plan – II 1995–2000', published by Planning Council, Central Tibetan Administration, Dharamsala 1994.

6. The terms 'exile' (*rgyang* bud *btang*) and 'refugee' (*btsan byol ba*) will be used interchangeably for a number of reasons. First, it comes out through the numerous conversations with Tibetans that the Tibetans commonly refer to themselves as both, although during political gatherings such as demonstrations the term 'refugee' is more often employed. Second, the use of both 'refugee' and 'exile' is legitimate since the entire population of Tibetan refugees in India does not in fact benefit from 'refugee' status since India is not a signatory of the UN Refugee Convention. First-generation Tibetan refugees and their India-born children have been granted 'refugee-like status' and a Refugee Certificate (RC) as proof of identity. However, more recently-arrived Tibetans are allowed into India, but not given legal residence here.

7. Toni Huber delivers the brunt of this critique, 'In my own experience, most Tibetan refugees are not like these persons and certainly do not live in Dharamsala but in rather non-cosmopolitan agricultural and craft communities. They tend to be humble and self-effacing, conservative, often uncritically devoted to their leaders, seemingly as avid about watching Hindi films as attending religious ceremonies and they have Hindi or Nepali not English, as their second language. Why are these many Tibetan exiles left backstage or merely out in the audience in the study of "Tibetan culture?"' (Huber 1999: 6).

2

Methodology and Imperatives in Refugee Research

Conceptual Considerations

The refugee problem is 'first and foremost one of categorization, of making distinctions. None of the discussions in the field – among politicians, policy makers or academics – can proceed without an idea of who exactly we are talking about when we use the label refugee' (Haddad 2004: 1). It seems obvious that 'refugees' are forced migrants who are accorded 'an internationally recognized legal status, given credibility by an international agency specifically charged to safeguard their interests, endorsed most powerfully of all by spontaneous philanthropy' (Zetter 1991: 40). As Haddad (2004: 2) asks, 'In a field linked to humans and human suffering, how can we avoid making the refugee simply an instrument of academic enquiry and instead ensure that the defining process serves the refugee herself?'

The semantic domain that the term 'refugee' covers is varied and complex. One can begin by considering the cognate concept, such as exile, which denotes the act of enforced separation from one's homeland. The other terms associated with refugee and exile are as Tabori notes, 'displace, send out, exclude with dislodgement, eviction, ejectment, deportation, expatriation, extradition and excommunication' (Tabori 1973: 23). The semantic complex surrounding the term exile is at once etymological, legal, having historical, psychological and ideological dimensions. Tabori goes on to define as an exile as 'A person compelled to leave or remain outside his country of origin on account of well-founded fear of persecution for reasons of race, religion, nationality or political opinion; a person who considers his exile temporary (even though it may last a lifetime), hoping to return to his fatherland when circumstances permit – but unable or unwilling to do so as long as the factors that made him an exile persist' (Tabori 1972: 27).[1]

According to Harrell-Bond and Voutira, the issue is not helped by 'the conceptual confusion surrounding our perceptions of displacement and the lack of rigorous classification for the different conditions, causes and patterns of refugee movements in time and space' (1992: 6). Zolberg writes, 'language serves to mystify rather than clarify the social processes it depicts', a tendency which is unusually pronounced in the refugee field since 'the standard refugee lexicon is highly normative and thus self-evidently legitimizing' (1989: 274). What is observed is a greater chasm between principles related to asylum prescribed in international law and the actual practice of granting asylum which is bestowed by the state. Asylum has become a scarce resource (in the political sense) in recent years since access to the international protection regime has become more and more restrictive with Western states erecting greater physical and bureaucratic barriers. Therefore increasing the definitional circle of who is included in the refugee category eliminates the 'conceptual assurance that the entitlement will remain within reasonable limits, a factor that States see as a threat' (ibid.: 36).

We need to recognise the fact that refugees and migrants are distinct categories, although 'large and complex migratory flows are blurring facile distinction between refugees and migrants.'[2] There is the voluntary element in a migrant's decision to move, whereas 'it is the reluctance to uproot oneself and the absence of positive original motivations to settle elsewhere which characterizes all refugee decisions and distinguishes the refugee from the voluntary migrant' (Kunz 1973: 130). Joly further notes that immigrants can be distinguished by their having been influenced by the hope for a better life while refugees are merely trying to rebuild the life they have lost (Joly 2002: 6). In search for a sociological definition, Kuhlman proposes labelling refugees as 'involuntary international migrants' (Kuhlman 1991: 6). Kuhlman states that 'the spatial and temporal aspects of migration are less important in relation to the refugee than the classification or type of migration, since spatially the refugee is assumed to be international and temporally refugee status is indefinite pending a change in circumstances back home' (ibid.: 6). Kuhlman points to the fact that the distinction between voluntary and involuntary migration can be blurred, since voluntary migration can sometimes be so heavily influenced by external forces that the individual has been left with little choice but to move. Is the answer then, asks Kuhlman, to look at the push-and-pull factors involved in any movement? Migrants would perhaps take both into consideration while refugees are influenced primarily by the push factors. He notes, 'It is not some paradise at the other end which they seek but merely an escape from hell in which they live' (ibid.: 8).

Since the formulation of the 1951 Convention, 'considerable terminological or conceptual flora has grown up within which refugee realities confront the language of the Convention' (Sztucki 1999: 64). The array of terms that has been added to the legal literature further befuddles the concept of 'refugee'. From the time of the inception of the Convention, 'mandate refugees' (those who have legal documents affirming their refugee status) individuals fleeing generalised conflict agreed to fall under the United Nations High Commissioner for Refugees's (UNHCR) ambit due to their need for international protection despite the absence of a persecutor as such. Since 1957, the UNHCR has come to incorporate 'refugees who do not come within the competence of the United Nations.' In 1975, the UN added 'displaced persons' to its list although this was to be applied at the time to externally displaced persons who failed to qualify as Convention Refugees (ibid.: 64–65). National legislation relating specifically to 'refugees' began to occur as early as the seventeenth century alongside the growing field of nationality laws.[3] The 1951 Convention definition is the culmination of a series of different attempts at defining and categorising various groups of specific 'refugees' in the inter-war period.[4] Hathaway has divided the pre-1951 definitions into three groups, according to which he claims it is possible to identify three distinct approaches to defining 'refugees': the 'juridical' approach of 1920–35, whereby the international community recognised that membership of a certain group deprived the refugee of governmental protection; the 'social' approach of 1935–39, which concentrated on providing international assistance to ensure safety of the refugee—in the majority of cases, those fleeing Nazi persecution; and the 'individualist' approach of 1938–50, which abandoned a determination procedure based on political or social categories in favour of an examination of the merits of each applicant's case on the basis of a perceived injustice or fundamental incompatibility with the home state (Hathaway 1991: 2–5). Hathaway's three approaches reveal much about what the concept of the refugee has meant to states and the international community as a whole at different times. The application of specific definitions relating to specific groups of refugees hints at the idea that states initially perceived the 'refugee problem' as one that affected very identifiable groups of people for particular reasons in certain places at certain times. The way to respond to refugee flows was to address them on a case-by-case basis. As Haddad points out, 'Yet when numbers reached hitherto unimaginable heights, something had to change—one refugee is an individual in need who should be let in, a thousand refugees are a threat and a burden and must be kept out' (2008: 31). Debates surrounding nation-states, their stakes and interests are inextricably intertwined with the prevailing approaches to defining a refugee in different periods.

Nevzat Soguk asserts that the paradox of the 'refugee discourse' is that it has no place for its very subject, 'When the refugee seemed to exhibit any sign of agency in the discourse, either as some kind of threat or as someone whose agency was manifested in her will to drag her body between distances, she hardly ever figured as a person but was part of an amorphous mass, faceless and speechless' (Soguk 1999: 242). However, in the humanitarian regime, the refugee is both the means and the end: it is the image of the refugee herself that will bring in the money for the relief programmes that will then assist and protect her (Harrell-Bond and Voutira 1992: 205). Having a refugee label for a diverse group of individuals can be difficult to justify. As Lammers notes, 'far too often the label of "refugee" artificially constructs and degrades people into a one-dimensional, homogeneous category yet except for their common experience of flight, they are an extremely heterogeneous category of people' (1999: 22). In most writings on refugees, the figure of a helpless victim is upheld. As a result 'an individual identity is replaced by a stereotyped identity with a categorical prescription of assumed needs' (Zetter 1991: 44).

The received notions of a bounded, authentic culture, which presumes an isomorphic link between people, culture and places, can be effectively challenged by studying groups of people who are deracinated from their places of residence and transplanted elsewhere owing to contingent reasons. Refugees are such people on the move. (Malkki 1998). Understanding refugee lives requires that we come to full terms with the 'give-and-take' process of cultural change that animates their lives once uprooted from their place of origin. The fetter on the freedom to borrow cultural elements is the stuff of refugee existence. Such a scenario complicates popular ideas of global flows where people mingle as they like and borrow as they please. 'Far from it, refugees living on the wrong side of the border are actually likely to be less free to innovate than others (a fact that further problematizes the celebratory view of multiculturalism and hybridity held by many outsiders and some innovative community members). Even though refugees are on the move they still live in communities that largely strive to keep their members in place' (Diehl 2002: 7). They are not, as Gupta and Ferguson put it, 'free-floating monads' (1992: 19).

Forced population movements have extraordinarily diverse historical and political causes and involve people who while all displaced, find themselves in qualitatively different situations and predicaments. As Malkki observed, 'it would seem that the term refugee has analytical usefulness not as a label for a special, generalizable kind or type of person or situation but only as a broad legal or descriptive rubric that includes within it a world of different socioeconomic statuses, personal histories and psychological or spiritual situations. Involuntary or forced movements of people are always only one aspect of much larger constellations of sociopolitical and cultural processes and practices' (1995b: 496).

Seeking refuge and sanctuary has been a human practice since time immemorial. However, the refugee as a social and a global category, a problem to be dealt with legally, acquired salience only by the end of the great wars. A whole new system of procedures for administering such populations on the move was devised on a scale undreamt of earlier. (ibid.: 498) It was towards the end of World War II that the refugee camp became emplaced as a standardised technology of power in the management of mass displacement.[5] The spatial concentration and ordering of people that it enabled as well as the administrative and bureaucratic processes it facilitated within its boundaries had far reaching consequences. 'The segregation of nationalities; the orderly organization of repatriation or third country resettlement; medical and hygienic programs and quarantining; "perpetual screening" and the accumulation of documentation on inhabitants of the camps; control of movement and black marketing; law enforcement and public discipline; and schooling and rehabilitation were some of the operations that the spatial concentration and ordering of people enabled or facilitated. Through these processes, the modern, postwar refugee emerged as a knowable and nameable figure and as an object of social-scientific knowledge' (Malkki 1995b: 498).

'In the last years of World War II and the immediate post-war years, displaced people in Europe were classified as a military problem and they were under the jurisdiction of the Displaced Persons Branch of the Supreme Headquarters Allied Expeditionary Force (SHAEF). Throughout much of the war, the control of civilians and refugees had already been widely considered as a combat problem and the benefits of organising refugees "for useful service behind the combat lines" had been recognised by the military forces. In spatial terms, this military model was important. The basic blueprint of the military camp and many of its characteristic techniques were appropriated by those new spatial and disciplinary practices that were emerging in the 1940s refugee camp in Europe' (ibid.: 499). By 1951, refugees began to appear more clearly as an international social or humanitarian problem than as a primarily military one. The refugee camps made people accessible to a whole gamut of interventions, including study and documentation.

'Refugee lives are inherently experimental and thoroughly modern' (Diehl 2002: 7). As informants, refugees are uniquely able to discuss the ways in which the cold, hard issues of politics and economics inform their personal and communal experiences, explicitly tied as these are to global forces. It would seem that these characteristics make refugee populations particularly well poised to receive attention from anthropologists and anthropologically-minded sociologists seeking to meet the challenge of moving beyond symbol and meaning ethnography and figuring out how to 'represent the embedding of richly described local cultural worlds in larger impersonal systems of political economy' (Marcus and Fischer 1986: 77). Marcus and Fischer go on to explain that 'this would not be such a problematic task if the local cultural unit was portrayed as it usually has been in ethnography as an isolate with outside forces of market and state impinging upon it. What makes representation challenging and a focus of experimentation is the perception that the "outside forces" in fact are an integral part of the construction and constitution of the "inside"' (ibid.: 77). Diehl further notes, 'As evidenced by the few fine anthropological studies of refugees that do exist, one is immediately obligated when working with displaced populations to put aside presumed inside/outside6 or traditional/modern distinctions and focus instead on the ways in which the local and the global are experienced by refugees' (2002: 8).

The very newness of the discursive domain of refugee studies makes difficult any attempt to give a comprehensive synopsis of its intellectual agenda. Case studies of specific refugee situations have grown, yet it seems to be generally agreed that a broader theoretical framework has been lacking. Malkki is of the view that it seems not so much that 'refugee studies' has lacked theory as that it has uncritically imported its main theoretical ideas often on an ad hoc basis from other scholarly domains (Malkki 1995b: 507). The functionalist model has been in vogue in 'refugee studies' and is evident in many works that deal with questions of identity, culture, ethnicity and tradition. One finds in this literature the assumption that to become uprooted and removed from a national community is automatically to lose one's identity, traditions and culture. Malkki stresses that the theoretical apparatus of anthropology has been biased in favour of studying 'indigenous peoples', 'local contexts', and 'closed systems', instead of studying the movement and traffic of people. This kind of sedentarist analytical bias is not unique to anthropology as the interdisciplinary literature in 'refugee studies' attests. Common notions of culture are biased, as Clifford has observed, 'towards rooting rather than travel' (Clifford 1997). The bare fact of movement or displacement across nation-state borders is often assumed a priori to entail not a transformation but a loss of culture and identity. Stein's work offers a particularly clear illustration of this sedentarist norm. He proposes that there is a generalisable phenomenon that can be called 'the refugee experience' and that this experience has characteristic 'stages', which are 'perception of a threat; decision to flee; the period of extreme danger and flight; reaching safety; camp behaviour;

repatriation, settlement or resettlement; the early and late stages of resettlement; adjustment and acculturation; and finally residual states and changes in behaviour caused by the experience.'[7] Talking about the initial 'stage' of exile for refugees in general, Stein predicts, 'The refugees will be confronted by the reality of what has been lost. From a high occupational and social status at home they will plunge downward in their land. They will confront the loss of their culture-their identity, their habits. Every action that used to be habitual or routine will require careful examination and consideration…' (1981: 325). Malkki differs from Stein as regards the basic assumptions of place, culture and identity one in which the latter displays a bias towards sedentariness. Malkki stresses the fact that 'it is doubtful that most people's social universe stops abruptly at the border of their own country or that the lifeworlds just across the border could be as axiomatically alien as Stein suggests' (1995b: 509). Further, one would imagine that mass displacements occur precisely when one's own, accustomed society has become 'strange and frightening' because of war, massacres, political terror or other forms of violence and uncertainty.[8] In the sedentarist scheme then, according to Malkki (1995b: 509), 'going home involves only the most minor cultural adjustment problems. To go home is to go where one belongs'.

There has, for long, been a tendency in refugee studies to naively employ concepts such as adaptation and acculturation to study transformation in varied aspects of refugee life. This stems from the overwhelming importance accorded to psychological interpretations of forced migrations. One must, while taking cognisance of mental distress and disorders caused in the wake of displacements, necessarily keep in mind the empirical or structural aspects that lead to such migrations. 'We cannot assume psychological disorder or mental illness a priori, as an axiom nor can we claim we know from the mere fact of refugeeness, the actual sources of a person's suffering' (Malkki 1995b: 510). Arguing that refugee problems are too often viewed by refugees and refugee agencies as 'temporary and unique events', Stein has proposed, 'If we are to move toward a comprehensive professional refugee assistance system then research must be encouraged and supported. The research should focus not only on the most recent arrivals or specific policy questions but general research, looking at refugees everywhere from a broad historical perspective that views them as recurring phenomena with identifiable and often identical patterns of behaviour and sets of causalities.... We must investigate broadly all of the stages of the refugee experience' (Stein 1981: 321). Malkki identifies the problem of defining 'the refugee experience', as she calls it, in that 'this intellectual project of defining posits a single essential, transhistorical refugee condition' (Malkki 1995b: 511). She further notes that, 'The quest for the refugee experience reflects a wider tendency, in many disciplines, to seize upon political or historical processes and then to inscribe aspects of those processes in the bodies or psyches of the people who are undergoing them. In this way, every mobile, unstable social phenomenon may be imagined as essential traits and characteristics attached to or emanating from individual persons' (ibid.: 511). Almost like any essentialised anthropological 'tribe', refugees thus become a 'culture', 'an identity', (Stein 1981: 323) 'a social world', (Marx 1990: 144) or 'a community' (Gold 1992). There is a tendency to proceed as if all refugees shared a common condition or nature (Malkki 1995b: 511). If the category 'refugee' becomes another 'culture', the refugees and the places where they are found come to appear as natural sites for field research.

Populations on the move have been under the disciplinary gaze, having coming under the domain of peace studies, security studies and international relations. Such populations have to be placed in a specific historical context in order to understand the particular social and political dynamics that they engender for military societies, civil society and political society within the boundaries of the nation-state as well as within regional and global sites of engagement (Loescher 1992). The influence of the international refugee regime on scholarship has been specially marked in the linked figures of 'refugees' and 'development'. The settlement of refugees and other displaced people especially in the Third World has shown a marked tendency to be absorbed in well-established forms of development discourse (Malkki 1995b: 506).[10] Development programmes targeted at refugees are often established in conjunction with the UNHCR and these programmes have offered points of entry for many social scientists. But the refugee–development link is more far-reaching than that. Hein has argued, 'Economic

Development and assistance to refugees are inseparable issues...because the "refugee" is an indicator of world system dynamics' (1993: 45). The world system perspective cannot explain how the historical processes of state formation and breakdown create refugees in particular countries (Zolberg 1983).

The history of refugees in the twentieth century began with the replacement of the old multi-ethnic European empires by the new world order of sovereign nation-states. Hundreds of thousands of people were forced to flee their homes because they did not belong, they did not fit the nationalist principle of 'one state, one culture' (Gellner 1983) and thus could not be accommodated within the European national state borders. Unlike such movements in the previous century, which in proportional terms were much larger, in this century there have been far fewer places for these extra or surplus people to go. The world population is increasingly divided into citizens protected by the state and people who are not members of a functioning nation-state (Hein 1993). Responding to the need for a coordinated international response, the League of Nations and later the United Nations (Skran 1995) labelled them 'refugees' (Zetter 1991) and introduced humanitarian law intended to ensure the protection of their rights. The organisations of the United Nations have played a decisive, instrumental role in consolidating 'the international refugee system' (Gallagher 1989) and what has developed is a network of national, international and relief agencies. Hein has observed that 'It is no coincidence that an organization functioning as a global state is forming to manage refugee problems' (Hein 1993: 47), and that the very 'concept of migration emerged from the growth of national bureaucracies' (Dowty 1987). This is the reason why Hein reiterates the need to bring in the state in order to explain the origins of refugee crisis (Hein 1993: 47).

Many have called for development-oriented strategies in the management of mass displacement in the Third World. The argument has often been made that rather than just providing immediate emergency relief in the face of new refugee crises, the agencies involved should also concentrate on setting up mechanisms for long-term development aid to improve conditions of life for everyone in impoverished regions of the Third World. It is in the arena of refugees and development that anthropology has been particularly visible (Malkki 1995b). Malkki traces precisely how the discourse of development has colonised refugee issues and what other intellectual or political connections have been erased and rendered unthinkable in the process. 'If nothing else, the development discourse on refugees has sometimes facilitated the continued depoliticization of refugee movements; for instead of foregrounding the political, historical processes that generated a given group of refugees and that reach far beyond the country of asylum and the refugee camp, development projects tend to see a whole world in a refugee camp' (Malkki 1995b: 507).[11]

Arrival in a host country is an inaugural event that sets the refugee diasporic thinking about prospects of settling permanently or creating new diaspora groups or aligning with an already existing one. Such decisions are not easy to come by for refugee migrants who emotionally and cognitively remain attached to their homelands (Gold 1997; Miles and Sheffer 1998; Van Hear 1998). Pinpointing that juncture in the personal history and collective history of migrants is critical not only for a proper understanding of development of particular diaspora but also for distinguishing among the various types of transient migrants and diasporans. Such distinctions can be useful because those who from the outset do not intend to settle in their first host country and those who later consider it unfriendly and therefore migrate to another host country and those who are determined to return to their homelands will not be interested in joining or establishing diaspora communities (Sheffer 2003: 77–78).

The readiness and capability of migrants to maintain their ethno-national identities in their host societies and to openly nurture their communities and support their homelands are two crucial features of the ethno-national diaspora. Most scholars have stressed how the structural, social and political environments can affect migrants' abilities to maintain their identities in their host countries.[12] Clifford (1997: 255) notes, 'The language of diaspora is increasingly invoked by displaced peoples who feel (maintain, revive, invent) a connection with a prior home. This sense of connection must be strong enough to resist erasure through the normalising processes of forgetting, assimilating, and distancing'. Diaspora cultures, thus, mediate, in 'a lived tension, the experiences of separation and entanglement, of living here and remembering/desiring another place'.[13]

Few works have shown the juncture in the personal history and collective history of migrants that is crucial not only for a proper understanding of the development of particular diasporas but also for distinguishing among the various types of transient migrants and diasporans (Sheffer 2002: 77). The menu of available strategies is large, beginning with assimilation, ranging through various modes of accommodation and ending with separation and in the case of stateless diasporas, including support for secession in an attempt to seize land from dominant societies and create their own nation-states in their own homelands. More specifically, this spectrum includes the following strategies: assimilation, integration, acculturation, isolationism, corporation, secession, separation and irredentism (Smith 1981, 1986; Weiner 1991; Sheffer 1994).

Researching Tibetan Refugees

Social scientists working on forced migration, having a penchant for theoretical analysis, cannot neglect the affective, the cathectic dimension of their research, for the object of their study—the refugees and displaced—are necessarily those who undergo tremendous 'suffering' . The intent of their research is to also influence policy but with a difference. As Jacobsen and Landau state in this regard, 'Most forced migration research seeks to explain the behaviour, impact and problems of the displaced with the intention of influencing agencies and governments to develop responses that are more effective. This policy orientation stems in part from the subject of research, the figure of the refugee, whose experience of violent conflict, displacement and human rights violations inhibits researchers from treating them simply as objects for research' (2003: 1).[14] This sentiment echoed by policy-oriented refugee researchers has led on the one hand to the growth of a large body of refugee literature, which consists of reports by human rights organisations like Amnesty International or Human Rights Watch, which document and expose human rights abuses with the intention of putting pressure on governments to protect and promote the well-being of the refugees. On the other and quite paradoxically, it has produced an image of the refugee as a victim and a client in need of assistance. As Dorsh Marie de Voe comments, 'Understanding the impact of the event of flight in the lives of refugees rarely enters the analysis of refugee needs, problems and programs. It is as if culture were a novelty easily dismissed in the face of events, which have turned persons into victims' (1981: 88).

At the same time, refugee-related social science seeks to attain methodological and theoretical rigour in order to justify its place in the academia and to attract scarce funding for social research. Refugee researchers like Karen Jacobsen and Loren Landau (2003) are led to believe that once academic sophistication is achieved, their work becomes ever more irrelevant to practitioners and policymakers. 'The fear that our analyses may not address current crises, that the language and concepts we use are too arcane or jargonistic or that the questions we ask (and purport to answer) are interesting only to other academics, not to those who work in the field or to those refugees and Internally Displaced Persons and war-affected people who live the situations we study. How do we address the dual imperative, which Jacobsen and Landau talk about, so that the work on refugees can be both academically rigorous and relevant to policy?' (Jacobsen and Landau 2003).

Revealing and explaining the research method at the outset is important from the point of view of understanding processes, events and structures that unfold over time. Recognising the limits and strengths of the concepts and method towards gathering data from the field is critical to any enquiry. What does come out most clearly through the review of existing secondary materials on Tibetans in exile and from the conversations with lay Tibetans is the increasing realisation among them that their ethnic identity or ethos is threatened not only by the event of flight but also its aftermath. The ensuing research study seeks as its object an understanding of this aftermath, which has meaning well beyond the functional, instrumental forms of physical survival.

Confronting the Problem of Refugee Numbers

Almost half a century into exile, Tibetan refugees find themselves in a protracted refugee condition. Camps have acquired a certain permanency and the refugee situation can be judged as relatively stable. Under such circumstances, knowing numbers is important from the point of view of policy and academic enquiry. Demographic profile, list of camps, camp inhabitants and resettled populations and the refugee–local divide are list of items that need documentation. At the outset, it is important to note that while statistics are central to the function of the international refugee regime, it has long been recognised that the collection of accurate data on displaced populations is confronted with some formidable obstacles.[15] Writing in the mid-1980s, Gaim Kibreab pointed out, 'there is a cloud of uncertainty and unreliability surrounding African refugee statistics' (1985: 10). According to a paper presented to UNHCR's Executive Committee, the world's most affluent states, with all of their resources and technological sophistication, have great difficulties in answering or are not able to provide an answer to the simple question, 'how many refugees are living in the country', and 'information is generally lacking on essential characteristics of the refugee population, for example, country of origin and sex'.[16]

Refugees are seen to arrive at times in large numbers to a host country in order to seek asylum. Borders are crossed at several points. The sheer number of refugees at the border makes the task of counting almost impossible. The UNHCR has no access to these areas which are kept out of bounds by the government for security considerations. As a refugee influx levels off and relief operations become more organised, the potential for the collection of accurate statistical data evidently improves. This was the case with the Tibetans who had to live in their country of asylum, India, for about three decades before they could come up with a comprehensive socio-demographic data of their own community in the diaspora (represented through the Tibetan Demographic Survey published in 1998 by the Tibetan government-in-exile).

The operational constraints on gathering quantitative information on refugee groups become more visible at the local level. As residents of India, Tibetan refugees move around freely within the territory of India, unlike foreign visitors to the country.[17] Tibetans are seen going in and out of a refugee camp to take advantage of seasonal economic opportunities in the towns and cities of India. Refugee households inevitably split up or regroup. Refugee populations are therefore dynamic social entities. However accurate they may have been at the time of their collection, statistical data about the size and composition of a refugee population can quickly become outdated. Updating this information is not a straightforward exercise, when the refugee population or host country concerned records births, deaths, ages and family size in ways that do not correspond with standard demographic practice. Tibetan refugees in Darjeeling, who are relatively free from the gaze of the authorities, happen to be mobile, making their way to the plains for various reasons. Therefore, those with legal documents are more often not traceable, men and women alike, except the elderly. Some of them choose not to live in designated camps or specially made housing, which makes the task of keeping track of them and their group challenging. Fieldwork among refugees of this kind is all the more challenging on account of their sheer 'invisibility', due in part to their mobile existence and their mixing with other ethnic groups in the town.

The Setting

Darjeeling district of the state of West Bengal provides a unique context for exploring not only 'local integration'[18] as a durable solution to the situation of protracted exile of Tibetans in India but also the experience of 'self-settled'[19] refugees who have lived outside the permanent settlements that were specially built under the rehabilitation scheme for Tibetans in India. For the purpose of illustration, it would be prudent at the outset to describe Darjeeling district as a whole of which Darjeeling town is a part before turning to the latter. The district falls under Jalpaiguri Division that consists of six districts. The district itself is divided into four sub-divisions: Darjeeling, Kalimpong, Kurseong and Siliguri with Darjeeling sub-division as the district headquarter. The total population of Darjeeling district is 1,695,900 comprising 826,334 males and 779,566 females with 23.54 per cent as the decadal growth rate according to the Census of India 2001, Provisional Population Totals, Series - I.

Darjeeling (*rdorjegling* in Tibetan) is a colonial creation of the nineteenth century. British imperial interest throughout this period was to foster trade with Tibet and Central Asia which prompted them to secure the northern border of India against Chinese intrusions. Tibet acted as a buffer and guided the making of British policy in Sikkim, north Bengal and Nepal that had profound ethnic and political implications. Sikkim was of special interest to the English rulers because of its strategic position. In 1828, Captain Lloyd, along with the Commercial Resident at Malda J. W. Grant, visited this area in connection with disputes between Sikkim and Nepal. They noticed the position of Darjeeling both as a prospective hill resort—a sanatorium for British troops and an outpost of strategic importance overlooking Tibet. Darjeeling was then part of Sikkim (*bras ljongs*) and inhabited by Lepchas—regarded as the aboriginal inhabitants of the area. The Raja of Sikkim was under obligation to the British for having restored the territories Sikkim had lost to Nepal and when the British approached him for taking Darjeeling on lease, he could not refuse. Darjeeling was gradually annexed to British India beginning 1 February 1835, marking the period of execution of a deed of grant by the Raja of Sikkim. With the annexation of Darjeeling from Sikkim and Bhutan and the containment of Nepal, the British started to increase trade with Sikkim, Nepal and Tibet through Darjeeling.

From 1850 onwards, trade with Tibet gradually developed. Kalimpong (*ka blon sbug*), also situated within Darjeeling district and ethnically similar to Darjeeling town, had become a thriving centre for trading activities. Traders found it profitable to invest in land, build houses and have some members of their families live there running guest houses and restaurants. For many Tibetans, the pleasant little town became in the course of time, an ideal second home because of its close proximity to their original home as well as the easy access it afforded to other Indian centres of trade and pilgrimage (Wangyal 1978: 11).[20] Indo-Tibetan trade came to an abrupt end with the Chinese occupation of Tibet by the middle of the twentieth century.

Bidhan Golay, while stressing on the need to study hitherto neglected aspects of migration in the region, wrote, 'Darjeeling was sparsely populated when the British set their foot there. The boundaries with its neighbouring territories were notional and people from adjoining places would come for grazing sheep and cattle or for cutting firewood.

With the discovery of Darjeeling by the British as an ideal retreat, this wild frontier was gradually normalized into a "hill station"' (2006: 34). Colonialism ended its fluidity by putting it firmly under the control of its knowledge system. The British, since the nineteenth century, began the process of collecting information about Darjeeling, (gazettes, for instance). The knowledge that was gathered about Darjeeling from out of the colonial gaze, as Golay relates (2006: 34) using Sudipta Kaviraj's phrase, led to the refiguring of the 'fuzzy' identities into an 'enumerated' community. What Nicholas Dirks called the 'ethnographic state', where knowledge is 'anthropologized', is seen at work by the beginning of mid-nineteenth century, in evidence by the proliferation of gazetteers and reports documenting the customs and manners of castes, tribes and religion of the Darjeeling region. Golay writes about how 'immigration was encouraged by the colonial state, as it required cheap labour for building infrastructure for its "hill station" and most importantly for its teeming tea gardens. It was within the matrix of race relations in the colonial situation that the colonial enterprise encouraged migration. The British planters did not fail in employing sardars (local appellation for agents) who would go to Nepal and bring back young and healthy labourers to work in their tea gardens. The sardars in return got commissions from planters' (2006: 38).

The most striking aspect of the history of Darjeeling is the issue of migration. The point of contention seems to be centred around a report by Dr Campbell, the superintendent of Darjeeling, who claimed to have raised the population from 'not more than hundred souls in 1839 to about 10000 in 1849 chiefly by immigration from the neighbouring states of Nepal, Sikkim and Bhutan' (O'Malley 2001 [1907]: 22). Interestingly, the framing of the debate here was along traditional lines such as the familiar use of the migration theory of push-and-pull factors or cause-and-effect. The contentious issue of original inhabitants or autochthony is somewhat laid to rest with regard to the Lepchas. The identity of groups placed within the category of Nepali or Gorkha should be re-evaluated from the standpoint of their immigrant or settler status. Writing about the ethnic history of Darjeeling, Tanka Subba remarked, 'The monument of belief about the so-called Nepalis is erected on shallow foundation and this must be shaken if not pulled down. This is not done to legitimize their claim over Darjeeling, as some may imagine but simply for the sake of truth' (Subba 1992: 37). The ethnic composition of the three hill sub-divisions of Darjeeling, which had, thus, undergone change since the middle of the nineteenth century till the present times was evidently caused by the waves of massive migration from Nepal which in turn emanated from three major factors:

i. First, the marginalisation of the non-Hindu Nepali Buddhist communities by the high-caste Hindu monarchy in the second half of the eighteenth century led to out-migration of non-Hindu Nepali communities such as Rai, Limbu, Gurung from the eastern region of Nepal. These Nepali communities found the hill sub-division of Darjeeling a convenient and accessible place for settlement.
ii. Second, the recruitment of Nepalis as tea plantation labourers by the British at low remuneration because of their poverty stricken backgrounds throughout the second half of the nineteenth century.
iii. Lastly, the need to recruit Nepalis for the Gorkha Battalions in the Indian army during the post–Sepoy Revolt period (Dasgupta 1999: 54–55).

The Nepalis consist of numerous distinct and interlinked tribes embracing different languages and dialects, costumes and rituals. Among some tribes, even different scripts and mutually unintelligible dialects can be found while in some cases, it is possible to find rare relationships of vocabulary with people of another distant area with whom the Nepali tribe had apparently no documented contact. There are references to show that the Limbus and the Mangars are among the earliest inhabitants of the region. 'Beyond a few Lepchas and Limbus with their little clearing in the forests, an occasional raid from Nepal or a stray visitor from the table-lands of Tibet, the Darjeeling Hills were practically uninhabited' (O'Malley 2001 [1907]: 22). Given the migratory nature of life in the Himalayas (Pinn 1986: 14) for many centuries before the arrival of the British, neither the term 'immigrant' nor 'autochthonous' can be appropriately applied in the strict sense to the Lepchas, not to mention the Nepali castes like the Limbus and the Mangars who are said to have had their roots in the Darjeeling region itself.

In order to understand the meanings that Tibetan refugees/diasporics give to their predicament in Darjeeling, it is appropriate to state clearly what entails doing fieldwork in the social settings of displacement. The fieldwork, which requires one to be physically situated at the site, was principally concentrated in the Darjeeling Municipal Area of the Darjeeling district. The district resembles an inverted wedge with its base resting on Sikkim, its sides touching Nepal, Bhutan and the Jalpaiguri district of West Bengal while its apex projects into the West Dinajpur district of West Bengal (Gazetteer of Darjeeling, West Bengal). The southern parts of the district (Siliguri and the terai) consists of foothills and flat lands (340 ft) and the northern parts (Darjeeling, Kalimpong and Kurseong) are mountainous (12,000 ft). Owing to this great range of altitude, the district possesses different climatic zones that support a wide variety of vegetation. The Darjeeling Municipal Area has an area of 10.57 sq km according to the 2001 Census of India. The total population of Darjeeling Municipality is 107,197 comprising 55,963 males and 51,234 females according to the 2001 Census of India, Final Population Totals, Urban Agglomerations and Towns, Series - 1. This can be compared to the total population of Darjeeling Municipality in 1991 which stood at 73,062 with 37,763 males and 35,299 females according to the 1991 Census of India.[21]

Darjeeling town is located in the Sadar subdivision of the district of Darjeeling which is also the headquarters of the district. The actual fieldwork while being based at the Darjeeling Municipal Area was also conducted at the TRSHC situated in the Lebong hillside at an average altitude of 2,143 metres above sea level. Darjeeling town is situated on a long, narrow mountain ridge of the Sikkim Himalayas that descends abruptly to the bed of the Great Rangit River. The town lies at an elevation of about 7,000 feet (2,100 m). On a clear day, Darjeeling affords a magnificent view of Kanchenjunga (28,169 feet [8,586 m]), and Mount Everest can just be seen. It was constituted a municipality in 1850. Chowrasta forms the town's main centre, the former being a broad open space on the saddle of the mountain-ridge and the most attractive promenade. Mall Road is a circular road running from the Chowrasta, northwards along the western side of the ridge reaching the gates of the Government House (formerly the summer residence of the Governor of Bengal during the colonial era) and then circling round the base of Observatory Hill and returning again to the Chowrasta along the eastern side of the ridge. Observatory Hill, the town's highest point (7,137 feet), houses the Mahakal Temple. Birch Hill contains a natural park and the Institute of Mountaineering. The Lloyd Botanic Gardens were laid out in 1865. Besides these attractions, Darjeeling has a zoo, a natural history museum, a racecourse, cemeteries and several hospitals. It is also the seat of the University of North Bengal, founded in 1962, with a number of affiliated colleges including a medical school in the town. Tourism is the mainstay of Darjeeling's economy. It was systematically organised for the first time in November 1975 when the West Bengal Tourism Development Corporation came into being. The important point to note here is that hotels and transport companies are owned by plainsmen. The local communities are engaged mainly in service occupations such as taxi-driving, selling of vegetables and other articles, and other government jobs. The only hill community which has a stake in this industry is the Tibetan (Subba 1988: 13–15).

Encountering the Field

In ethnographic fieldwork, Liisa Malkki writes, 'methodology rarely means a set of standard tools and techniques applicable independently of contexts....The settings in which the anthropologists find himself or herself shape the day-to-day practices and the tool kit of field research' (1995a: 47). Such was certainly the case with the conduct of this research study. The field study was spread over a period of two years (2004–06), totalling six months: October–November 2004 in Darjeeling; May 2005 in Darjeeling; April 2006 in Dharamsala; October–November 2006 in Darjeeling. I also seized opportunities to converse with Tibetans (some from Darjeeling) in Kolkata and Asansol (which do not have any refugee settlements), and in the Delhi settlement (this was mainly during the winter season). Intricate and often long historical processes are at the heart of nearly all refugee situations (Asad 1973; Said 1984; Said 1989). Since 'refugee' is a category often seen as politically sensitive, doing field research among Tibetan refugees in Darjeeling raised problems of ongoing access, representation, trust, sampling technique and therefore warrants the use of a flexible research strategy.

Access

Gaining access to a site that is relevant for pursuing a research problem constitutes one of the most difficult steps to be undertaken in ethnography. In humanitarian situations, access to refugees who do not live in camps is a major problem both for researchers and practitioners and large numbers of the displaced are often omitted from studies. Difficulties of access to refugee communities stem from logistics—remote areas, bad roads, hidden communities, security problems and lack of trust. In any refugee community, there are also groups of people who are difficult to reach due to norms of refugee communities that may debar their members from being too outspoken, or simply due to their work and living conditions. Researchers tend to concentrate their activities in camps where refugees are more easily accessible and where they can be identified by officials or aid organisations. Refugee camps are, however, not a routine site for ethnographic fieldwork and displaced people are not the usual 'native informants' of anthropologists. Yet, fieldwork among refugees almost necessarily speaks to profound riddles and questions that live at the very heart of the discipline. One classic analytic arena, the anthropological study of classification and categories, has much to say about some key dynamics in the social construction of refugeeness in the contemporary world (Malkki 1995a: 5).

The people who appear as refugees in the present research study have lived in the Darjeeling township situated in the Darjeeling district since May 1959. These refugees were Tibetans (those who fled from Tibet after 1959 and their heirs) who were far from leading a physically-isolated existence. Regular bus services or hired vehicles connect Darjeeling town with Siliguri and the neighbouring towns of Kurseong, Kalimpong and Gangtok. Land Rovers are the most popular means of transport as they can easily navigate the steep slopes in the region. Travelling to this site (by the 80-km long Darjeeling Himalayan Railway from Siliguri or by the Hill Cart Road or National Highway 55 that follows the railway line) was not a difficult proposition, unlike a number of refugee camps around the world, which are situated in remote areas. However, rail and road transport often get disrupted during the monsoon season due to landslides. On arrival in Darjeeling town, the most favoured means of getting to the TRSHC was by walking down the winding hill slopes either from the Chowrasta side or on the other end, from the Hermitage, or by using two wheelers and hired taxis, used more often by tourists.

Key Informants

Once key informants[22] residing at the site were fortuitously identified, the need to take recourse to formal channels of entry into the field was no longer there. It requires particular mention that the first of my key informants was not a Tibetan refugee but an Indian national of Tibetan descent and a Buddhist. His predecessors, he mentioned, had come to the Darjeeling hills from Tibet before 1959 for purposes of trade and other economic pursuits. Bhutias made India their home and soon acquired Indian citizenship with Scheduled Tribe (ST) status under the Indian constitution. Locally, they were known as Bhutia (those who traced their origin to Tibet (Bhot) or a province in Tibet, a term sometimes used derogatorily by dominant Nepalis but understood as such by the Bhutias there.

My key informant, although dependable, could not be the only source of data, for such over-reliance can lead to one-sidedness in data collection. Seeking additional and different perspectives warranted that new informants be contacted through the help of the key informant without jeopardising his trust. His Tibetan ancestry came of great help in finding refugees at the TRSHC. He led me to a Darjeeling-born Tibetan refugee who lived most of his life in the refugee camp (40 years in all). He became, in a way, my second key informant from the Tibetan refugee community and the problem of access to the refugee community was resolved. His local knowledge and erudition about the place and the past proved highly beneficial and also, his many encounters with locals and visitors gave a certain outlook to refugee issues. My refugee informant had a phenomenal memory and I would eagerly take down notes while he recounted events from his childhood to the present. I needed information that went beyond direct observation that could come through sustained in-depth interviews. The two key informants were childhood friends and the revealing fact was that my Bhutia informant's grandmother had provided shelter and support by way of cash and kind to the refugee informant's mother, who had fled Tibet. This vital information provided the backdrop for my research enquiries into the refugee–host dynamic in Darjeeling town.

Role as a Researcher in the Field

Related to the issue of 'ongoing access' is the question of the kind of role the ethnographer adopts in relation to the social setting and its members. In the present research study, the principal role that has been followed is that of observer-as-participant. Opportunities for genuine participation were few in refugee contexts and there were situations that were not amenable to the immersion that is a key ingredient of the ethnographic method. 'Hanging around' (Bryman 2004: 298) was another access strategy that was used. It entailed loitering in the TRSHC and also in the marketplace in Darjeeling town in order to get noticed so that unsolicited information could be extracted. For the conduct of this research study involving an observer-as-participant role, Gold's classification of participant observer roles with their respective advantages and risks was duly considered, which has greater potential for a broader meaning and applicability to refugee research contexts than either participant observation or ethnography (Gold 1958: 217–23).

My observer-as-participant role in the context of this field study largely involved interviewing. Initiating the interview process required establishing rapport with the respondents so that they are prepared to participate in and persist with the interview. In the context of this research study on refugees, this rapport could not be established quickly because of the difficulty of establishing trust involved in the relationship and the gulf that already exists between the refugee 'lifeworlds' and that of the researcher. Familiarity brings with it its disadvantages, leading to the problem of 'reactivity' or replying to keep the interviewer always feeling good about the interview. The familiar phrase often heard in conversations with Tibetans is that which harped on their supposed unity or oneness in the face of extreme odds. One such reply was, 'We Tibetans believe....' or, 'We Tibetans are Buddhist, so therefore....' Replies like these reflected the desire on the part of the Tibetans to convey a certain ethic in exile, one that is rooted in the Buddhist cultural ideal or to show an image of an 'ideal Tibetan refugee'. Frontal acknowledgment of this aspect to one's research on the refugees is crucial in order to avoid any misrepresentations or to know how and when such misrepresentations can arise in the first place. Establishing rapport in the classical anthropological sense is an ongoing accomplishment, requiring tact and empathy.

Use of Interview Schedules

An interview guide consisting of a list of questions and the specific topics to be covered was used having an appearance of an unstructured or semi-structured interview schedule. Interview schedules were designed to capitalise on the knowledge of the interviewees about local issues and conditions as well as about issues regarding Tibet and the Tibetan diaspora. The strategy was to give enough space to the interviewee to reply to queries in a manner they desired, in which 'rambling' was given preference. Open-ended questions and in-depth interviews meant that the conversations were picked up from what was last said by interviewees. Capturing the uniqueness of the refugee experience meant that interviews were directed towards individuals as well as settings where respondents were seen in groups, both at the TRSHC and in Darjeeling town.

Issue of Trust

Crucial to developing relationships in the field, which involves refugees, is the establishment of trust between the researcher and the researched. Securing access is in many ways an ongoing activity. Refugees whom

I encountered at the beginning seemed to adjust their behaviour in my presence (problem of reactivity), which is symptomatic of the levels of trust or mistrust that existed in the relationship. Daniel and Knudsen's (1995: 1) contention that 'the refugee mistrusts and is mistrusted' therefore cannot be ignored. A large part of what Emmanuel Marx (1990) calls the 'social world' of refugees remains unknown to a researcher even till the end of the research study and therefore the strategy in the present field research was to desist from making an ambitious claim that a particular set of research questions and methodology deployed would reconstitute trust and would rather regard mistrust as something inherent in the refugee system. People from all walks of life frequent the TRSHC. Tourists, NGO members, donor agencies, administrators and, less frequently, politicians are a familiar sight. They had their curiosities in knowing about the lot of refugees. I tried to be as 'unobtrusive' as I can, so that my presence as a researcher, although acknowledged by the refugees at first, would not be noticed in due course. Trust could only be built gradually and with great caution. Initially, I was accompanied by my key informant during all visits to the TRSHC and in Darjeeling town. The preliminary introduction to the administrative staff of TRSHC tended to be officious but my presence did not arouse any suspicion or fear, which is generally the case in conflict-prone refugee settlements in Africa and West Asia. Gradually, when the refugee settlement became more familiar, it was possible to start visiting the TRSHC alone. Conducting fieldwork without the assistance of the key informant is deemed crucial, since it was observed that the presence of the key informant did affect the respondents.

'Trust' and 'mistrust' between the refugee respondent and an interviewer like me had to be negotiated, and the problem was particularly more stark in the town. Respondents were busy shop-owners who had little time to spare. Conversations did get interrupted in the middle, even when conversations could be initiated. I had to come at a designated time of the day as agreed upon, or else I had to wait patiently for closed days on account of any festival. I chose to be an observer—a bystander—then. Tibetan refugees preferred to call themselves Bhutia at first. They revealed their refugee identity on further probing and much depended on the level of trust and confidentiality that I could strike with my refugee respondents, and the time taken to build this trust varied with each respondent. The claims to Bhutia identity made by the refugee respondents were testified by others from different ethnic backgrounds such as Nepalis, Bhutias and Tamangs, among others, who lived alongside. My Bengali-cum-researcher identity surprisingly allayed any hesitation in their minds about my intent. This happened, I realised, since refugees have always valued education in exile as a means to upward mobility, and the fact that several Bengalis, in the remote past, have contributed to the growth of Buddhism in Tibet—Atisha Dipankara and Sarat Chandra Das were among a few that they could relate to.

Sampling Strategy

The sampling of informants in the present study of refugees is a combination of convenience and snowball sampling methods. However, deploying the convenience sampling method to the study of Darjeeling town refugees is difficult since the majority of them are self-settled among host populations. Convenience sampling has had its advantages in refugee settings. The self-settled nature of refugee life in Darjeeling town, with fluid boundaries and high mobility among youths (specially during the winter) made convenience sampling the most effective strategy in refugee settings of this kind. Locating people and identifying them requires considerable effort and some basic knowledge about the demographics of the place.

The gradual creation of trust and friendship with key informants eventually led to the use of the snowballing sampling technique that could be deployed in refugee settings. Initiation of conversations with friends, neighbours, kin of the key informants living close by eventually led to conversations being struck with others living in faraway places. Access problems mean that most refugee researchers rely on snowball sampling approaches. Although the specifics vary, the researcher almost always begins by contacting a local body, such as a religious or refugee organisation or an aid agency that is familiar with the refugee community, and requests their assistance in identifying and approaching potential research subjects in the community. This initial core group of subjects is then interviewed and asked to name others who might be willing to be interviewed, and thus the snowball sample is built.

The pitfall of using the snowball sampling approach is that it is liable to produce a biased sample. A snowball sample draws respondents from a certain section of a target group or community, very different from a random sample which gives everyone an equal chance for getting selected. The sample drawn from snowball also tends to be similar in social characteristics, like a denomination or a social network. It tends to peripheralise and exclude those in the group who are not part of group which is studied. Awareness of the ethical dimensions of snowballing is essential to keep trust intact not only between the respondents and interviewers but also between the respondents themselves.

Establishing contacts with a respondent through a key informant is, to begin with, a necessary rite of passage. However, any attempt to crosscheck sensitive information about income data or religious or personal affiliations between the concerned respondents who happen to know each other can create animosities amongst the group members. Sharing of such data can be potentially damaging to the reputation of everybody involved and much discretion is called for on the part of the researcher so that trust and cooperation are maintained. Researchers must, therefore, be explicit in recognising the limits of their claims to representativeness. Doing otherwise can mean that policies recommended for one group can, on the assumption of representativeness, end up harming other refugees (and hosts) not included in the sample.

The unruly nature of the Tibetan refugee population prompted me to administer unstructured interview schedules in order to draw out qualitative data. About 80 respondents coming from diverse backgrounds were interviewed on an individual basis in Darjeeling town and in the TRSHC. Of the 80 respondents, 60 belonged to the Tibetan refugee community and 20 were from the host groups (15 from the Bhutia community and five from the Nepali community). Furthermore, discussions took place in groups involving members from the Tibetan refugee community, Bhutia community and Nepali community. The members of each group (comprising a maximum of four individuals) belonged to the same community. Over and above the 80 respondents who were part of the individual-based interviews, about 40 respondents were involved in the group-based discussions. Of these 40 respondents, 20 belonged to the Tibetan refugee community, 10 to the Bhutia community and 10 to the Nepali community. In total, the number of respondents taking into account the individual-based interviews (80 respondents) and group-based discussions (40 respondents) would be 120. The respondents were mainly shop-owners, craftsmen and entrepreneurs; a few were scholars, administrators, activists, teachers, students and monks. The age group of the Tibetan refugee respondents was 18–50 years. They comprised those Tibetans who were born in exile on and after 1959. The reason for keeping this broad age range is that in the exile context, the idea of the new-generation Tibetan refugees is rendered vague by the stretch of the diaspora. As Topden Tsering (2007) writes:

> In the exile context, the idea of youth is rendered convoluted by the fleeting stretch of the Diaspora. The expiry tag on the process of being young comes with a sooner date in India than in the US. In New York at 35 you can still be a freelancer but in Dharamsala shame on you if you are not by then comfortably married complete with a kid or two to make up for the family portrait!. On the exile shore, youth takes on a kaleidoscopic visage. Exile Tibetan youth is the 27-year-old girl in some northern Indian city of her family's seasonal sweater-selling destination, where from a makeshift store, she retails woolen garments, hand-knit scarves, and the like, to local customers, while her aging parents ponder over her childhood swiftly passed and wonder if she will grow old to be like them. Exile Tibetan youth is the 40-year-old man, a father of three back home in Bylakuppe, who upon arriving in New York, finds himself in a dormitory-like situation he had never known, sharing a room with three other Tibetans in their twenties, all of who when not slaving under the weight of the American dream steal moments of reprieve from playing cards, joking around, sharing grocery bills, and getting drunk on the money left over from purchasing gifts back home of Nike Shoes, and sweatshirts.

Other Methodological Concerns

The fact that Tibetans are scattered across the globe requires one to undertake what George E. Marcus (1995: 95–117) called multi-sited research. It was difficult to conduct multi-sited research in the context of Tibetan refugees, since it was not physically possible to go to other sites both in and out of India where Tibetans reside (except the Delhi and Dharamsala settlements) in order to conduct ethnography. Using multi-sited research, albeit in a limited way, did expand the scope of the field. I could interview the same persons in different locales and at different times across India. I could also interview Tibetan government-in-exile officials at Dharamsala with the many sweater sellers in Kolkata. Darjeeling provided a microcosm of the Tibetan exile world, one which Tibetans came to embrace, only to explore new horizons and new possibilities in exile. The other way to offset the limitations of travel to multiple sites in the Tibetan diaspora was to use the Internet in order to interact with Tibetan refugees settled in the United States but who were born in India. As Thubten Samphel notes, 'The power of the internet to create virtual communities has fascinated Tibetans in exile. This fascination is intensified by the fact that the ability to create a cohesive community, across international borders, has been denied to Tibetans in Tibet by an internet-shy China' (2004: 167). Other Internet sites frequently used by Tibetans, like phayul.com (for news updates); tibet.net which is the official website of the Tibetan government-in-exile; Tibet.ca (Canada Tibet Committee); tibetlink.com (Canada); tibetsearch.com (USA); tibetwrites.org; and tibetwrites.org (where refugees share their experiences in the forms of prose and poetry) were referred to in order to gain access to the Tibetan diasporic world.

The fluency with which the new-generation Tibetans in Darjeeling spoke English, Hindi and Nepali in Darjeeling made it easy to strike long conversations and elicit significant data (although I could speak only in English and Hindi with them). A translator belonging to the Tibetan Bhutia community was employed for interviewing some members of the older generation in exile. The *English-Tibetan Dictionary of Modern Tibetan*, compiled by Melvyn C. Goldstein with Ngawangthondup Narkyid, published by the Library of Tibetan Works and Archives, Dharamsala 1999 was consulted on numerous occasions. Apart from ethnographic interviews, the source material for the research work constituted a wide spectrum such as secondary literature on Tibet and the Tibetan diaspora; subject of refugees; on diaspora in general and on Darjeeling district.

The other set of publications consulted are: one, the CTA's White Papers obtained from tibet.net and its Integrated Development Plan 2004–07; two, publications of the Department of Information and International Relations (DIIR) on political and human rights issues, and environment and development issues; three, the Tibetan Demographic Survey 1998; four, Tibet Under Communist China, and Indian Leaders on Tibet; five, International Resolutions and Recognitions on Tibet (1959–97); six, report brought out by the TRSHC, 1999; seven, reports and documents brought out by the Tibetan Centre for Human Rights and Democracy (TCHRD); eight, Tibetan Parliamentary and Policy Research Centre (TPPRC) and resources at the Library of Tibetan Works and Archives (LTWA). Besides, articles published in newspapers and journals such as the Tibetan Bulletin (available online); Tibetan Review, Rangzen (Tibetan Youth Congress magazine) and Tibetan Affairs (published from Darjeeling) have been referred to.

For several decades, anthropologists concerned with the inherent power dynamics of the Western practice of anthropology (Asad 1973) have questioned the way in which ethnography is written. Ethnographers are now increasingly held accountable by people about whom they write. At issue are the related questions of the situatedness of the researcher and the representation of the researched subject. These are results of the changing political and economic dynamics. Awareness of this state of affairs has brought about new forms of ethnographic writing with emphasis in some cases on a dialogical approach and others that highlight the author's subjectivity (see Nowak's ethnography on Tibetan refugees). The present work does not neatly fit into either of these styles of writing. The attempt has not been to tell the story of Tibetans through the single voice of one of my informants as in a Life History method which has been depicted as documenting 'the inner experience of individuals, how they interpret, understand, and define the world around them' (Faraday and Plummer 1979: 776). Wherever possible, the voices of Tibetans are represented through the use of direct quotations. Some of the sub-headings represent the collective voice or opinion of the respondents. Writing of this kind of research has involved the insertion of a personal narrative in the form of one's arrival at the field site, the initial reception by the inhabitants, the process of overcoming language barriers and resistance. Though these personal narratives exist only in the margins of the formal ethnographic descriptions, these conventional opening narratives are not trivial. As Mary Louise Pratt remarks, 'They play the crucial role of anchoring that description in the intense and authority-giving personal experience of fieldwork.... Always they are responsible for setting up the initial positionings of the subjects of the ethnographic text: the ethnographer, the native and the reader' (1986: 32). Aware of the experiential side to the field-based study, the inclusion of the personal narrative is done in order to reconcile the 'contradiction within the discipline between personal and scientific authority', a contradiction that had taken an acute turn 'since the advent of fieldwork as a methodological norm' (Pratt 1986: 32). As Clifford and Marcus state, 'Anthropological fieldwork has been represented as both a scientific laboratory and a personal "rite of passage". The two metaphors capture nicely the discipline's impossible attempt to fuse objective and subjective practices' (1986: 109).

In the context of the present research study, concerns for an appropriate style of writing were complicated by some of the political realities that contextualised the research process and the existential conditions of Tibetans in exile. 'Despite its frequent ahistorical – its synchronic – pretense, ethnography is historically determined by the moment of the ethnographer's encounter with whomever he is studying' (Crapanzano 1986: 51). Fear and caution informed refugee relationship with strangers. The fact that my ethnic background came to my aid in establishing rapport with the Tibetan refugees needs to be reiterated. Opening up to the researcher served their purpose of disseminating the refugee problem to the outside world. This study of the Tibetan refugees does assume that a chasm exists between the 'life-world' of the researcher and the researched subject (refugees). The belief is that this chasm would remain even till the end of the research process. It is prudent therefore to proceed towards making the relationship easy for the respondents at the fieldwork stage of the research process. The aim of the fieldwork has been to ferret out that much of data which is felt worthwhile to be taken notice of without being too intrusive.

Notes

1. Haddad (2004) in her paper contests the assumption of the refugee as a contemporary cousin of the pre-modern exile, arguing instead that refugees are a creation of modern territorial states bounded by clear political borders. Refugees rely for their existence on clearly defined ideas of inside and outside and as such are only fully intelligible within the pluralist system of separate sovereign states.

2. For an elaboration of this aspect, see United Nations, Office of the United Nations High Commissioner for Refugees, 'The State of the World's Refugees 1995: In Search of Solutions,' Oxford: Oxford University Press, 1995: 197.

3. For a detailed account of the history of legislation concerning refugees, see Grahl-Madsen 1966–72.

4. For a comprehensive analysis of refugee legislation leading up to the 1951 Refugee Convention, see Skran 1995.

5. These practices have connections to earlier forms of confinement; for example, quarantine and concentration camps.

6. For more on the inside/outside distinction, see Samaddar 2000: 200–14.

7. For an outline of the 'stages' of the refugee experience, see Keller 1975.

8. This realisation is the starting point for Daniel and Knudsen's essay on refugeeness and breach of trust (1995).

9. Positing a transhistorical refugee condition or experience becomes especially problematic when we think about displacement in relation to children, childhood and questions of memory and witnessing, asserts Malkki (1995).

10. For more on the connection between refugees and development discourse, see Harrell-Bond 1986.

11. Another interesting view into the development–displacement link in the African context is provided by the African Charter on Human and Peoples' Rights adopted by the Organisation of African Unity (OAU). According to Article 22 of this charter (known as Banjul Charter), '1. All Peoples shall have the right to their economic, social and cultural development with due regard to their freedom and identity and in thee equal enjoyment of the common heritage of mankind. 2. States shall have the duty, individually and collectively, to ensure the exercise of the right to development.'

12. For more on this, see Gold 1992.

13. Role of mediating cultures has been discussed by Ulf Hannerz in his analysis of the transnational urban swirl in *Cultural Complexity: Studies in the Social Organization of Meaning*, New York: Columbia University Press, 1992.

14. David Turton's admonishment that research into other's suffering can only be justified if alleviating that suffering is an explicit objective is worth noting while undertaking research on refugee groups. See Turton 1996: 96–110.

15. Scholars have generally been content to rely on figures offered by the two leading producers of refugee statistics—UNHCR and the US Committee for Refugees (USCR). Some limited discussion of the politics of refugee numbers can be found in 'The State of the World's Refugees: In Search of Solutions', UNHCR and Oxford University Press, 1995: 244–46.

16. See for instance 'Refugee Registration and Statistics', UNHCR Executive Committee paper, August 1998.

17. The legal conditions that govern movement of refugee populations in India and operative upon Tibetan refugees are complicated and will be discussed in Chapter 6.

18. The concept of integration is a problematic one. The UNHCR's definition of integration as 'the process by which the refugee is assimilated into the social and economic life of a new national community' is clearly unsatisfactory since it is tautological as it merely replaces the term to be defined with another word which is presumed to be synonymous. Barbara Harrell-Bond's definition is more suggestive here as it refers to 'a situation in which the host and refugee communities are able to co-exist, sharing the same resources – both economic and social – with no greater mutual conflict than that which exists within the host community' (1986: 7).

19. It has been claimed that self-settlement is inevitable for two reasons. First, all refugees could not possibly be accommodated in organised settlements because of insufficient funds. Second, organised settlements have largely failed to achieve the objective of economic self-sufficiency: the so-called land settlements have been unable to provide enough land for the settlers to make a living and 'wage earning' settlements provide only seasonal employment (Kok 1989: 420).

20. For more on the history of Indo-Tibetan trade, see Markham 1875: 299–315.

21. For more on the distribution of rural and urban population in the district of Darjeeling for 1991 and 2001, see District Statistical Handbook 2004 Darjeeling, pp. 17–22, published by Bureau of Applied Economics and Statistics, Government of West Bengal.

22. In the folklore of participant observation, key informants are almost heroic figures. They are the researcher's best friend in the field. Whyte's (1955) Doc is a notable example.

3

The Tibetan Exilic Paradigm*

In the introduction to the edited book *Exile as Challenge: The Tibetan Diaspora,* Bernstorff and Von Welck have remarked that the Tibetan community in exile since 1959 has performed three remarkable feats, notwithstanding the historical fact that they remained secluded from the rest of the world during the period known as the 'Great Game'[1] in the late nineteenth and early twentieth centuries. These are

> First, individual Tibetans and their families stand on their own feet economically and able to maintain themselves. Second, a school system has been built up which has transformed a large illiterate society into a fully literate society within two generations-a testament to the political will. Finally, the Dalai Lama introduced democratization and reduced his own power step by step, so much so, that in 2001 the prime minister of the Government in exile (Chief Kalon) is no longer appointed by the Dalai Lama but directly elected by the Tibetan diaspora. (Bernstorff and Von Welck 2004: 1)

The general perception about the Tibetans in India is that they are hardworking (Saklani 1984) and the reason for their success is that 'a part of the Tibetan society has been transplanted to South Asia with their own internal organisation, their culture and their leader' (Arakeri 1998). The decision to create settlements where the refugees could rebuild their lives has been exemplary (Bernstorff and Von Welck 2004: 1). This contrasts with other refugee groups who have lived in provisional camps for decades entirely dependent on assistance.[2] Such commendations are not uncommon and have been a consequence

* Previously published as Sudeep Basu, 'Generating Meanings in Exile', *Seminar: The Monthly Symposium,* April 2013, pp. 78–79 and as 'Reflections on the Tibetan Paradigm of Exile', available at http://refugeewatchonline.blogspot.in/2010/06/reflections-on-tibetan-paradigm-of.html. These articles have been modified by the author for the current volume.

of the general tendency to take sides in writing about Tibet and the Tibetan diaspora at the expense of a critical assessment of the Tibetan issue. Such a tendency has arisen partly from the importation of the functionalist model to the study of refugees (Stein's and Keller's works are an apt example of this tendency). As Liisa Malkii (1995b: 508) says, 'The implicit functionalism of much work in "refugee studies" is especially clear when one is dealing with questions of identity, culture, ethnicity, and "tradition." Again and again, one finds in this literature the assumption that to become uprooted and removed from a national community is automatically to lose one's identity, traditions, and culture'. This has had a marked categorical effect upon the study of Tibetan refugees wherein any cultural re-emergence or the presences of past cultural practices is interpreted as evidence of cultural continuity that gives an image of a refugee society that is supposedly stable and orderly. In this sedentarist analytical scheme, then, 'going home involves only the most minor cultural adjustment problems' (Stein 1981: 324). Malkki further problematises the notion of 'home'. 'First, one thinks of how this sedentarist bias unintentionally mirrors the increasingly elaborated nativism of anti-immigrant or xenophobic violence that often relies on the slogan "go home!" But if "home" is where one feels most safe and at ease, instead of some essentialized point on the map, then it is far from clear that returning where one fled from is the same thing as "going home". Second, recent work in other theoretical domains has shown how fraught the concept and lived experience of home can be and how little studied it is' (Malkki 1995b: 509).[3]

The field of refugee studies is dominated, for the most part, by functionalism which is based on the presumption that the loss of homeland is tantamount to the loss of cultural identity (Malkki 1995b). Another aspect is the uncritical use of the concepts of 'adaptation' and 'acculturation' to analyse processes of transformation in identity, culture and cultural tradition (Berry 1988; Gold 1992; Stein 1981).[4] In comparing Tibetans to other diaspora communities, Methfessel (1995: 19) makes the point that, 'at present, exiled Tibetans do not show the typically negative aspects of certain other diasporic groups living in a state of perpetual apathy', which Goldstein and others have termed the 'refugee syndrome' (1978: 397). He goes on to explain that among the many factors that have contributed to Tibetan's great accomplishment in exile is religion. He states that, 'Buddhist tenets proved to be very helpful in enabling to participate fully in the economic activities of their host societies' (1995: 19). When compared to many other refugee groups in Southeast Asia or in Africa, it seems that the Tibetans belong to those who have least suffered from the physical and psychological stress of uprooting (Morgan and Colson 1987: 6). The prominence of the psychological interpretations of displacement has been noted by Malkki who stresses that 'although many displaced people might benefit from the therapeutic interventions of psychiatry and psychology, psychologizing modes of knowledge and therapeutic forms of relationship have too often been unreflectively imported into the disciplinary toolkit of sociocultural anthropology or sociology, subtly reinforcing the depoliticizing and dehistorizing tendencies of the implicit functionalism that has been already noted' (Malkki 1995b: 510).[5]

The 'Shangri-La' imagery, as we have noted earlier, predominated any attempts at representing Tibet. The imagery implies a mythic place, figment of imagination, a real desire, an abode of peace, among others. Those writing on Tibet at present have to take cognisance of its rich and variegated legacy. This legacy has had deep implications in terms of the constructions of the self and the nation for Tibetans vis-à-vis their interlocutors. 'Western and Tibetan accounts have together played an important role in the development of an ideal Tibet and by transference, of an ideal Tibetan refugee' (Diehl 2002: 20). Much of the current discourse about self and representation is influenced by these styles of thinking and imaginings about Tibet. These have had a marked bearing on the way Tibetans are understood, being in exile. The rhetoric of solidarity, success and cultural preservation that is associated with Tibetan refugees is largely a product of the 'idealised' imagery of Tibet.[6] The romanticised imagery of Tibet and Tibetans tends to carry over into exile and in consequence, turn our attention away from the varied experiences that Tibetan refugees have in hostlands. Keila Diehl's work anticipates this lacunae in exile scholarship. Understanding silences in the exile community is crucial for her. In undertaking this exercise, she puts forward her intention, which is to avoid the representational pitfalls by giving a more balanced account of the Tibetan refugee experience. She points out that her task is to 'make more believable the accomplishments of this group by complementing those accounts with the tales of disillusionment, in-group tensions and change that make those accomplishments meaningful'. (Diehl 2002: 20).

The Shangri-La imagery brought with it a clear bias in scholarly attention towards understanding monastic orders in pre-exilic Tibet. Those materials which were brought by Tibetans into exile were carefully preserved to be assessed and translated for purposes of dissemination within the Tibetan populace and those interested in the study of Tibet and its people. These materials also happened to be predominantly religious in nature. The consequence of such a condition is reflective of the general orientation of those in exile who give priority to religious life over the non-religious realm of lay existence. However, decades in exile have produced a signal change in this way of looking at the Tibetan world in exile.[7]

While retaining the focus on the religious aspect, there is a growing anthropological and sociological interest in Tibetan culture in exile since the mid-1970s. Almost two decades into exile, refugees from Tibet came to realise that their exile was a protracted condition. They began to grow roots in their country of arrival and the camps were to stay, at least for the time being. Tibet was out of bounds for all up until the end of the Cultural Revolution and the death of the Mao Tsetung in 1976. This scenario changed with the opening of the borders which paved the way for some Westerners to visit Tibet. Shangri-La is being examined from the inside out as a rhetorical trope employed as frequently by Tibetans themselves as by Westerners. According to Kiela Diehl, 'After four decades in exile, many Tibetans realize not only that the utopian dream is still an important source of hope but also that it can be a source of disappointment and frustration that has very real effects on individuals and communities who are raised to feel responsible for its actual, though unlikely realization' (2002: 24). A shift in interests is notable, as Kiela Diehl stresses that the 'new scholarship on Tibetans critically examines not only the effects of scholarly biases but also the particular effects of the dominant paradigm of "cultural preservation" espoused by the Tibetan government-in-exile in Dharamsala on the everyday lives of refugees' (Diehl 2002: 24).

Forced Migration and Its Empirical Rendering

'Any study of refugee culture...necessarily problematizes the culture concept by exploring the processes of cultural maintenance and reconstruction required when a group of people (and their practices and beliefs) are unhooked from the reinforcing context of "their" place' (Diehl 2002: 8). In the 1990s, 'Displacement' became an intellectual metaphor with tremendous momentum. Clearly, much of the literature of this period pointed to uprootedness, transgression, multiculturalism, boundary crossing and hybridity following from the notion of global flows. These notions singularly challenged the disciplinary assumptions about boundedness and the maintenance of social order. Keila Diehl takes note of the same and recognises how few ethnographic works on refugees have been undertaken so far in the academia.

Diehl, who was aware of the distance between scholarship on displacement and the people whose experiences actually inspired and generated the current trends, stated, 'My own prioritization of ethnographic detail is in itself a statement of concern regarding the overwhelmingly theoretical nature of the attention being paid to displacement in the social sciences and humanities. This study of echoes between cultures foregrounds a muffled dialogue between anthropology and cultural studies by examining the current interest in, even fetishization of displacement, marginality and multiculturalism; the normalization of expectations about how those conditions will be experienced and the colonization of the spaces of exile and diaspora by theories that are it sometimes seems losing touch with the histories and conditions of existence of displaced people in today's world' (Diehl 2002: 5). A few studies have addressed the local significance of and reactions to the flux and transience of exile. Diehl observed in her study, 'While the lives of Tibetan refugees could certainly be described in terms of hybridity and pastiche, these characteristics were often regarded as the very unfortunate consequences of refugee life, as embarrassing failures rather than as sources of pride. These natives were proving themselves to be far more conservative that I had been led to expect to find in a study of "culture on the road"' (ibid.: 4).

Liisa Malkki claims that displacement has in fact been pathologised as an aberration in our persistent 'national order of things' causing refugees in turn to be regarded as an abomination (in Mary Douglas's sense) that has been 'produced and made meaningful by the categorical order itself, even as they are excluded from it' (1995a: 6). She states, 'The construction of a national past is a construction of history of a particular kind; it is one that claims moral attachments to specific territories, motherlands or homelands and posits time-honored links between people, polity and territory…It is precisely the interstitial position of refugees in the system of nation-states that makes their lives uniquely clarifying and enabling for the anthropological rethinking of nationness, of statelessness and of the interconnections between historical memory and national consciousness' (1995a: 1). Likening the 'structural invisibility' of displaced populations to that of Victor Turner's liminal personae, Malkki makes the observation that refugees are 'no longer unproblematically citizens or native informants. They can no longer satisfy as "representatives" of a particular local culture. One might say they have lost a kind of imagined cultural authority to stand for "their kind" or for the imagined "whole" of which they are or were a part' (1995a: 6). A counter to this position is the unique social and cultural location of the Tibetan refugees. The Dalai Lama's presence in the diaspora provides cultural authority, by virtue of which many Tibetan refugees regard themselves as more Tibetan or more authentic than their counterparts living in Tibet, who are getting sinicised. In this connection, Emily Yeh's paper, 'Will the Real Tibetan Please Stand Up! Identity Politics in the Tibetan Diaspora' (2002) brings a strong reflexive perspective to how Tibetans in both their homeland and in the diaspora in San Francisco, California attempt to categorise her and each other. 'Looking' Tibetan appears to be an all-important means of establishing solidarity in Tibet among the citizenry. Her research suggests that the Tibetan self is envisioned as an intuitive process, as defined by actors.

Diehl points to the tendency in Western scholarship of presenting exile as a 'literary, bourgeois state' (Said 1986: 121) or portraying it as a space having 'people without culture' (Rosaldo 1988: 79). Consequentially, theoretical exercises treat 'the displaced people as if they are out of mass politics' (Diehl 2002: 11). Support from sponsors has its flipside. Receipt of material and moral support from aid agencies and governments require that Tibetan refugees have had to show how well they have continued to maintain their identity and unique culture in exile until their return.[8] Accessibility to aid and sympathy requires acts of coping, adjustments and innovation.[9]

Even before the fascination with global flow took hold, the 'liminal' (Turner 1967) and 'marginal' enjoyed a privileged status in anthropology. Earlier structuralist efforts in ethnography celebrated and sought to decode the systemic unity of cultures and were therefore focused on the 'typical' or the 'normal' while today, culture making is generally understood in terms of a dialectic between creativity and constraints. The experience of displacement by refugees and other marginalised renders their 'taken-for-granteds' into highly negotiable practices in their new environments. They are therefore forced to acknowledge at some level that culture is constructed rather than 'natural'. Since they feel at odds with the status quo, they are better able to tell us what it is. Victor Turner articulated the seminal position on this notion of the special vantage point offered by marginality in his classic study of Ndembu ritual when he noted that the 'phenomena and processes of mid-transition expose the basic building blocks of culture just when we pass out of and before we re-enter the structural realm' (Turner 1967: 110).

Drawing from Turner's notion of the liminal that has 'set the agenda for the study of creativity in culture', Kiela Diehl elucidated the role of music in the lives of Tibetan refugees, exploring the connection between creativity and marginalisation, in particular the connection between artful expression and place. According to Kiela Diehl, 'The arts play a central role in officially choreographed and privately initiated efforts to entertain and "place" Tibetan refugees, to negotiate an essential or shared Tibetan identity in exile, to celebrate and preserve the diversity of Tibetan culture and to publicize the Tibetan cause internationally' (2002: 14).[10] She shows how in exile, for example, Tibetan performances such as public stagings of traditional folk operas (*Lhamo*) reminds exiled Tibetans that they are not at home. At the same time, Tibetan exiles participate in a moment in which sounds, images and feelings fleetingly coalesce to create a place that feels like home, so that, potentially, 'the expression of the desire for home becomes a substitute for home and embodies the emotion attendant upon the image' (Seidel 1986: 11). According to Kiela Diehl, 'Many exilic performances comprise a continual ritual reenactment of the memories of displacement, violence and loss that are central to the shared experience of exile, memories that bond the Tibetan diasporic community together' (2002: 14).

Constructing the Rich Cultural Heritage of Tibet

Various studies point to how Tibetans in exile have successfully maintained their traditional culture in the midst of an alien host environment, by resisting assimilation, the Dalai Lama's leadership and continued support from international aid agencies and sponsors (Diehl 2002: 64).[11] Since 1959, one of the primary concerns of the exiled Dalai Lama and the Tibetan refugee community has specifically been to preserve the 'rich cultural heritage of Tibet'.[12] This attention to the preservation of linguistic, religious and artistic knowledge through both documentation and education (Nowak 1984) was prompted by two legitimate threats: the disappearance of Tibetan culture in the homeland under Chinese rule[13] and the disappearance of exiled Tibetans into their host societies. Generally, the 'preservation' rhetoric informs policy-making emanating from the Dharamsala administration, as well as the everyday exilic life in the matters of habits, rituals, and language use.

Innumerable policy dictates by the Tibetan government-in-exile have had conservative predilections. Oftentimes, this has spilled over into the 'private' domains of making choices in one's daily life, including language use, habits of dress, marriage ceremonies and food preparation. The apparatus of the exile government has been geared towards preserving culture as a means to maintaining the hope of returning[14] to the homeland. Tibetan refugees born in exile are taught to remember the experiences of others in order to keep alive the memory and lived experience of 'Tibetanness' and to cultivate a shared sense of loss and victimisation. For these Tibetans, Tibet is an idea of a land inconsistently informed by official efforts in exile to preserve and teach traditional culture, images from foreign-made documentary films and coffee table books, political and economic information from newspaper clippings, and the firsthand stories from older relatives, tourists and new arrivals.[15] In Tibet, the memories of Tibetans struggle against the 'forced forgetting' (Connerton 1989: 15) imposed by the Chinese; in exile, Tibetans deal with self-protective, opportunistic or time-induced forgetting by developing what Diehl calls 'tutored mindfulness' (Diehl 2002: 66).

In exile, as Keila Diehl states, 'the sense of history, identity and responsibility is conveyed to young Tibetans and is reinforced in others through narratives and performances in schools and other institutional settings...While a great amount of traditional knowledge is still transmitted in refugee homes, it is in the public sphere that such casual tacit or explicit articulations of the "old ways" are confirmed and consolidated outside the homeland' (2002: 66). The entire effort on the part of the community in exile is to emphasise and display endurance, connections and stability as an immediate response to their uprooting. Protracted exile produces gaps in shared memory and difference, which make Tibetans even more conscious of their self in everyday exilic life. Here, one is bound to, as Naficy states, 'reassure the self that it will not disappear or dissolve in exile' (1993: 118) through performances. The efforts of many native and foreign commentators to document Tibetan culture in exile have been descriptive evaluations based on a time and space-bounded notion of the 'rich cultural heritage of Tibet' that is itself dependent on a binary of 'preservation' and 'loss'. 'This framework, which ignores or devalues nonhegemonic, hybrid and popular foreign practices or points them out only as evidence of cultural decay does little to account for the complex mosaic of cultural practices that are continually being constructed in exile through the choices and circumstances of even the most "traditional" Tibetan refugees and that constitute their everyday reality' (Diehl 2002: 67). This popular framework with its interest in 'pure survivals' does little to account for the rich diversity of pre-1950 Tibetan culture and is closely related to the attachment to the image of Tibet as an unchanging, medieval 'Shangri-La'. According to Kiela Diehl, it 'ignores the fact that appearing "unchanged" in keeping with dominant understandings of the "originary" or "traditional" often requires making significant and ongoing changes' (2002: 67).

Presenting Tibet in Exile

In her important ethnographic work with Hutu refugees in Tanzania and her theoretical reconsideration of the notion of 'uprootedness', Malkki describes Mishamo, a refugee camp, as a 'site that was enabling and nurturing an elaborate and self-conscious historicity among its refugee inhabitants' (1995a: 52). She goes on to explain that the Hutu history represented in the camp (not unlike that generated through public performances in Dharamsala) was 'not only a description of the past, nor even merely an evaluation of the past, but a subversive recasting and reinterpretation of it in fundamentally moral terms. In this sense, it cannot be accurately described as either history or myth. It was what can be called a mythico-history.... The mythico-history was . . . a process of world making because it constructed categorical schemata and thematic configurations that were relevant and meaningful in confronting both the past in Burundi and the pragmatics of everyday life in the refugee camp in Tanzania. In both cases, the mythico-historical world making was an oppositional process; it was constructed in opposition to other versions of what was ostensibly the same world, or the same past' (1995a: 54–55). It appears that the experience of displacement, of multiple physical, social and emotional transformations, has fuelled in Tibetan refugees a certain 'consciousness of historicity', to use Gramsci's term. Gramsci maintained that such consciousness spurs self-knowledge, disallows passive acceptance of the status quo and creates a resistance to processes of 'naturalization'. Diehl (2002: 81) notes how exile fuels among the Tibetans a certain 'consciousness of historicity, using Gramsci's felicitous phrase. In the face of relentless Chinese onslaught, Tibetans have become conscious of their Tibetanness and have continually rejected Chinese claims on Tibet, particularly the more vociferous Tibetan Youth Congress'. She further observes that, 'owing to political pressure to maintain a unified force in the diaspora and/ or out of desperation for community and continuity, the experience of extended displacement has, in fact, increased their acceptance of the status quo in Dharamsala and their dependence on official public representations, despite an increase in historical self-consciousness. One result of this pressure to present a unified image and to feel unified has been the development of not only a shared master narrative about Gelugpa history and the events leading up to the Dalai Lama's flight from Tibet in 1959, but also a widely shared aesthetic sensibility regarding the "authentic" and the "traditional"' (ibid.: 81).

Although there is diversity within the core of the Tibetan refugee community, shared understandings of the 'traditional' and the 'authentic', essentially the 'Tibetan', lead to ways of getting to or sorting out what is meaningful or ideal for the community and what is not. 'This sorting-out process can lead to a notion of ethnicity imagined along a continuum between purity (ethnic integrity) and pollution (hybrid identity)' (Diehl 2002: 85). The older generation in exile, those who escaped from central Tibet more than 40 years ago, embody the old ways in their language, dances, religious practice, garments and lifestyles. 'They include the majority of individuals for whom personal experience and lived knowledge are in synch with the dominant memory selected and promoted within the official paradigm of preservation' (Diehl 2002: 85). The *chang ma* singing at weddings, the goldsmith who drinks his everyday tea out of an elaborate silver and porcelain goblet worthy of the aristocrat in old Lhasa, the heavy felt boots and wool *chuba* worn right through Indian summers are the ways that are revered as fundamental to the 'continual distillation and disciplining of ... categorical purity'.[16] Malkki's observations concerning how displacement can become a 'form of categorical purity' (1992: 35) are also helpful in understanding how and why many Tibetan refugees perceive themselves as 'more Tibetan' than Tibetans in contemporary Tibet and further assume the authority to imagine what a modern, free Tibet should look like in the future.[17] In the Hutu case, Malkki observed, 'being a refugee, a person was no longer a citizen of Burundi and not yet an immigrant in Tanzania. One's purity as a refugee had become a way of becoming purer and more powerful as a Hutu. The "true nation" was imagined as a "moral community" being formed centrally by the "natives" in exile' (1992: 35). In this connection, in an article comparing the performances and motivations of Tibetan drama troupes from Chinese-run Tibet and Tibetan-run Dharamsala, Calkowski articulates the grounds on which each group respectively bases its authority to represent Tibetan culture.

Using Malkki's notion of 'mythico-history', Diehl writes, that, 'the production and transformation of the mythico-history[18] of Tibetan refugees involves judgments and a degree of consensus regarding how the "past" should be articulated within the present' (1992: 96). The inevitability of exile is change—sudden and, at times, transformative. This has, as Kiela Diehl observes, a direct impact on traditional Tibetan art and performances, which has as its purpose the need to preserve that which threatens to disappear in exile. (1992: 96). Based on his research with Tibetan refugees, P. Christiaan Klieger has concluded that 'it is the context of interaction, not the content, which in appearing to remain traditional, provides a perceived continuity with the past' (1989: 366). While the context and the impression of continuity are certainly crucial, few works have shown which cultural practices are and are not acceptable to whom. This study seeks to clarify the limits of the remarkable adaptability[19] noted in this refugee community.

Traditionality and the Tibetan Institutional Structure in Exile

Corlin has observed that the 'refugee administration is consciously endeavouring to incorporate traditional institutions in the refugee organization (this being in line with their general policy of guarding Tibetan culture)', and that the political organisation of the exile communities is 'largely founded on traditional customs under an apparently modern clothing' (Corlin 1975: 144). The CTA has, however, also been instrumental in the establishment of new institutions, such as the parliament, the Assembly of Tibetan People's Deputies and the modern Tibetan school system. Until now, the emphasis of most of the works on Tibetan society in exile has been to highlight the role of the CTA in the reestablishment and maintenance of traditional institutions with little consideration given to refugee agency in the creation of new viable Tibetan communities in exile. This is reflective of a general trend in the representations of refugee problems in which the narrative of 'victimhood' predominates. Pradip Bose, in the introduction to the edited book *Refugees in West Bengal* states, 'The fixed identity that the narrative of victimhood seeks to impose upon the refugees is in fact unstable, because in their multiple efforts to come to terms with the new situations, the agentive subjects have to negotiate a very complex arena of possible give and take and choices' (2000: 1). He has also noted that the central institutions related to the aspirations and an expectation of the refugees is the state and its agencies deployed for the care and welfare of the refugees. In this connection, Karen Jacobsen's (1996) article discusses the policy responses of asylum governments to the mass influx of refugees, which have varied considerably. The article explores why some host governments respond in relatively generous ways while other governments act restrictively. The policy alternatives available to governments are classified which include costs and benefits of accepting international assistance, relations with the sending country, political calculations about the local community's absorptive capacity and national security considerations. Host governments also struggle with bureaucratic politics, the position of refugees in domestic politics, power struggles among government ministries and among policymakers, and paucity of information that must be teased out at the empirical level.

In the case of the independent communities (that is, communities not under the administration of the CTA), these are, to a greater extent than the centrally administered settlements, organised on the basis of the regional origin of the inhabitants and the aim of their establishment has been to create social environments where traditional interaction could be perpetuated (Strom 1995).[20] According to Strom, 'When a group of people are displaced and transferred to a radically different natural and social environment, the threat of social disintegration and cultural discontinuity are strongly imminent and the task of establishing new, viable communities is therefore a great challenge' (1995: 32). Within a span of a few years, the refugees from Tibet became self-supporting and emerged as 'one of the most successful refugee communities in the world'.[21] This estimate has been corroborated by social scientists who have studied the Tibetan refugees since 1966.

Melvyn Goldstein's (an American anthropologist working on Tibet) arrival at Bylakuppe in Karnataka, India, in early 1966 to undertake fieldwork among Tibetan refugees was a significant event, as Dawa Norbu (2004: 190) notes. Documenting early life in exile has its benefits from the point of view of policy and research. Goldstein's observations were that the refugees at Bylakuppe had 'become a tremendous economic success' (1978: 399). Goldstein notes that pathological behaviour in the form of mental or emotional disorders or alcoholism was absent (ibid.: 403). He observed very little manifestation of the dysfunctional behaviour commonly associated with the 'refugee syndrome'. There was little incidence of mental and emotional disorders, and no incidence of alcoholism (Goldstein 1978: 403).[22] Girija Saklani did extensive fieldwork and research among Tibetan refugees living in Dharamsala, New Delhi and Dehradun and her findings are similarly positive. She wrote that Tibetans have, on the whole, 'successfully emerged from a self-sufficient barter economy into a competitive economy and have adjusted to the new situation which is a tribute to the Tibetan community in exile' (1984: 216). She gives three reasons for the Tibetan success in India. First, the Tibetans are hard-working people. Second, their womenfolk also work as hard as men, if not more. Third, the Tibetans have a natural instinct for trading (Saklani 1984: 219).

That the new communities in the diaspora are characterised by a remarkably high degree of cultural continuity is noted by Strom (1995: 32). There is a definite conception of 'continuity', which Strom brings to his study of Tibetan refugees. According to Strom,

> Continuity necessarily implies change and this is all the more so in a situation where people are exposed to alternative worldviews and social forms. As cognitive and social contexts change, so does the significance of customs and institutions. Continuity is thus a process, an outcome of the interplay between conceptions and experience. The development of institutions must therefore be analyzed with reference to their past as well as to their present situation; namely, their former and contemporary natural, social and cognitive context. (1995: 34)

This allows us to rethink notions of place and space in theorising about refugees. Tibetan educated youths relate to the contexts of tradition and modernity in ways that are different from non-refugees. Works that identify the problems in delineating the contours of these contexts as they pertain to exile are few.[23]

The idea of Tibet is a mental concept, what Anderson (1991) has designated an 'imagined community', serving as a context for an emerging national identity among all groups of refugees. Anderson's imagined community has been referred to by Corlin (1975) as the 'Nation in your mind', a phrase which is preferred by Strom for its applicability to the Tibetan case. What is brought out perceptively is that the 'imagined' context is conceptualised in different ways by those who were brought up in Tibet and those who were born in India. 'The difference is related to the issues of experience, memory and habitus[24] on the one hand versus reflexivity and cultural construction on the other' (Strom 1995: 35). One needs to keep in mind the complex web of meanings associated with culture and tradition, even when they are museumified and institutionalised. The traditionality is as much a result of conscious elite strategy as it is of habitus (Anand 2000: 278).

Monastic Institutions in Exile

Sherab Gyatso in his article 'Of Monks and Monasteries' writes, 'In the exiled community despite the undoubted decrease in wealth and political influence, the monastic visage whilst perhaps battered and bruised remains both recognizable and supremely visible. Reinvention and reform are definitely not the order of the day here. Rather, it is in very familiar guises that the Tibetan monk and the monastery have re-established positions for themselves at the very heart of the new society' (2003: 213). Continuity is the core concept in the monastic traditions. In the monastic context, the notion of spiritual transmission serves as an assurance of the validity and authenticity of doctrines, social organisation and ritual practice.[25]

Tradition is an embodied experience in the monastic order of things. Much of what existed as monastic life in Tibet, which was ritually ordered, continues with little modification. As Axel Strom (1995: 36) notes, 'The novices are brought up by older monks, many of whom were raised in Tibet and a dominant feature of their socialization into monastic life is the memorization of the ritual texts which form the basis of their future ritual practice. Collective prayers and recitations are performed daily in monastery or in the home of the sponsor. Large rituals are performed on special occasions in honour of the protective deities and the lineage ancestors of the various orders. In the institutions for higher education, particularly those of the Gelugpa order, the traditional, ritualized debate (*rig lam*) is the major method of learning'.[26]

Strom observes that the most significant impact of sociocultural change in the diaspora is an altered pattern of recruitment of monks, as proportionally fewer parents are sending their sons to become monks. Another seems to be an increasing defection of young monks who have been recruited as children.[27] According to the latest census figures,[28] which exclude native monk populations in places such as Ladakh, Spiti, Sikkim, Nepal and so forth, the combined Tibetan monk population of India and Nepal is 11,067. The number of Buddhist monasteries of the same group is 218. It is a truism that monasticism was accorded the highest value in pre-exilic Tibet. It was desirable for a family to send at least one male to the monasteries, a practice that has eroded over time in exile. Few members of the refugee community are part of the monk order. However, the new arrivals from Tibet since the 1990s, most of whom are monks, continue to provide fresh recruits into the monasteries, after settling into host conditions.[29]

Strom observes (1995: 40) that, 'In the first decade after their reestablishment, the monastic institutions in India had a relatively small population but they were not affected by a decline in recruitment or defection. The reasons were that the processes of sociocultural change in the diaspora had not gained momentum and that they recruited many monks from the Buddhist societies of the Himalayan region (who prior to 1959 were sent to Tibet for higher education).' The Cultural Revolution (1966–76) sealed off Tibet from the rest of the world. All the Tibetans in exile could do was to create a society where they could live the Tibet of their imagination. As Sherab Gyatso observes, it is 'in the diaspora that the lay community and the monks were thrown together. As time progressed, the monks gradually extricated themselves once more with the surviving member of many of the former monasteries in Tibet re-establishing their old centres' (2004: 215). This situation was not to remain; by the 1980s, there was a steady trickle of people, particularly monks, from Tibet into exile with the partial opening up of the border between India and China (Gyatso 2004).

Strom observes that the monks from Tibet now constitute the majority whereas the monks from India are proportionately reduced to a small and decreasing minority. The monks from Tibet are predominantly youths or adults who have chosen monastic life as are the majority of the monks recruited from the diaspora (1995: 41). These groups are set apart from each other in terms of background, habits and experience. The Indian-bred monks are more urbane, having received modern or monastic education, whereas the monks arriving from Tibet since the 1970s had a rural upbringing, not having received elementary school education in Tibet. Therefore, in general, newcomers accept the status quo of the institutions; that is they voice no need for structural changes, the introduction of new subjects and other modifications. In this sense, they represent no challenge to the institution and its dominant elders. Strom noted that some of the young diasporic monks even voice the suspicion that a segment of the newcomers had been sent by the Chinese in order to make trouble. The difference between the two groups is augmented by the fact that most of the newcomers are relatively old when they come to India. They are then too old to join the monastic schools and therefore rarely introduced to subjects other than Buddhist philosophy. As few of them learn Hindi, English or other modern subjects, they remain isolated from Indian society.

Tibetan monastic institutions in India are small in size, unlike the huge monasteries dotting Tibet such as the Drepung, Sera and Ganden monasteries, among others. As an institution, these monasteries in India try to replicate the organisational and ritual practices in vogue prior to 1959, although in a miniaturised form. The latter are institutions devoted to higher education. These are of several kinds, which may be classified as follows: 1) The Gelugpa monasteries: Ganden, Drepung and Sera (Densa sum); 2) a) The Nyingmapa, Kagyupa and Sakyapa *shedra*, b) The Institute of Buddhist Dialectics (IBD). Whereas the other shedra are specialised schools for higher education, Densa sum[30] are also monasteries with particular ritual traditions as well as communities consisting of houses constituted on the basis of the regional origin of members. Densa sum are large independent institutions with a highly decentralised internal structure. These are crucial differences which account for the fact that the shedra of the three oldest orders have undergone much greater changes in India than Densa sum, particularly in terms of educational organisation (Strom 1995: 42).[31]

In contrast to the traditional education of the monastery proper, the education of Sera Je school is organised according to modern principles of school administration. However, it also functions as a traditional monastic school aimed at the memorisation of religious texts. The school thus represents an interface between the two contexts: the old and the new, or Tibet and the West.

Tibetan Government-in-Exile

Government and administration were set up in a relatively short time. Phuntso notes the train of events following the Dalai Lama's arrival in India. 'On 25 April 1959, the Dalai Lama called an emergency meeting of the few senior Tibetan officials who had accompanied him from Tibet into exile and those who had arrived earlier in India to discuss the situation and plan for the reconstruction in exile. The meeting was held in Mussoorie, which served as the Dalai Lama's initial headquarters. The meeting identified a few areas of concentration: rehabilitation of the Tibetan refugees, education of Tibetan children, preservation of Tibetan culture and identity, gathering and disseminating information regarding Tibetans both inside and outside Tibet, pursuing the Tibetan question at the United Nations and preserving and promoting unity among the Tibetan refugee community' (Phuntso 2004: 134). Soon after the meeting, the Dalai Lama re-established the Tibetan government-in-exile[32] to meet both the immediate and long-term needs of the Tibetan people. The Dalai Lama said, 'In 1959, when I escaped with a few cabinet ministers, the Tibetan government, which has a history of three hundred years also came into exile. The exiled Tibetan government is not a new creation. Wherever the Dalai Lama resides, the Tibetan people consider that as the seat of the Tibetan government'.[33] The Tibetan government-in-exile is the official face of the Tibetan independence movement, dedicated to both representing Tibetan exiles and presenting the Tibetan case for independence or 'genuine autonomy' (Ardley 2002: 42). The principal concern of an exile organisation is how to create and expand national loyalty and international support (Shain 1989). In 1960, the Dalai Lama established the Assembly of Tibetan People's Deputies (ATPD). This legislature was to replace the diarchy of equivalent monastic and secular offices that had existed in pre-exilic Tibet, as well as removing all hereditary privileges from government. In principle, the CTA was based on a democratic principle. The CTA faces problems in securing national loyalty with the exile Tibetan community. Their support for the CTA is more determined by loyalty towards the institution of the Dalai Lama. The exile administration has to manoeuvre within a complex political situation (Roemer 2008: 183).

Exilic Orientations

For Tibetan refugees, the dominant framework for thinking about and attempting to understand exile is the Buddhist doctrine of reincarnation and its promise of eventual release through good action and compassion. The idea of 'taking refuge' is also, in addition to beliefs in reincarnation, a cornerstone of Tibetan culture. Since the 1950s, the idea of taking refuge has taken on a highly politicised level of meaning for Tibetans. Buddhism encapsulates Tibetan life so much so that for Tibetan refugees, the idea of living in exile , of 'taking refuge', was made sense of through the idiom of religion; in particular, the doctrines of reincarnation, karma and compassion. It took on a politicised form later. Nevertheless, spiritual practice provided the inner resources, exemplified in the figure of the Dalai Lama in facing the odds.

In an effort to characterise how Tibetan refugees deal with the experience of exile, it is not sufficient to stop at the formal Buddhist belief and practice. According to Kiela Diehl, 'Assuming a correspondence between the philosophical ideals of a culture's religious paradigm and the attitudes of the general population is neither ethnographically accurate nor fair to lay Tibetans, as such expectations are virtually impossible to meet. Such assumptions which are not uncommon in contemporary accounts of Tibetans may well be an act of transference that says more about the desires of Western Tibetophiles than about Tibetans themselves' (2002: 113).

While the Dalai Lama asserts that when you are a monk, any place that is habitable becomes your country, most lay Tibetans in exile, as Diehl has observed in her study, feel deeply out of place and often fearful in India.[34] In exile, Naficy has written 'Home colonizes the mind' (1991: 111). The Tibetan case is no exception to this tendency since the orientation towards homeland has dominated most scholarship and discourse about Tibetan refugees (Diehl 2002: 110). Few studies grapple with or even acknowledge the Indian context in which the exile experience takes place. Most works written about Tibetan life in exile fail to bring to the fore the Indian context, both at the local and supra-local levels, in which the exile experience takes place. Analysis is comparative in nature, where a Tibetan refugee settlement in the diaspora is described in relation to pre-exilic Tibet (Palakshappa 1978; Saklani 1984).

Saklani selected 265 respondents from three scattered communities in north India (Dharamsala and Clement Town in Himachal Pradesh, and Majnukatila in Delhi) to look at changes in social structure and institutional patterns. Although Saklani makes general conclusions about the settlements in India, the selection of these three locations is not representative of the Tibetan refugee community. Both are descriptive studies and data is only analysed as frequency tables. With a focus on the host society, Kiela Diehl elsewhere writes,

> The shared disdain of many westerners and Tibetan refugees for the day-to-day realities of India-hardship, corruption, poverty and filth is an important ingredient in the often-romantic collusion between these groups. Focused as Tibetans and their Western supporters are on preserving and gaining access to an ideal Tibetan way of life, India must it seems be suppressed and reduced to a temporary and unfortunate backdrop for the struggle with the result that a blind eye has been turned to the myriad

> ways in which India and Indians are in fact integral to any understanding of contemporary Tibetan culture or identity in exile. (2002: 110)

Following along the lines of P. Christiaan Klieger's observation, 'it is the oppositional process which has kept Tibetans Tibetan' (1989: 4), Diehl focuses on some of the ways Dharamsala refugees oppose themselves to otherness within the Tibetan population itself.[35]

Hamid Naficy has noted that refugee narratives often have 'dual and apparently contradictory roles to communicate and celebrate continuity and to highlight discontinuities, to authenticate the past and point to its legacy and to discredit the present' (Naficy 1993: 151). Kiela Diehl's attempt in her study has been to highlight the effects of the accompanying 'discrediting of the present'. Based on her observations, she continues,

> While events like the annual spring opera festival in Dharamsala bring most members of the community together, the round dances and songs that always follow special religious events, mark holidays, bless weddings and welcome in new years more often reveal and confirm the camaraderie of smaller communities within the larger exile community. Indeed the hesitancy of most Tibetans to jump spontaneously into a dance during a public celebration may point to a general professionalization of traditional Tibetan arts over time due to a learned sense that these forms of expression are so important, even sacred, that ordinary folk cannot be trusted to do them correctly. (2002: 98)

Calkowski elsewhere voices a fear of unclear boundaries or undesirable influences typical of conservative preservation efforts. 'Contemporary tape recordings from Tibet, India, Switzerland and the United States offer conflicting examples of inscribed tradition and various stage performances in the West mixing Tibetan artistes who embody tradition with those who pursue Eurasian pop and with those reflecting their Chinese musical training, blur genres for uneducated Western and Tibetan audiences' (1997: 57). Since 1959, Tibetan refugees have been engaged in an ongoing 'confrontation of representations' (McLagan 1996) with Chinese officials in which the two sides compete to legitimise their own representations of Tibetan history as well as current events in Tibet. In recent years, a new dimension to the confrontation has emerged with the display of culture becoming one of the most important means through which Tibetan and Chinese claims to legitimacy are contested. Tibet activists' use of cultural and religious performances for political purposes reflects the global emergence of 'culture' as a favoured idiom of political mobilisation for indigenous, minority and diasporic groups (Turner 1993). The foremost objective of the Tibetan refugees in exile was to preserve Tibetan Buddhism not only as a way of life, but also as a mode of preserving Tibetan identity. The Dalai Lama exhorted Tibetans to maintain their traditions for the sake of Tibetans living in Tibet. This narrative of nurturing and preserving culture was also voiced by the Tibet House.

Early encounters with sympathetic aid workers in India and Nepal and with Western travellers reinforced Tibetans' awareness of their culture as an asset and as a potentially important resource in the struggle to gain independence.[36] Dorsh de Voe has observed, 'the refugee context has provided a chance for Tibetans to experience themselves as unique and to observe how widely sought after are the products and precepts of their religion and cultural heritage' (1987: 60). McLagan notes that following this logic, the Dalai Lama has repeatedly claimed that for him, the Tibet issue is not a political matter but a spiritual struggle. The Dalai Lama states, 'For more than a thousand years Tibetans have been custodians of the full range of the Buddha's teachings. These have been analysed, refined and most important of all put into practice, becoming the mainstay of Tibetan culture. We have had a responsibility to preserve our living culture, not just to our brothers and sisters who remain in Tibet, but also to the world at large' (Council for Religious and Cultural Affairs of H.H. the Dalai Lama 1991: 5). By equating the Tibet issue with the preservation of Tibet's spiritual heritage, a particular construction of Tibetan culture itself becomes the object of political action (McLagan 1995: 73).

Notes

1. The Great Game involved the countries of British India, Russia and China.
2. One is reminded of the refugee camps in parts of Africa, such as Sudan and Tanzania, where refugees have to live out their lives for decades in camps.

3. For more on the question of 'home', see Bammer 1992; Massey 1992; Peck 1995.

4. The application of the concepts of adaptation and acculturation to the study of Tibetan refugees is marked; see, for example, Subba 1990; Arakeri 1998; Saklani 1984; Methfessel 1995.

5. For more on the psychological disorders among refugees, see Sandler and Jones (eds) 1987; Keller 1975.

6. Tibet was for many a 'forbidden' land by virtue of its vague political status nestled among three great empires, its naturally enclosing topography and conscious efforts by Tibetans to remain uncontaminated by the outside world.

7. For more on the role of religious institutions among exiles, see Gellek Tsering, 'The Role of Buddhist Institutions in the Tibetan Diaspora', in Feinstein International Famine Center, Working Paper no. 4, September 2001.

8. Many Tibetan refugees, especially schoolchildren, monks and nuns, receive financial support from individual Western sponsors either privately or through institutionally managed arrangements; see de Voe 1983 and Klieger 1992.

9. Meg McLagen (1996) examines the kinds of 'willful misunderstandings' that exist between Tibetans and their Western supporters in the activist context. She argues that both groups operate with sets of assumptions, perceptions, constructions of the other that are often incorrect but serve to advance their mutually shared goal of promoting the Tibetan Cause.

10. The Chinese have also aggressively harnessed the energy and appeal of Tibetan style folk performances (Lhamo) for their own political ends; see Calkowski 1995: 51–57.

11. Dorsh Marie de Voe, in her article 'Framing Refugees as Clients' (1981), discusses the historical roots and the mutually beneficial dynamics of contemporary Western financial support of Tibetan refugees. In Christiaan Klieger's analysis of Tibetan nationalism as a modern manifestation of 'patron-dyad', it is argued that the refugees have been able to retain their status by converting the whole exile community as belonging to client category.

12. Soon after his arrival in exile, the Dalai Lama founded a number of institutions at several levels for the preservation of Tibetan culture. The Tibetan Institute of Performing Arts was the first one established in 1959; the Central Institute for Higher Tibetan Studies in 1969; the Library of Tibetan Works and Archives at Dharamsala since 1971; the Norbulingka Institute and the Tibet House in Delhi (1965) represent Tibetan culture in the Diaspora.

13. For an insight into the Tibetan government-in-exile's perspective on contemporary Tibet see 'Tibet under Communist China', Department of Information and International Relations, Central Tibetan Administration,

Dharamsala 2001; see Adams (1996) for a discussion of karaoke and modernity.

14. For more on the problem of 'return', see Zetter 1994: 307–22. He argues that the ambiguous identity of the refugees as both insiders and outsiders and the protracted political uncertainty of their status give contradictory messages about the likely scale, processes and success of their return.

15. Recently, there is a growing interest towards the effect of the Internet on Tibetan attitudes; see Samphel 2004: 167–85.

16. This is the notion used by Malkki (1995a: 223) in relation to the Hutu refugees in Tanzania, which is akin to Diehl's notion of 'perceived ethnic integrity'.

17. This is evident from the many booklets that come out from the Department of Information and foreign Affairs, Planning Commission and the Department of Home, Tibetan government-in-exile and the Tibetan Parliamentary and Policy Research Centre (TPPRC).

18. The term 'mythico-history' is not, as Malkki explains, 'mythical in the sense of being false but in the sense of being concerned with order in a fundamental, cosmological sense' (1995a: 55).

19. Methfessel (1995: 16) mentions the three stages of socio-economic adaptation: physical survival, ethnic survival, and economic and social integration. The concept of 'adaptation' has also been used by T. B. Subba (1990) in his study of the Tibetan refugees in the Sikkim Himalayas.

20. One such example of an independent community is The Tibetan Refugee Community in Darjeeling. However, a Welfare Officer from the Tibetan government-in-exile is posted in Darjeeling town.

21. See The Dalai Lama, 'Inaugural Speech' in Conference-Cum-Workshop on Tibetan Refugees in India: A Report, Council for Home Affairs, Central Tibetan Secretariat, Dharamsala 1986.

22. For an elaboration of the theme of dysfunctional behaviour among refugees, see Cohon 1981: 255–75.

23. Strom uses the terms 'tradition' and 'modern' with reference to how they are currently employed by Tibetans in India.

24. What Strom considers fundamental to cultural continuity is the notion of the habitus coined by Bourdieu which means 'generative dispositions which produce "regulated improvisations" of conventional practices in accordance with the situation' (Bourdieu 1977: 72). Nowhere is habitus as predominant as in the monasteries, where a strong emphasis is laid on the continuity of ritual practice and doctrinal transmission.

25. For an elaboration of this topic, see Strom 1995.

26. For more on the monastic way of life among Tibetans in general, see Tucci 1980; Samuel 1993.

27. The cause of the latter problem has, by members of the clergy, been placed either in the attitude of the parents who sometimes take the children back because they need them or in the 'temptations of the modern world'.

28. See Planning Council, Central Tibetan Administration, Tibetan Demographic Survey 1998, vol. I, Dharamsala 2000: 106, 215. Monks and nuns combined are 12,297, that is, 12 per cent of the refugee population.

29. Saklani (1984), in her study, noted that 69 per cent of Tibetans continue to draw sustenance from their conviction that they left their country for the sake of 'saving their religion'.

30. Densa sum, the 'Three seats of learning', are in fact six monasteries since each of the three consists of two distinct 'colleges' (*tratsang*) which have separate economies and (apart from a common body) administrations as well as different curricula (as regards commentaries to the basic texts) and ritual traditions (Strom 1995).

31. For more on the monastic schools in general, see Dungkar 1993: 3–48.

32. For a detailed account of the Central Tibetan Administration, see Phuntso 2004: 125–35.

33. See His Holiness the Dalai Lama's keynote speech to the Second International Conference of Tibet Support Groups, Bonn (Germany), 14 June 1996, text in: A. A. Shiromany, 'The Political Philosophy of His Holiness the XIVth Dalai Lama', New Delhi: Tibetan Parliamentary and Policy Research Centre, 1998: 118.

34. Kiela Diehl arrives at this conclusion despite the results of one of Saklani's survey questions to which 75 per cent of the Tibetan refugees who responded chose 'India Only' as their choice of country of domicile (1984: 356).

35. The widespread evidence of this fact is the marginalisation of newly-arrived refugees in Dharamsala.

36. Among diasporic Tibetans, this awareness of 'culture' exists more strongly in Dharamsala than in any other Tibetan settlement in India. Several factors account for this, as Marcia Calkowski argues, 'The fact that Dharamsala's economy has become inseparable from the presentation and promotion of Tibetan culture' (1991: 645).

4

The Tibetan Question*

A Reappraisal

ARTICULATING TIBET

More than five decades have lapsed since the flight of the Dalai Lama from Tibet in March 1959 following the Chinese invasion of Tibet.[1] The Tibetans who accompanied him in large numbers to India and its neighbouring countries have now lived a major part of their lives in exile. Their children have been born and educated in their adopted lands, depending solely on the memories (Nora 1989) of the older generation for their knowledge of the 'Land of Snows'. Conway, who wrote in the mid-1970s (1975: 74) about the predicament of Tibetan refugees, stated, '... the Tibetans like other refugees have been confronted with two mutually contradictory pressures. If the Tibetan exiles seek to keep alive the idea of return, they must somehow prevent their thorough dispersion, in the hope that political conditions change in their favour. On the other hand, if refugees willingly accept the generous contributions of relief agencies and by their own endeavours, succeed in rehabilitating themselves in their host countries, they would inevitably be subject to pressures to assimilate with their host populations.' In the 1970s, the Dalai Lama had the hope and the belief that the political circumstances would change in favour of the Tibetans and it would not be long before he and his exile followers would be able to return to Tibet. As he told an audience at Bylakuppe, one of the Tibetan agricultural settlements in

* Previously published as Sudeep Basu, 'Interrogating Tibetan Exilic Cultures: Issues and Concerns', in *Readings in Indian Sociology Volume 9: Culture and Society*, Susan Visvanathan, ed., New Delhi: Sage Publications, 2013, pp. 58–81; and Sudeep Basu, 'Interrogating Tibetan Exilic Culture: Issues and Concerns', in *Sociological Bulletin: Journal of the Indian Sociological Society*, vol. 61, no. 2, 2012, pp. 232–54. The articles have been modified by the author for the current volume.

south India, a year before Conway published his article: 'It appears that within three to six years situations may be likely to change. We are now in a hopeful situation. Therefore, I urge you that everyone should struggle continuously for our common interest as we have done in the past and we should not lose our morale. In Tibet, not only the older people, but the younger people who accept communist ideology are opposed to Chinese aggression and thus have great moral strength to get Tibet back for the Tibetans. The whole Tibetan people have one common goal: the independence of Tibet'. However, the political events in the succeeding decades belied this hope and the Tibetans had to face squarely with the prospect of a protracted exile that necessitated, among other things, a reformulation of their strategy in exile centred around the idea of 'return'.

From the middle to the end of the twentieth century, the Tibet question has been one of the most controversial international political issues. This should not preclude our attention from the fact that Tibet had, for long, been the object of myth-making in many Western texts in the nineteenth and the twentieth centuries. To study fantasies about Tibet is to understand often mystifying and ideological processes. Also through these moments, when an image of Tibet is mobilised, a window is opened onto Western fears, hopes and desires. Metaphor and fantasy are revealed at every level of the construction of a text. Indeed, these and the participation in myth are inevitable aspects of any attempt to make meaning, to sustain belief and experience, irrespective of whether the perspective comes from scholarship, popular culture or personal experience. The notion of myth-making must be deepened beyond simple notions of right or wrong. Importantly, the kind of texts selected for study is deemed crucial. Opening ourselves to the diverse influences that Tibet exerts on our imagination requires not only a careful examination of select novels and short stories that provide an account of Tibet, but also newspapers and magazines that refer to Tibet (Dodin and Rather 2001). Notwithstanding the exploitative projections and ideological manipulations of the very idea of Tibet in fiction, we should not judge Tibet as a 'silent other' (Said 1979). Portraits of Tibet in fiction with its inevitable correlation between knowledge and power are often exploitative projections, ideological manipulations within an Orientalist milieu. With the turn of the twentieth century began a new kind of encounter between Tibet and the West, conjuring up a new set of fantasies.

James Hilton's classic of 1933, *Lost Horizon,* is the first Western novel to be located mainly in Tibet.[2] At this time, Western fantasies about Tibet and its religion had achieved their most coherent form (Bishop 1989). It was imagined as a land outside space and time. Tibet was like a fantasy world. Entering it was like going backwards in time and becoming ahistorical. It seemed to offer wisdom, guidance, order and everything that the West found wanting within its own civilisation. It is precisely within this order of thinking that Hilton's Shangri-la belongs. 'This complex utopian fantasy was however overshadowed by a sense of loss, a belief that traditional Tibet was doomed. The main threat was imagined as coming from an unstoppable process of globalization, producing a uniform, dreary materialism. In such an imaginative climate the utopian spiritual could no longer be entrusted to the literal geographical place. "The myth of Shangri La" was born, the hidden valley into which the essence of Western fantasies about Tibet was alchemically concentrated and distilled. In a period of environmental and cultural anxiety, Tibet as Shangri La was a fertile paradise in the midst of a global wilderness' (Bishop 2001: 209).

The romanticisation of Tibet gradually ceased by the mid-1960s, particularly in the West. Shangri-la was no longer a fantasy as before. The demystification of Tibet was underway with the coming of the technological age. It became difficult to keep a coherent view of Tibet in the Western imaginative framework with the exile of the Dalai Lama and lay Tibetans gradually getting ensconced in host lands. Only traces of pre-exilic Tibet remain. Yet, Tibet continues to serve as a productive site for Westerners to think about their own cultures and selves. As McMillin states, 'Western travellers have often expected something from Tibet... Thus when Pico Iyer writes about certain magical moments in Tibet in 1988 or Frederick Lenz dreams of spiritual transformation and snowboarding in "Surfing the Himalayas of 1997", they are participating in the myth of epiphany in Tibet' (McMillin 2001: 3).[3]

Donald Lopez (2001: 200) takes note of the 'various forms of overt fictionalizing about Tibet – novel, short stories, film and travel writing seem to follow their own specific, imaginative trajectories and the "new visuality" of Tibet (in works such a R. Jones Tung's *A Portrait of Lost Tibet*, 1980) that occurred in the 1930s, a break from the earlier practice of using aids such as sketchings and etchings for depicting Tibet that prevailed for over two hundred years'. By no means has Tibet always been portrayed simply as a Shangri-la. Since the 1940s, there has been some ambivalence towards Tibetan culture, generally refusing to characterise it either as a utopia or as a simple answer to Western problems and anxieties.

Political Representations of Tibet: Juxtaposing the Old and the New

Barnett (2001) observes that there is a tendency to view statements produced by political institutions in terms of outcome and policy rather than as images or representations. Instead, one should look at representations in terms of their functions and intended effects, for such political representations, he says, differ from literary works in that they include an implicit offer of certain benefits for their supporters if their proponents are able to acquire the power to put them into action.

As Barnett states, 'Statements produced by political institutions are often viewed in terms of outcome and policy rather than as images or representations. The prudent approach would be to look at representations in terms of their functions and intended effects. Political representations differ from literary works in that they include an implicit offer of certain benefits for their supporters if their proponents are able to acquire the power to put them into action, but they share the features of other forms of representation, among which is their tendency to contain contradictions that expose them to weaknesses and instabilities of one kind or another' (2001: 270).

Barnett tried to show how this process of inherent disintegration is especially marked and significant with regard to political representations and how it has led Tibetan leaders to seek constantly to adapt and modify the Western circulation of these views. Barnett was responding to the reductionist depictions of Tibetans engaged in the contemporary political and cultural domains as more or less trapped subjects of Western constructions.[4] Vincanne Adams elsewhere questioned contemporary Tibetans' 'authenticity', describing many of them as 'engaging in scripted simulations, becoming the sort of Tibetans desired by Chinese and Westerners by reproducing and enunciating the scripts of authentic Tibetanness produced by outsiders' (Adams 1996).

Admittedly, the 'Tibetan Question' has not generated a debate in the strict sense of the term, in which evidence-based arguments are put forward by opponents in the debate so that the most persuasive one prevails. Chinese and Western claims on Tibet differ from each other to begin with, but each side presents its case based on a strongly-held ideological position shared by members belonging to each group. No one is willing to hear the other speak. In the Chinese case, the appeal is made to the constituency which imagines China as a nation-state with its clearly-defined borders, while tracing its origins to some historical past.[5] In the case of Western sympathisers to the Tibetan cause, their appeals is based on some general human rights principle that puts premium on notions such as autonomy, self-determination of a people and religious or cultural freedoms that are lost due to foreign occupation.

Barnett points out that, 'Western political discourse about Tibet, in the sense of formal statements by political bodies and representatives, was quiescent throughout the 1970s, once China had achieved its rapprochement with the United States and had been readmitted to the UN in 1971; until then Tibet had been part of an anti-Chinese, Cold War agenda. Since the 1980s, the dominant form in which Tibet has been put forward in Western and exile political discussions has involved the image of a zone of specialness, uniqueness, distinctiveness or excellence that has been threatened, violated or abused' (2001: 273). The circulation of this image in recent political discussion seems to have stemmed largely from decisions made by the exile leadership at a series of meetings held between 1985 and 1987.[6] At these meetings, which followed the collapse of negotiations with the Chinese in 1984, the exile leaders for the first time asked the Dalai Lama to give political speeches abroad.[7] The representations of Tibet that emerged in Western discussions following the Dalai Lama's speeches[8] in the late 1980s focused on the uniqueness and violation of Tibet. In some more recent cases, the violation is seen as a result of advancing modernity or commercialisation in general, a view that implicitly exonerates the state as a perpetrator of abuse. Usually, this violation is identified with acts of violence or desecration that have been carried out by the Chinese authorities. That Tibet was a land increasingly getting violated was the stuff of many of the representations around Tibet that emerged in Western discourse. It is truism borne out of many of the reports on human rights violations that acts of violence and desecration have become all too common in Tibet's villages and towns. The other view is that it is the rapid urbanisation and the spread of Chinese forms of modernisation in general which are exclusionary, that violate the social body of Tibet. Echoing Donald Lopez's *Prisoners of Shangri La,* this idea of violation, as Barnett states, is linked to 'a perception of the place or the people as previously unimpaired and now desecrated for the first time. The images ensuing from this idea tends to disempower its subjects by implying that they are either victims who are incapable of standing alone, or collaborators in the act of violation' (2001: 273). Chinese representation views the barbarity of Tibet as requiring civilising. The paramount imagery in Chinese official and unofficial writing about Tibet's relationship with China is found in its purest form in the frequently repeated accounts of the marriage of the seventh-century Tibetan ruler Songtsen Gampo with the Chinese princess Wencheng who brings with her to Tibet ink, music, agriculture and other Tang dynasty technologies.[9] 'Overall purpose is to strive to construct a united, wealthy and civilized New Tibet!' as the Chinese reformer Hu Yaobang put it in 1980 (Barnett 2001: 274).[10]

The image that 'the Tibetans are intrinsically non-violent people' was less preferred among politicians in the West during the 1990s. Instead, they opted for a less essentialist phraseology about the 'path of nonviolent resistance' pursued by the Tibetans, which suggests a choice rather than an inherent quality.[11] Even this phraseology has led to occasional embarrassment for less careful politicians who had suggested that non-violence has been the Tibetans' sole strategy rather than a recent choice, since the history of recent Tibetan armed resistance and some accounts of internal political violence are now well known.[12]

Many of the representations about Tibet began to move away from asserting about the uniqueness of Tibet in terms of its religion and culture to that of its environment, which was thought to be pristine and needed to be preserved at any cost. A European parliament resolution was passed in 1992, 'deploring the destruction wrought on the natural environment of Tibet by the ruthless exploitation of the country's natural resources', which it said, had 'resulted in major deforestation around the upper reaches of Asia's greatest rivers with catastrophic implications for the future of the region'.[13] Much of this language also came from the Dalai Lama's own writing about a primordial Tibet, 'Prior to the Chinese invasion, Tibet was an unspoiled wilderness sanctuary in a unique natural environment. Sadly, in the past decades the wildlife and forests of Tibet have been totally destroyed by the Chinese.... What little is left in Tibet must be protected and efforts must be made to restore the environment to its balanced state'.[14] The view that Tibet is special in terms of its unique topography is carried forward, as Barnett writes: 'It is a view of Tibetans as an endangered species or of Tibet as a threatened habitat. All the representations of Tibet as special share this sense of an unindividuated collectivity or zone that is unique and at risk. This is again important in a political analysis of these representations because it reproduces the colonizing type of relation between the writer and the subject that can be seen in literary texts of the romanticizing type and has disabling implications' (2001: 278).

The models presented by Chinese and Western political texts are very similar: the phrase 'Tibet's unique natural environment' is standard in Chinese official texts.[15] Both the authorised Chinese and Western conceptions regarding the 'specialness' criteria of Tibet which Barnett talks about differ in that the Chinese version treats uniqueness as backwardness, whereas the Western version treats specialness as a quality that needs to be preserved. Yet, we do find how Chinese and Western political texts are very similar in their emphasis on 'Tibet's unique natural environment' (Barnett 2001: 277). The more recent work by Andrew Fischer draws attention to how Han labour migrations into Tibet are leading to divisions between urbanising Tibet, dominated by

Han Chinese, and the increasing marginalisation of the rural Tibetan population. This is part of the forced Sinisation strategy of the Chinese state to bring about further unity or to realise its assimilationist agenda (Fischer 2011).

Robert Barnett, in writing about the Human Rights thematic with respect to the Tibetans, states: 'Tibetan exile leaders realized that foreign governments had no strategic interests in raising the Tibet issue by 1980s, they turned for support to former colonizers rather than to the formerly colonized and chose public relations rather than political alliance as its form of politics' (2001: 279). Nevertheless, most representations of the Tibetan situation in official discourse continue to be highly politicised and, therefore, bereft of an objective standpoint. The fantasy of a non-violent Tibet runs counter to the reports on the Tibetan armed resistance against the Chinese (McGranahan 2005). Any attempt at presenting an idea of Tibet as having a unique culture is attended by a clear tendency to ignore Tibet's cultural world apart from political Tibet, as well as the Bon, Muslim and communist atheistic elements. Nevertheless, as Lopez states, 'Tibetan leaders continue to use the notion of Tibetan uniqueness as a principal tool for the Tibetan leadership' (2001: 273).

The trope of modernisation is frequently used in most political texts by the Chinese state to legitimise their rule over Tibet and it has come to replace the earlier legitimating device that stressed on the duty of the Communist Party of China to liberate Tibetans from the yoke of feudal oppression. As Barnett (2001: 277) states, 'This means that there are two or more interpretations of the same modernization; of the same fax machines, mobile phones, metalled roads, computer links that line the streets of Tibetan towns. To the Chinese state, these facets of modernization represent progress, while to some foreign writers and the Tibetan exile members they represent modernization as encroachment, depravity or the erosion of distinctiveness and tradition. Some of these writers raised the question as to how modernization should be considered and recognized that interpreting this process was problematic'.[16]

The most pervasive threat to Tibetan culture comes from the immigrant entrepreneurs in the figure of Chinese men to the Tibetan towns including Lhasa and this view is appropriated by the Tibetan exile administration and widely disseminated. It is particularly important because it is often adopted by Western governments as well as parliamentarians albeit in more restrained terms. Thus the 1996 report of the US department of State on Human Rights noted that ethnic Han and Hui immigrants from other parts of China, encouraged by government policies and new opportunities, are competing with and in some cases displacing Tibetan enterprises and labour. Rapid and ecologically-inappropriate growth has also disrupted traditional living patterns and thereby threatened traditional Tibetan culture.

The Dalai Lama as a Representational Issue

In recent years, there have been a number of attempts to circulate counter-representations within the contemporary discussion of Tibet, most of them attacks on the personal credibility of the Dalai Lama.[17] Western counter-representations focused more on the notion that the Dalai Lama's authority was in doubt because of his association with film stars, disputes among Tibetans in exile and in Tibet over the use of armed resistance[18] or his ban of the sectarian protector-deity Dorje Shugden. The persistent Chinese representation of the Dalai Lama as an unreliable negotiating partner has come to dominate the consideration of the Tibet issue for Western policymakers.[19] Notwithstanding this in the political domain, especially in governmental documents, the dominant representation of the Tibetan issue in the late 1990s has thus become the representation of Tibet as the Dalai Lama.

According to Barnett (2001: 299), 'It is no mean achievement to have exported the perception of Tibet and the Dalai Lama as one into foreign discourse because there is a constant tension between his role as a traveling teacher representing spirituality in general and his role as a representative of a country in crisis'.[20] How the Dalai Lama has come to represent the Tibetan people and how his personal biography is seen as a collective biography of the exiled Tibetans remains a mystery to Westerners. They therefore construe this as the prevalence of the theocratic element in Tibet's socio-political arrangements, one which is at odds with the Dalai Lama's recent position with regard to his role in Tibet's politics in exile.[21]

Of all the elements of Tibetan tradition that survive today, none is more critical to Tibetan self-definition than the Dalai Lama. In his own words, which represent his reflections before leaving Tibet and lack of fear at dying at the hands of the Chinese, the present Dalai Lama has expressed his awareness of what he means to his people: 'I felt then as I always feel that I am only a mortal being and an instrument of the never dying spirit of my Master and that the end of one mortal frame is not of any great consequence. But I knew my people and the officials of my government could not share my feeling. To them the person of the Dalai Lama was supremely precious. They believed the Dalai Lama represented Tibet and the Tibetan way of life, something dearer to them than anything else. They were convinced that if my body perished at the hands of the Chinese, the life of Tibet would also come to an end' (Dalai Lama 1962: 195).

The evocative strength of the symbol of the Dalai Lama is directly counterpoised by a corresponding vulnerability: the unitary character of a summarising symbol allows little possibility for adaptive reformulations when the social matrix that originally produced it undergoes radical change. This singularly remains the challenge of the Tibetan diaspora.

The present Dalai Lama has impressed even non-Buddhists with his realism and openness to democracy and has given his avowed pledge to respect the will of the Tibetan people regarding the continuation of the political aspect of the institution. What the Dalai Lama has said, in this respect, is: 'As early as the 1960s, I have repeatedly stressed that Tibetans need a leader, elected freely by the Tibetan people, to whom I can devolve power. Now, we have clearly reached the time to put this into effect. During the forthcoming eleventh session of the fourteenth Tibetan Parliament in Exile, which begins on 14th March, I will formally propose that the necessary amendments be made to the Charter for Tibetans in Exile, reflecting my decision to devolve my formal authority to the elected leader' (https://www.dalailama.com/news/2011/statement-of-his-holiness-the-dalai-lama-on-the-52nd-anniversary-of-the-tibetan-national-uprising-day; downloaded on 24 May 2017).

But no Tibetans, not even the most vocal critics (members of the Tibetan Youth Congress, for example) of the Tibetan diasporic community desire to see this happen. All feel a very real need for the continuation of that one Tibetan symbol that can transcend the potentially destructive factionalism of political groupings. The rapidly-changing circumstances in the diaspora and the Dalai Lama's advancing age do pose a great challenge to the future generation of Tibetans living at home and in the diaspora.

Interpretive Results on Tibet's History and Geography

Powers, in taking up the case of conflict being waged between Tibetan exiles and the People's Republic of China, writes, 'In the past, effective control over the production of historical narratives was generally held by governments that had the power to determine what version of history would be widely circulated and that controlled the means by which this information might be disseminated. However in modern times, one of the hallmarks of conflicts between competing groups is an ideological battle over the production of historical "truth" that often continues long after military subjugation has been achieved' (2004: 3–4). A case in point is the conflict which is being waged between Tibetan exiles and the People's Republic of China (Powers 2004: 4). Differences in the respective claims to the Tibetan plateau for both the sides stem from the differences in historical interpretations about Tibet's past and Tibet–China relations down the ages. Indeed, questions of history and historical claims have profound implications for the lives and futures of Tibetans in exile, many of whom learn to 'live the present historically' (Malkki 2002).

Linked to the central issue is also the question of the political or cultural geography of Tibet, which again has implications for the Tibetan exiles in shaping the contours of their imaginings about Tibet, many of whom have not directly experienced their homeland. The issue of contention is what constitutes 'Tibet'. The Chinese government generally limits Tibetan territory to the Tibet Autonomous Region, which consists of the central provinces of U and Tsang. As Powers notes, 'The issue of contention is what constitutes "Tibet". The Chinese government generally limits Tibetan territory to the Tibet Autonomous Region, which consists of the central provinces of U and Tsang. The Tibetan government-in-exile, however, claims that Tibet includes these central provinces as well as ethnically Tibetan areas of eastern parts of the Tibetan plateau that have been made parts of other neighbouring Chinese provinces by the PRC. Traditionally, the Tibetan government has claimed ownership of the "three Provinces" (Cholkhasum): i. U and Tsang which extend from Ngari Corsum in the west to Sokla Gyao; ii. Do Do, which extends from Sokla Gyao to the upper bend of the Machu river and includes Kham; and iii. Do Me, which incorporates an area ranging from the Machu river to the traditional border with China marked with a monument called the 'White Chorten'. Over the centuries, ownership of border areas has shifted between the Tibetan central government and China and although Kham and Amdo for example were claimed by modern Tibetan governments as part of their territory prior to the Chinese invasion in the 1950s, actual control was either in Chinese hands or in those of local hegemons' (Powers 2004: 164).[22]

As Ashild Kolas, in giving a description of what she calls the pre-communist Tibet, writes, 'The notion of the "religious land" is reflected in the Tibetan concepts of the dual religious and secular system of government and of chosrgyal, the king as protector and patron of religion. Chosrgyal is a Tibetan expression for the Buddhist conception of Dharma king. This conception of polity and political legitimacy has a widespread canonical basis in Buddhism throughout Asia' (1996: 52–53).[23] The Tibetan state appeared theocratic in character with religion (Buddhism) and polity, all rolled into one, epitomised in the figure of the Dalai Lama, where, in Ashild Kolas's words, 'The Dalai Lama was understood as chosrgyal in the dual role of political leader and earthly manifestation of Tibet's protector deity Chenrezig, the Buddha of Compassion... The clerical Buddhist traditions of Tibet draw on a vast array of oral and ceremonial as well as scriptural transmissions, whereas Tibetan folk religion is based on oral rather that on scriptural tradition.'[24] Tibetan 'folk religion' is based on oral, rather than scriptural traditions (Stein 1972). In these 'little traditions' of popular beliefs, every community had its own sacred spots, mountain deity, stupa, shrine or temple specific to the locality. These sacred centres defined the local communities, while Tibet in its entirety was defined by the sacred centre of Lhasa, where the Potala Hill was associated with the sacred mountain at the centre of the world (Kolas 1996: 53). Dawa Norbu maintains that the distinction between Tibetan and non-Tibetan was a Buddhist differentiation between believers and non-believers and that sub-national identity prevailed in Tibet before the Chinese invasion (Norbu 1992: 10). Norbu, in his interviews with elderly exile Tibetans, discovered that foreigners such as Nepalis, Chinese, Hui and Mongols were distinguished as separate groups but so were Amdowa, Tsangpa and other regional identities. There was no clear distinction between national and other identities based on place of origin. According to Corlin, 'The concept of bod (Tibet) describes the area of the Tibetan way of life, whereas chos (religion) describes the cultural instrument that provides the symbols of collective identification. In other words, "Tibet" describes a particular territorial unit identified with and integrated by the Buddhist doctrine' (1975: 150–53).

There is a growing corpus of work in Western languages that explores the contested history and debates surrounding Tibet. Many Western writers on Tibet advocate for either the Chinese or the Tibetan position and they often present the issue in absolute terms, as conflict between truth and falsehood, good and evil, oppression and freedom (Powers 2004: 4).[25] Both the Chinese and the Tibetan authors, Powers considers, view history as an independent voice of truth. 'All the Chinese works published in China accompany their assertions about the nature of Old Tibet and the improvements subsequent to the Chinese takeover with pictures that either claim to represent the brutal system of Old Tibet or the current happiness of its people. The covers of Great Changes in Tibet and Tibet: No Longer Medieval, for example, juxtapose these cheery titles with photographs of smiling Tibetan women; the implication appears to be that they are smiling because Tibet has leaped forward and because they are no longer medieval' (Powers 2004:15).

Rhetoric and passionate advocacy is the stuff of most works on Tibet – Western and Chinese. The brutality and crackdown on Tibetans by the Chinese is frequently reported and retold by Westerners sympathetic to the Tibetan cause to the audience worldwide. As Powers notes, 'Many of them indicate that they have personal connections with Tibetan refugees and are deeply concerned about their plight, but they also state that their analyses are balanced and authoritative and that their conclusions are derived entirely from the facts of Tibetan history and not from bias or personal feelings. Some claim to possess authority to tell the truth of the situation because of direct contact with Tibet and their own eyewitness experiences; others have not visited Tibet or Tibetan refugee settlements but assert authority on the basis of extensive study of available written sources on Tibetan history' (2004: 15).

Hugh Richardson states in *Tibet and its History* that he decided to write an introduction to Tibetan history after listening to a debate regarding Tibet's status during the fourteenth session of the General Assembly of the United Nations in 1959. 'I was struck by the need for a guide to Tibetan history which had regard not only to its continuous development over thirteen centuries but also to the Tibetan background and character and to the Tibetan point of view. That is what I offer in this book' (Richardson 1984: Preface). We see the proclivity among Western writers like Richardson to influence readers by showing how qualified they are in reporting on Tibet on account of having lived many years in Tibet and having acquaintances from many spheres of Tibetan life, prior to the Chinese takeover of Tibet.

Following the works of Richardson, Powers states, 'a supreme belief that he is telling a story that Tibetans themselves are unable to tell and that he perceives himself to be advocating on their behalf. He straightforwardly reports the main events of Tibetan history but in a number of places he heaps contempt on what he characterizes as Chinese fabrications and distortions' (2004: 16). Intriguingly, Western authors sympathetic to the Chinese view of events, such as Grunfeld, too have the supreme confidence that their accounts are also meant to reveal the truth of Tibetan history and the real nature of the Chinese takeover. Aware of the criticism, Grunfeld states that his analysis is balanced and authoritative. It is a 'search for a middle ground….I have made every effort to use materials from the most if not all contending points of view. I therefore choose to call this book "disinterested and dispassionate" history and I present it as an attempt at historical interpretation without political, religious, economic or emotional commitments to either side but rather with a commitment to furthering historical understanding and even truth' (Grunfeld 1988: 5). Grunfeld's book betrays a clear pro-Chinese bias, leaving the reader unsure of its use of original sources in writing about Tibet (see Powers 2004: 167).

On the other hand, Powers commends Melvyn Goldstein's monumental study, *A History of Modern Tibet,* as an exemplary work in Tibetan scholarship, in attempting to be, as stated by Goldstein, 'neither pro-Chinese nor pro-Tibetan in the current sense of the terms. It attempts to explicate a dramatic historical event: the demise in 1951 of the de facto independent Lamaist State. It examined what happened and why and it balances the traditional focus on international relations with an emphasis n the intricate web of internal affairs and events' (Goldstein 1989: 20). However, in his subsequent study, *The Snow Lion and the Dragon,* he betrays a bias in favour of the Chinese position in a number of places. For example, he portrays the fourteenth Dalai Lama as a devious but inept politician who continually exasperates China's leaders with his duplicity and intransigence (Powers 2004: 17).

The most vehement pro-China text is *Tibet Transformed* by Israel Epstein (a naturalised Chinese citizen of Polish descent), a lengthy book published by the New World Press in Beijing that uses the sort of rhetoric found in works by Chinese authors on Tibet and reflects the Chinese government's party line. Epstein asserts that his book is based on his own observations during three visits to Tibet and that it reports the truth of what he saw and was told by ordinary Tibetans, 'given largely in the words of hundreds of people who were there all along – mainly Tibetans within a frame of historical background from any sources' (Epstein 1983: 7).

The most contentious focus of the use of language by both pro-Chinese and pro-Tibetan authors is the nature of pre-1950s Tibet. The language they use is clearly persuasive – intended to convince the readers of the correctness of their authors' respective historical narratives and the conclusions they draw from them. Powers (2004: 18–19) notes some key words that occur over and over again in both Chinese and Tibetan sources. Chinese sources uniformly describe pre-1950s Tibet using the terms 'feudal', 'serfdom', 'backward', 'cruel', 'brutal', and others. Tibetan sources refer to it as 'peaceful', 'happy', 'religious', and so on. Chinese sources portray their takeover of Tibet as a 'liberation' that freed the 'serfs' from their feudal oppression and that has resulted in dramatically-increased prosperity for the Tibetan people. From a state of 'Mediaeval backwardness'[26], Tibet has leaped forward in all significant areas and now its grateful people happily celebrate their full reintegration into the motherland.[27]

Tom Grunfeld endorses the Chinese version of events and paints a picture of pre-exilic Tibet as brutal, exploitative and primitive. Powers elucidates upon Grunfeld's version of Old Tibet, a country that was 'rigid and ossified feudal society' (2004: 20), in which torture was widespread. He provides lurid descriptions of 'brutal forms of punishment' and states that 'a British resident of two decades reported seeing countless eye-gouging and mutilations' (Grunfeld 1988: 16, 24, 33, 129). Powers writes, 'In Grunfeld's view, those Westerners and Tibetans who reported positive impressions of Tibet were either blind to its squalid realities or deliberately obfuscating. Grunfeld's book contains many harsh judgments about Old Tibet but he gives no indication that he has ever visited the country or that he has fieldwork experience among his subjects. Despite these apparent limitations, he indicates throughout the book that he is confident of having ascertained the reality of the conditions in Old Tibet. He achieves this mainly by rejecting accounts of Tibetans who lived in Tibet and Western travellers who paint a positive picture and by privileging Western accounts that portray Tibet in a negative light.' (2004: 20–21).

Goldstein was more ambiguous with regard to pre-exilic Tibet in his insistence that Old Tibet enjoyed a certain de facto independence, but it was largely a semi-feudal theocracy and most rulers were corrupt and slothful.[28] In Goldstein's view, 'The Tibet Question is about control of territory – about who rules it, who lives there and who decides what goes on there' (Powers 2004: 21). Like Grunfeld and Epstein, Powers, in elaborating on Goldstein's view, asserts that, 'In a number of places that the Chinese pursued a "gradualist policy" in Tibet and that they showed tremendous patience and moderation despite prevarication and mendacity of Tibetan officials who tried to hold on to their positions and privileges in an attempt to delay what he apparently views as an inevitable process of historical change' (2004: 22).

The picture of Old Tibet painted by Epstein, Grunfeld and Goldstein stands in marked contrast to Richardson's version. He admits that the country was poor and technologically backward, but he contends that the populace was generally happy and content and he agrees with the Tibetan authors examined in this study that it was a deeply religious land with little difference between rich and poor. Richardson reports that there was a traditional aristocracy that along with the monasteries controlled most of the land, but the land itself was poor and most landowners were only slightly better off than the peasants who did most of the work. Mobility was present and if a particular landowner became too exploitative it was relatively easy for workers simply to move somewhere else. Warren Smith adopts a strongly polemical tone and uses highly emotive language in his denunciations of Chinese actions in Tibet. He indicates that his decision to write was a result of his extensive contacts with Tibetans in Nepal, Tibet and India and that a five-month trip to Tibet allowed him to see the reality of Chinese rule. Smith is convinced that prior to the 1950s, Tibet was an 'independent country' and that Chinese takeover was an invasion that violated international law. He contends that the Chinese and the Tibetans are two distinct ethnic groups and that despite Chinese attempts to destroy their culture and to assimilate them into their own, Tibetans remain convinced of their distinctiveness. Smith portrays the Chinese as thoroughgoing chauvinists who implicitly believe that they are both racially and culturally superior to their minority populations, including Tibetans (Smith 1996: 16, 402).

On Histories of Tibet

By delving into the literature of Tibetan history, limiting it to those produced in English by Tibetan and Chinese authors, two things are clear: first, publications on Tibet tend to be highly polarised. There is little ambiguity or nuance in most contemporary works about Tibet and some of the most emotionally-charged rhetoric is found in studies of Tibetan history. Second, both sides believe what they say and there is an uncompromising tone to those that support the Tibetan exile view and their opponents in the pro-China camp. History is viewed by both sides as being crucial to their claims and both invest a great deal of energy in producing works that purport to tell the 'truth' about Tibet's past. According to Michael Aris, Tibetans 'by comparison with many other peoples of the east or west … maintain a high level of historical consciousness and deep sense of the vitality of the living past … Mythical events were remembered and recorded as "history" … to serve as the basis for their re-enactment as ritual' (Aris 1997: 9–10).[29] The way Tibetan exiles imagine their past is by beginning their narrative with origin myths which form the basis of their subsequent histories and their interpretation of the 'here and now'. One popular story which is often repeated by Westerners as well is that the Tibetan race began thousands of years ago as a union between a monkey, who was the physical manifestation of Avalokiteshvara, the Buddha of compassion, and an ogress living in the mountains of Tibet. Their progeny were the forbears of modern Tibetans. From their father they inherited the qualities of gentleness and compassion, while their mother's passionate and violent nature also became a part of their psychological makeup.[30] For Tibetans, this legend provides an explanation for why they have fervently embraced Buddhism but also often engage in negative actions.[31] According to another origin myth, the earliest settlers on the Tibetan plateau were refugees who escaped the conflicts described in the Indian epic Mahabharata. The Indian connection is important in this context because contemporary Tibetan histories develop a narrative in which India, particularly Indian Buddhism, was the main source of the development of Tibetan culture and China played at most a peripheral role. Shakabpa cites both of these origin myths and states that some anthropologists believe that Tibetans are related to Mongoloid races. Most of the Chinese histories, on the contrary, downplay Indian influence and do not even mention these origin myths. Wang Furen and Suo Wenqing do state that many Tibetans consider their progenitors to have come from India but contend that 'this presumption ... is again opposed to truth'. The truth as they perceive it, is that Chinese tribes settled in Tibet and so the Tibetans are related to the Han. They assert that Neolithic human remains '... are free from such physical features of the Indians of the Aryan race as prominent noses and deepset eyes' and that 'the Neolithic culture of these areas was closely related to that of the interior of China'.[32]

Certain episodes and periods of Tibetan history are emphasised by Tibetan and Chinese authors, who often attribute to them a significance out of all proportion to their actual impact at the time they occurred. But such historical emphases do produce a 'mythico-history', which is animated in the minds and lives of Tibetans in exile, albeit in certain settings. It should be immediately pointed out that the historical and political antecedents that have led to the creation of the Tibetan diaspora in the latter half of the twentieth century still remain to be clarified. The issues involved here are part of an exceedingly tangled web of centuries of policies, politics, precedents, and legal ambiguities (Nowak 1984: 12). The production of Tibetan histories is closely connected with the question of how things came to be as they are (the fact of mass exodus following the Chinese invasion), who the Tibetans are as a people and the nature of their claims to the land of Tibet. What follows is an explication of few important episodes in Tibetan history, of those that have determined the structure of Sino–Tibetan relations over the ages; of how they are so important in the evolution of the self-identity of the Chinese and specifically diasporic Tibetans and how they form part of their respective national narratives at present.

The Marriage of Songsten Gampo and Wencheng

Contemporary Tibetan histories state with considerable pride that from the seventh to ninth centuries, Tibet was a major military power in Central Asia (Norbu 1997). During this period, Tibet attacked China a number of times and at the height of its territorial expansion, conquered and annexed large portions of Chinese territory. Under the kings of the Yarlung dynasty, a significant empire was created and

Tibetan fighters enjoyed a fearsome reputation among their neighbours. During the early period of expansion, Songsten Gampo's forces attacked and defeated several Chinese tribes and as a sign of his growing power, in 634, a mission was sent to the Chinese emperor Taizong requesting a marriage alliance. This is described in Tang dynasty chronicles as a tribute mission but the message it delivered was an ultimatum and not a gesture of subservience by a vassal. When the request was denied, Tibetan troops attacked and defeated the armies of tribes affiliated with the Tang in 637 and 638. In 638, an army camped on the border with China and again envoys were sent to the Chinese capital to request that the emperor give Songsten Gampo a princess of the royal family in marriage. The envoys were attacked by Chinese troops but because of the size of Songsten Gampo's army, the emperor subsequently changed his mind and in 640 agreed that the princess Wencheng would marry the Tibetan king.[33] Powers narrates (2004: 31) and examines the course of events from the beginning, in the following words:

> During the early period of expansion, SongstenGampo's forces attacked and defeated several Chinese tribes and as a sign of his growing power, in 634 a mission was sent to the Chinese emperor Taizong requesting a marriage alliance. This is described in Tang dynasty chronicles as a tribute mission but the message it delivered was an ultimatum and not a gesture of subservience by a vassal. When the request was denied, Tibetan troops attacked and defeated the armies of tribes affiliated with the Tang in 637 and 638. In 638 an army camped on the border with China and again envoys were sent to the Chinese capital to request that the emperor give SongstenGampo a princess of the royal family in marriage. The envoys were attacked by Chinese troops but because of the size of SongstenGampo's army, the emperor subsequently changed his mind and in 640 agreed that princess Wencheng would marry the Tibetan king.

Events are subject to historical interpretation, with Chinese historians preferring to emphasise the diplomacy side rather than the military version alone. Marriage was, according to the Chinese interpreters, a strategic move to bring the recalcitrant and barbaric Tibetans within the Chinese universe of meaning. The emphasis was less on how Songsten Gampo prevailed upon the Chinese, but instead, that the princess was given to by the Chinese emperor out of his own choosing. The process of the inevitable transformation of Tibetan culture was seen to have begun with a cultural intrusion, through the figure of a Chinese princess and justified as such.[34] The annals of Chinese imperial history explain, using facts and myths, the sheer absorptive capacity of Chinese culture in bringing the barbarians—the Tibetans—into their fold. The notion that Wencheng converted the Tibetans to Chinese culture is now part of folklore passed down from generation to generation. Tang chronicles state how 'since Princess Wencheng went and civilized this country, many of their customs have been changed'.[35]

Powers notes that the trend in contemporary Tibetan historical narratives has been general lack of acknowledgement of the influence of China in the formation of Tibetan culture (Powers 2004: 35). Dawa Norbu cites unnamed Tibetan chronicles which assert that Songsten Gampo's intention had nothing whatever to do with politics but was solely motivated by religion. Powers further recognises that 'many Tibetan writers also emphasized that Tibetans were strongly aware of their cultural and religious differences with the Chinese and never considered themselves to be part of China' (Powers 2004: 36). Norbu and other Tibetan writers also emphasised that Tibetans were strongly aware of their cultural and religious differences with the Chinese and never considered themselves to be part of China. In the study of the Tibetan accounts, Richardson concludes that Wencheng was 'a dim figure who made no mark on either Tibetan or Chinese history in the remaining thirty years of her life (following Songsten Gampo's death) and whose religious affiliation is uncertain' (Richardson 1998: 212).

Recounting Trison Detsen

While there is some doubt regarding Songsten Gampo's level of interest in Buddhism, it is clear that some of his successors became ardent Buddhists. In the eight century, King Trisong Detsen (740–98) devoted considerable resources to the importation of Buddhist culture and the building of Buddhist monasteries and temples. As Powers, in narrating Trisong Detsen's influence on subsequent developments, writes, 'Like Songsten Gampo, he is regarded by Tibetan tradition as an incarnate Buddha and is characterised as the second of Tibet's religious kings (chos rgyal). In traditional histories, Trisong Detsen is said to have invited a number of Indian Buddhist teachers to Tibet, the most prominent being Santarakshita, the abbot of Vikamshila, one of the great seats of Buddhist learning in India. Upon his advice, Trisong Detsen invited the tantric master Padmasambhava to Tibet because his magical powers could subdue the demonic opponents of the dharma. From that point on, Tibet began a wholesale importation of Buddhism, primarily from the great monastic universities of northern India and tantric lineages that mainly derived from Bihar and Bengal. According to Tibetan histories in 767, Trisong Detsen, Santarakshita and Padmasambhava officially consecrated the first Buddhist monastery in Tibet, which was called Samye and located in the Yarlung valley. In the following decades, Buddhism began to attract increasingly large number of adherents. The government allocated significant funds for the import of Buddhist literature, teachers and artifacts and increasingly, numbers of Buddhist missionaries travelled to Tibet to spread their version of the dharma.' (2004: 38–40). In foraging into Tibet's past, Powers (2004: 42) also suggested that there was growing influence of Indian version of Buddhism at this time and a slow marginalisation of all other competing versions, such as Hashang Mahayana Buddhism, which Trisong Detsen declared as heretical and subsequently banned. The pervasiveness of the rift between Tibet and China grew with the ever-growing influence of Indian Buddhism. This development has had a marked implication on Indo-Tibetan relations, almost a millennium later, albeit under completely different circumstances[36] (1984: 141, 147).

Buddhism continued to get state patronage under Trisong Detsen's successors. The dharma reached its zenith during the reign of King Ralpachen (815–836), regarded by Tibetan tradition as the third of the religious kings. The ascendancy of Lang Darma, who was an adherent of the Bon religion, following the assassination of Ralpachen did not augur well for Buddhism. Atisa Dipamkara Srijnana[37] (982–1054), the Indian scholar-monk, travelled to Tibet in the eleventh century and was influential in restoring and reforming Buddhism, which had degenerated over time. A revival of sorts began soon after he came to Tibet with the introduction of both traditional Indian Mahayana gradualist Buddhism and Tantrism. Buddhism declined in influence with the ascendancy of Lang Darma who ascended the throne following the assassination of Ralpachen. Together with his disciple Dromdon, he founded the first Tibetan order, the Kadampa. This school was later absorbed into the Gelukpa which became the dominant tradition in Tibet.

Tibet and the Mongols

Tibet's state of political disunity persisted into the thirteenth century when the country was annexed by the Mongol Empire. Beginning in 1207, Tibet began paying tribute to Genghis Kahn. In exchange, he did not invade Tibet nor did he interfere in its administration. This situation changed with the death of Genghis Khan in 1227 when Tibetans stopped paying the yearly tribute. This situation was not to last for long. Godan, the son of Genghis Khan's successor Ogedai, summoned a senior lama of the Sakya order named Sakya Pandita to his court in Liangzhou (modern day Gansu province) to formally submit the country to Mongol overlordship. Sakya Pandita had little choice and yielded to the demands of the Mongol ruler. Tibet became part of the Mongol Empire and in return, the khan had expressed an interest in converting to Buddhism. According to Tibetan accounts, this was the beginning of an arrangement referred to as the 'priest-patron' (*mchod yon*) relationship in which the Mongols agreed to leave Tibet fully under indigenous Tibetan control and the Sakya hierarchs became the religious preceptors of the khans and rulers of Tibet.

Powers, in writing about the Tibet and Mongol encounter during the age of empires, points to the Tibetan exile government's official version of Tibetan–Mongol relations as outlined in a publication entitled, 'The Mongols and Tibet: A Historical Assessment of Relations between the Mongol Empire and Tibet', which claims to be based on Chinese language sources, although a number of its assertions are found only in Tibetan chronicles (2004: 48). He elaborates, 'According to its version of events, Godan does not appear to have been particularly concerned with military expansion; rather, his primary interest was in religion. After encountering Tibetan Buddhism during his military excursions, he decided to seek a spiritual teacher to lead the Mongolians in a desirable moral direction… (Godan) was convinced that no power in the world exceeded the might of the Mongols. However, he believed that religion was necessary in the interests of the next life. Thus, he invited Sakya Pandita to Mongolia' (2004: 48).[38] Shakabpa and Norbu's reading of this period involves a careful distinction between Mongols and Chinese in which the two are at odds. An example cited by Shakabpa is Sakya Pandita's lobbying of Godan Khan to desist from throwing large numbers of Chinese into a river. This was being done to reduce the Chinese population so as to negate the potential Chinese threat to Mongol power (Shakabpa 1984: 63).

Tibetan authors' belief in the equality of the two parties in the priest–patron relationship reflects their assumptions about the role of Buddhism in Tibet's interactions with its neighbours. Because of the importance they ascribe to Buddhism and the profound effect it has had on their society, they tend to view the world through a lens coloured by Buddhist perspectives. The Mongols benefited by receiving religious instruction from their court chaplains and the Sakya lamas were able to gain influence in Tibet and Mongolia and to spread the dharma. 'What Tibetans generally ignore is the fact that the arrangement may well have benefited the Sakyapas, but it left ultimate authority over Tibetan affairs in the hands of foreigners' (Powers 2004: 54). This pattern persisted during later centuries, particularly during the period when Tibet was ruled by the Dalai Lama. Following the unification of Tibet under the authority of the fifth Dalai Lama, Ngawang Losang Gyatso (1617–82) in 1642, every subsequent Tibetan ruler relied on foreign patronage and military protection to support and maintain his power. The fifth Dalai Lama was installed as sovereign of a unified Tibet by the Mongol ruler Gushri Khan who used his armies to defeat the Dalai Lama's rivals. Powers writes, 'As Buddhist monks, the Dalai Lamas were generally reluctant to maintain powerful armies or personally order the use of force. Under their regime, Tibet became militarily weak and thus vulnerable to attack. From the time of the Sakya regency, no Tibetan ruler held power without at least the implicit military backing of a foreign power. This created a murky situation in which indigenous Tibetan governments led by the Dalai Lamas or their regents were effectively rulers of their country but were unable to officially declare their independence from China and risk losing its military support' (2004: 54). Tibetans commonly characterised the priest–patron arrangement as a workable model based on the principle of equality, but it was actually an unequal relation. In an age of empires and the 'Great Game', Tibet could no longer hold fort and found no patron to rescue it from its predicament and eventually fell to the People's Liberation Army.

Tibet and China during the Ming Dynasty (1368–1644)

When Mongol power waned in the fourteenth century, the Sakyapa were unable to retain their position of authority and in 1358 were overthrown by Jangchup Gyeltsen (1302–64) of the Phakmo Drupa branch of the Kagyu order who had been one of their governors. The Mongols were conquered by the Han Chinese who subsequently founded the Ming dynasty. In an attempt to assert an authority they were unable to exercise in fact, the Mongol court recognised Jangchup Gyelsten as their viceroy in 1351. During his reign, as Powers writes, 'he attempted to reverse the dependence on foreign rulers that had characterised Sakya rule. He instituted a programme of proto-nationalism that hearkened back to the traditions of the Yarlung dynasty's religious kings. After the Ming dynasty was founded, he refused to acknowledge subordination to it, but the Ming rulers still claimed Tibet as part of their territory' (2004: 56). As Goldstein notes, however, the Ming emperors 'exerted no administrative authority over the area', but still sought influence by giving presents and titles to prominent Buddhist teachers (Goldstein 1997: 4–5).

One way the Ming emperors attempted to influence Tibetan affairs was by encouraging powerful Buddhist leaders to participate in the Chinese tribute system.[39] As Powers (2004: 56–57) writes, 'According to Chinese imperial mythology, everyone who was a tributary explicitly acknowledged subservience to the emperor and vassalage to China but in reality, the system was a sophisticated bribe that was designed to purchase loyalty. Assuming that their superior civilisation and technology were attractive to their barbarian neighbours, Chinese rulers invited them to come to the imperial court and acknowledge their inferiority and subservience; in exchange, they received gifts and grandiose titles. In this process, the barbarians would come and be transformed, that is, they would naturally be drawn to Chinese culture and manners and be impressed by Chinese leaders. Through such contact, they would become more and more sinised and eventually come to view themselves as Chinese. In traditional Chinese views, the main difference between Chinese and barbarians was not race but culture.' As June Dreyer notes, 'From their ethnocentric view ... the Han do not believe that the culture and territorial claims of minority groups are equal to that of the superior Han civilization' (1976: 17).[40]

Elaborating on Tibet's relations with its neighbours, Powers writes, 'the priest–patron relationship which became the model for its foreign affairs policy. The Tibetans assumed that the gifts and military aid they received were acts of devotion by their religious clients that did not imply that the recipients were in an inferior position. However, Chinese imperial imagery conceives of China as the cultural and military center of the world' (2004: 55). As Dodin and Rather (2001: 113) state,

> These self-images not only constitute a self-contained sense of identity, they serve also as a transethnic cultural consciousness that considers all groups who lie outside the cultural "center" to be, according to such logic, culturally inferior. Because Chinese central power and culture have continued for two thousand years, traditional ethnocentric notions dominate the patterns of behaviour toward non-Han people and the expectations of how they should behave toward the central power. Imperial China understood itself as the cultural center of the world and its culture as the culture of humanity. Accordingly, in traditional perceptions it was acknowledged that numerous other people had well-defined areas but only one people were entrusted with the mandate of ruling humanity. This people inhabited the earth's epicenter, the Middle Kingdom.

Tracing the Dalai Lama's Gelugpa Sect (1640–1950)

The Gelugpa history is in several aspects a continuation of the post-Sakya period characterised by political instability and consequent power struggles. Dawa Norbu notes a significant difference: '... a polarization of conflicting forces into a direct confrontation between Gelugpa and Kargyupa forces by the 1530s. In the regions there was a series of conflicts between U (where Gelugpa influence predominated) and Tsang (where Kargupa influence predominated). This Gelug-Kargyu struggle for power and sectarian hegemony continued for over 100 years (1537–1642)'.[41]

A unique relationship developed between the Mongol Khans and the Tibetan spiritual leaders, more in the nature of priest–patron relations, in which the Mongols left Tibet undisturbed and the Tibetan spiritual masters such as Sakya Pandita gave religious instructions to the Mongols in return. The Gelugpa–Mongol relations began in the 1570s, when Altan Khan of the Tumat Mongols invited the third Dalai Lama, Sonam Gyatso. At this meeting, Sonam Gyatso was given a seal with the inscription 'Dorje Chang' (Vajradhara). He also received the title 'Dalai Lama' which ever since, has been used by the highest religio-political hierarch of the Gelugpa sect. 'Dalai' is Mongolian for 'ocean' and metaphorically connotes the depth and width of the Lama's knowledge and wisdom. The Dalai Lama, in return, gave the Mongol Khan the title of 'Dharma king'.

The beginning of Chinese imperial interest in the Gelugpa sect may be traced to the lifetime of its founder, Tsongkhapa, when the latter received invitations on two occasions from the Ming Emperor Yung Lo in 1408 and 1414. The fifth Dalai Lama's Beijing visit of 1653 signified the Qing China's recognition of the Gelugpa regime in Lhasa. Such occasions were characterised by complex layers of what we today call protocols that signified the hierarchy of authority relations and the relative distribution of power among the Chinese, the Tibetan and the Mongols.

For most of the seventeenth century, the closeness and affinity of the Dalai Lama was more with the Mongols than the Chinese. Part of this century was under the sway of the Great fifth Dalai Lama, much revered, who attained a great deal of autonomy with respect to temporal and spiritual matters. The type of lamaist polity, first created by the fifth Dalai Lama with Gushri Khan's armed help, remained an ideal Gelugpa model of government, even though its actual operation was by no means constant throughout the 300 years of the Gelugpa–Lamaist lineage. As Norbu (2001) states, 'It was characterized by a high degree of decentralization and even of distancing the autonomous units that supposedly composed the government'. In Gelugpa political theory, the Dalai Lama occupies a supreme spiritual and political place in their political system. His function is essentially to legitimate and morally support the government he presides over. But since his spiritual influence is not confined to Tibet, his powerful reign extends beyond Tibetan borders to the Mongol and Manchu world. This factor, even if it is not a religious reason, has traditionally compelled the Chinese emperors to respect the person and institution of the Dalai Lama (Norbu 2001: 80). These powerful factors sustained the Dalai Lama as a fairly permanent institution in the Gelugpa political system. As Dawa Norbu (2001: 75–76) observes:

> To the Tibetan lama, as to the Qing emperor and his Manchu officials, the relations were first and foremost of a religious nature and secondarily of a politico-military nature, What the Dalai Lama was looking for was Qing patronage of his sect and protection of his non-coercive regime as it was with the Mongols. Chinese involvement with Tibetan affairs grew in the years 1690–96 when the Qing waged a campaign against Dgalden, a Tibetanized Qosor Mongol living near Amdo who was a Gelugpa convert and closely allied with the then Tibetan ruling class. In 1696 China annexed Ta-chien-lu to the Manchu empire. This was the beginning of a gradual Chinese nibbling of Eastern Tibet territory (Amdo and Kham) which culminated with the Communist incorporation of Amdo and large parts of Kham into the neighbouring Chinese provinces of Qinghai, Gansu, Yunnan and Sichuan.

This mutuality between China and Buddhist Tibet did exist from this time on till the Communist revolution in 1949. These historical developments raise interesting questions about what constitutes the territorial claims of Tibet vis-à-vis Tibet before the Chinese takeover, since such claims impact the way Tibetans view their topography in historical terms and their history in topographical terms.

As Dawa Norbu elaborates, 'Next in the hierarchy of the Gelugpa political system as it operated during the fifth Dalai Lama's rule was the Mongol warrior whom the Lama called Bstan-zin chos-rgyal – defender of the faith and Dharmaraja. The role of the Mongol Khans was particularly crucial and visible during the early formative stages of the lamaist regime which was to defend the faith and ensure the security of the country. However, military dependence on an external power constitutes a fundamental and inherent weakness of the lamaist regime, particularly as it is a dependence without which the non-coercive lamaist regime could not survive. This weakness became more serious with the decrease in the power of the traditional lamaist protector, the Mongols and the penetration of Asian countries by Western imperial powers. The role of the Desid had been a much more pervasive and somewhat permanent institution in the history of lamaist regimes. This title means 'Chief Minister', and the office holder could exercise, as a matter of routine, considerable executive power. This was particularly true during the eighteenth and early nineteenth centuries' (2001: 81). The Gelugpa period saw the institution of the Dalai Lama getting firmly entrenched. What did change over time—and especially in modern times—was, as Dawa Norbu notes, 'the non-Tibetan component of the system, namely the protector, who historically has been an external power—Mongol, Manchu, Chinese, Russian, British, Indian and the United States' (2001: 83).[42]

The Rise of the Han Nation and Tibet

Confucian China did not appear to be either expansionist or imperialist. However, there is a deeply internalised sense of territoriality that necessitates boundary-building and boundary-maintenance of what was initially ancestor-worship sanctified territory (Norbu 2001: 86). The typical way in which imperial China spread her influence and power along the frontiers was by using the institution of indirect rule, which has been expressed with terms such as 'suzerainty' or 'protectorate' at different times.[43] During pre-modern periods, Imperial China had rarely sent any uninvited armed expedition into Tibet and only then upon the request of the ruling Lama to protect his non-coercive regime in extreme cases of internal rebellion or external invasion. Tibet, to the traditional Chinese mind, was always a separate country, foreign yet intimate territory. The subject matter of interstate relations discourse underwent a change. It was no longer dominated by traditional subject matters like tribute exchanges, announcement and acclamation of lamas and princes. By the middle of the twentieth century, there emerged in the Lifangyuan (Chinese foreign office) a new breed of scholar-officials who began to talk in a new language. Their new discourse made tribute relations and patron–priest relations irrelevant and obsolete. They began to press for Chinese sovereignty over Tibet as signified by the 1905 Anglo–Chinese talks in Calcutta, the Shimla Convention of 1913–14 and General Huang Musong's Lhasa negotiations of 1934 and finally by the communists in the 1951 Sino–Tibetan agreement. Medieval Tibet was totally unprepared for the 'modern' change in Tibet's status that was demanded by the 'newly' educated Chinese.[44]

By the turn of the twentieth century, the orderly and symbolic tribute relations were transformed into power politics especially in relation to Tibet. China's encounter with Western powers from 1895 to 1939 proved beyond doubt the Western supremacy over the previously assumed Confucian superiority. This created among the Confucian literate a complex politico-cultural crisis, shaking the foundations of their Chinese self-image and concept of Confucian world order. The Chinese elite came to the stark realisation that it was not virtuous behaviour as ancient sages advised, but power that made the critical difference to the nation's survival and world politics. Chairman Mao could formulate how that power was to be achieved: 'Political power grows out of the barrel of the gun' (Schram 1969: 290). The most striking thing about the change in Sino–Tibetan relations is the increasing use of force to fit Tibet into the Han scheme of nation-state,[45] such as signified by Chao Erh-feng's 1904–11 military campaigns in eastern Tibet and above all, the communists' armed 'liberation' of Tibet in 1950. Strictly speaking, Tibetan territory did not constitute a part of the ancestor-worship sanctified territory of

Confucian China. However, because the late Qing officials and early Han nationalists claimed Tibet to be a part of the five-race[46] based nation-state or republic, both Koumintang and Chinese Communist Party officials declared and demanded Tibet to be 'an integral part of Chinese territory'.

The Birth of Tibetan Autonomy

The entry of Western colonial powers on the Asian political scene altered the traditional balance of power centred on Buddhist Tibet and its military dependence on successive non-Tibetan regimes across the ages. British policy towards Tibet was characterised by two conflicting imperatives, which throughout their rule in India, they sought to reconcile. From early on, the British rulers realised their importance of Tibet as a buffer between India and any external power on the north, be it France, Russia or China. But to support or even encourage a completely independent Tibet was to damage a much larger commercial interest in China. Therefore, the British government recognised what they called Chinese 'suzerainty' but not sovereignty in Lhasa. As early as 1775, the British rulers tried to establish contact with Lhasa, but the latter studiously adopted a closed-door policy right up to 1904.

The images of Lhasa as the 'Forbidden City' and Tibet as the 'Hermit Kingdom' are of recent origin – probably dating from the nineteenth century. Prior to that, Lhasa was, by traditional standards, a fairly cosmopolitan city where Mongols, Nepalese, Bhutanese, Sikkimese, Ladhaki pilgrims and scholars, Kashmiri Muslim traders and Christian missionaries from Europe came together and mingled. Various types of influence – Indian, Chinese and West Asian – had gone into the making of Tibetan civilisation (Snellgrove and Richardson 1968; Stein 1972). What caused Lhasa to tighten its door to Westerners was the rise of imperialism in South Asia which since the 1840s had expanded into the Himalayan region, traditionally the Tibetan sphere of influence. The Tibetan-speaking peoples inhabiting the Himalayan region saw Lhasa as the centre of their faith and in terms of the trans-Himalayan religio-political relations, Lhasa wielded considerable influence over the lamaist culture areas in the Himalayan region. In fact Ladakh, Sikkim and Bhutan used to pay tri-annual tributes to the Dalai Lama until the Communist takeover of Tibet in 1950.[47]

Dawa Norbu recognised the tragic irony in Tibet's decision to remain isolated. It did so because of its incurable fear of colonisation of the country by the British. The British, after preliminary exploration, found out that it was not worth colonisation.[48] Under the circumstances, the only viable option for the British was that China had suzerainty over Tibet but on the understanding that Tibet was autonomous. The Simla Convention of 1914 gave the fullest expression to British strategic designs and Tibet's place in them. The British were interested in a relatively stable government because the theory of the buffer state has never worked properly except where the buffer state was strong enough to keep up an efficient government and administration and to make encroachment by either neighbour a risk. While the British insisted that China's historical status in Tibet was suzerain, the Chinese learnt to speak in the same political language but, of course, did not agree with the British proposition; they claimed their status was sovereign in Tibet.

The Europeanisation of Sino–Tibetan relations between 1905 and 1913 marks a major discontinuity in the history of Sino–Tibetan relations. As Ghosh (1977: 44) puts it, 'the terms of reference had changed by which issues are defined, relationships maintained or contentions resolved'. Anglo–Chinese negotiations regarding Tibet dictated that the Chinese representatives express themselves in modern terms of nationalism even though there was no appropriate English equivalent for patron–priest relationship in Tibetan. Tibet remained purely pre-modern in its outlook until 1950. The Europeanisation of Sino–Tibetan relations between 1905–13 mark a major discontinuity in the history of Sino–Tibetan relations: 'the terms of reference had changed by which issues are defined, relationships maintained or contentions resolved' (Ghosh 1977: 44). The terms of reference are no longer the Qing emperor and the Dalai Lama nor relations between two distinct though hierarchical civilisational realms. They are now the territorialising and nationalising Chinese nation-state. From a comparative perspective, feudal inter-state relations, in both theory and practice, were much more tolerant and subtle than the modern political and legal doctrine of state-centric sovereignty, as far as small states are concerned. There is no middle ground arrangement such as the one that fitted pre-1912 Tibet (Norbu 2001).

As far as the British were concerned, the term 'autonomy of Tibet' implied the following conditions: i. the absence of Chinese troops other than the specified suitable escort to the Amban; ii. no interference in the Tibetan administration which meant the absence of Chinese officials in the said administration; iii. no transfer of Chinese colonists into Tibet; iv. that neither China nor Tibet was allowed to permit any foreign power into Tibet (Norbu 2001: 167). Neither Chinese 'suzerainty' nor Tibet's 'autonomy' were acceptable to Lhasa. The Simla Convention was a logical culmination of an attempt to discuss Tibet's status among all the actors involved – India, China and Tibet.[49] With the decline of Chinese power in Tibet, British India tended to progressively relax its constraint on Lhasa from 1912 onwards, even encouraging Tibetan operational independence. On the whole, Britain appeared to be cautious even during this period about recognising Tibet's de facto independence (1912–50). On the whole, British diplomatic pressure and the occasional threat to use force sufficed to protect the fragile Tibetan autonomy from Chinese intervention for nearly 35 years.

The 1959 Revolt

When the Chinese communists passed through eastern Tibet during the Long March in 1935, they at once established a 'people's government' there; they even managed to recruit two or three young Tibetans into the Red Army who later became high-ranking officials.[50] However in Edgar Snow's words, '... the Reds for the first time faced a populace united in its hostility to them' (Wilson 1971: 220). The absence of a peasant rebellion in Tibetan history is in stark contrast with China's turbulent history, especially since the nineteenth century. Mao summed up the situation in Tibet when he said, 'We have no material base in Tibet. In terms of social power they are stronger than us, which for the moment will not change'.[51]

The 1959 revolt was only the culmination of a revolt that started in Eastern Tibet in 1952–53, when widespread fighting broke out in Kham and Amdo. Dawa Norbu (2001: 215–16) writes, 'Tibetans living in Eastern Tibet or what the Tibetans call Kham, which was considered de jure Chinese territory, enjoyed an incredible degree of independence both from Beijing and from Lhasa. While these Khampas were hostile to the Tibetan government and in particular to the lay aristocratic ruling class, their loyalty to the Dalai Lama as an incarnation of the Buddha of Compassion...was unquestionable'. In referring to George Patterson's 1960's account, Norbu writes, 'over 80,000 rebels were involved in the initial rebellion, out of which some 12,000 were deserters from the Kuomintang. The revolt, however, died down with no immediate help forthcoming from either India or America and because the Chinese at the persuasion of East Tibetan leaders relaxed their policy of immediate land reforms' (Norbu 1979: 82).

The strong military action in eastern Tibet was necessitated by China's high political stakes in Central Asia (Norbu 2001: 220). As the People's Liberation Army (PLA) carried on its extensive suppression campaigns all over eastern Tibet, the majority of the Khampa rebels who survived began to march slowly towards central Tibet. The Tibetan government, as a rule, completely dissociated itself from the rebellion. Meanwhile, the simmering discontent of the local people in central Tibet grew into open resentment and hostility against the Chinese, particularly in Lhasa. From all contemporary accounts, it would appear that the whole atmosphere in Lhasa and central Tibet was charged with anger, fear and suspicion.

Dawa Norbu chronicles the events, 'There was a Chinese invitation to the Dalai Lama to attend a theatrical show at the PLA headquarters on 10 March 1959. Tibetan suspicions were supposedly aroused by the timing of the invitation, which coincided with the Great Prayer Festival in Lhasa, and by the Chinese insistence that the Dalai Lama and his entourage come unescorted by Tibetan troops to the PLA headquarters.[52] Thousands of Tibetans from all walks of life had gathered what they regarded as the symbol and essence of Tibetan civilisation and Tibet, the Dalai Lama, to protect and defend and fight for all that he symbolised to the Tibetans. What was so striking beneath this strange medieval, religious and folkish behaviour was a resolute sense of anti-Chinese and anti-Communist feelings' (2001: 224). On 31 March 1959, the Dalai Lama arrived at Chuthangmo, an Indian checkpost on the eastern border of India; and from there he reached Tezpur in the north-eastern state of Assam.

The 1959 revolt which erupted could not sustain due to the vastness of Tibet and its rugged terrain. There is no disputing the fact, as Dawa Norbu notes, that, 'The rebellion was initiated and led by the Khampas, Tibet's warrior class, but had other participants too including most of the Tibetan army on only a little more than 3,000 men, most of Lhasa's 20,000 monks, a great number of the 30,000 public that surrounded the Dalai Lama's palace. In course of the suppression of the revolt, the Chinese killed over 87,000 Tibetans' (2001: 226). For Tibetan exiles today, the uprising of 10 March 1959 has come to function as a potent symbol of the dawning of a national consciousness and it is commonly presented as the spark that ignited a nascent awareness of Tibetanness among their people. It is commemorated by Tibetan exiles all over the world every year. In Tibetan exile communities, most of the population gathers and recounts the events of 10 March and their aftermath. The Dalai Lama and other Tibetan leaders make speeches which are disseminated on the Internet.

Exilic Metaphors

Understanding the concept of *rangzen* – self-determination, independence or freedom – is essential to understanding the framework of young Tibetan refugees' lives and the choices they make in the process of the creating a distinct Tibetan identity. In her doctoral study of Tibetan refugee youth, Nowak explores rangzen as the 'root metaphor' for Tibetan refugees. Nowak maintains that the concept of rangzen fits well with and even enriches certain traditional Tibetan feelings and ideas nurtured in school: compassion (*snying rje*), respectful behaviour (*ya rab cho zang*), patriotism (*gyal zhen*) and avoiding shame (*ngo tsa*) (Nowak 1984: 137–38). Striving to uphold all of them has led to a certain amount of frustration and 'psychological anguish' for many young Tibetans trying to integrate old traditions and ideology with new ways of thought derived from their own lived experiences. The Strasbourg proposal brought home the fact that there exists a lack of unity amongst Tibetans, which does not augur well for the Tibetan independence movement (Ardley 2002: 170). The predominance of the Shangri-la perspective has meant that all Tibetans agree with the Dalai Lama and believe that he acts in their best interests. Therefore, it is presumed that when the Dalai Lama took the decision at Strasbourg to aim for autonomy, this was the general wish of the Tibetan people. Jane Ardley, in her work, pointed to several problems with this proposition. First, there are no indications from inside Tibet itself that the people who continually protest against Chinese rule are fighting for anything less than independence.[53] Second it is not uncommon for Tibetan people to state that while they support the 'Middle Way' position of the Dalai Lama, they also wish for an independent Tibet. In the Tibetan exile community, no such formal channels exist for aspirations to be formulated into policy. While unity exists in theory, it is clear that while the Dalai Lama officially champions autonomy, many Tibetans such as those belonging to the Tibetan Youth Congress or the newly-formed Rangzen alliance disagree and still wish to fight for independence. This issue of the Dalai Lama's dual religious and political role is central to the Tibetan independence movement and according to Ardley, constitutes one of the most profound obstacles to its progress (Ardley 2002: 170).

According to Nowak, 'The neologism rangzen, for example was coined by compounding already existing Tibetan morphemes: rang meaning "self" and btsan meaning "power"' (Nowak 1984: 32). In this connection, the annual commemoration of the Lhasa uprising in March 1959[54] has become for refugees the archetype that sustains a recurrent but deeply meaningful new secular ritual. Many of the activities repeated annually by Tibetans on 10 March can be seen as a re-enactment or reaffirmation of key elements of the original drama that took place in Lhasa in March 1959. The commemoration for 10 March celebrations is a collective event held assiduously by Tibetans in the diaspora. The pattern is that a crowd gathers in a central square in the city. Speeches and demonstrations take place with the ritual of wearing the national dress, singing the national anthem and the display of the Tibetan flag and pictures of the Dalai Lama, as well as posters condemning atrocities on Tibetans in Tibet. The Dalai Lama delivers his annual address where the emphasis is on Indo-Tibet ties that go back centuries. The Dalai Lama delivers an annual 10 March address in places other than Dharamsala; his prewritten speech is read out by a local Tibetan official and the theme of India, the host country, is played up by frequent mention of the long centuries of Indo-Tibetan historical ties and friendly relations. According to Nowak, 'With such a repertoire of symbolic elements, the March 10 commemoration can indeed be seen as a key scenario, that is, as a ritual that publicly dramatizes both an ideal goal (proudly affirmed national identity) and the strategy for achieving it (self-conscious proclamation of 'Tibetanness' to and in the midst of others who are not Tibetan)' (1984: 35).

The Strasbourg proposal underlined the lack of unity amongst Tibetans. The Dalai Lama's overwhelming influence prompts large sections of the Tibetan people to go with his position with regard to autonomy for Tibetans, thereby believing that the Dalai Lama can do no wrong and is interested in their welfare and is committed to the cause of Tibet. Ardley (2002: 170) points to several problems with this idea.

> First, there are no indications from inside Tibet itself that the people who continually protest against Chinese rule are fighting for anything less than independence. Second, it is not uncommon for Tibetan people to state that while they support the Middle Way position of the Dalai Lama, which essentially calls for compromise, they also wish for an independent Tibet. This problem could be linked to the lack of democracy in the Tibetan exile polity; if a truly representative government in exile existed then such confusion may not arise. In the Tibetan exile community no such formal channels exist for aspirations to be formulated into policy. While unity exists in theory, it is clear that while the Dalai Lama officially champions autonomy many Tibetans, such as the Tibetan Youth Congress or the newly formed Rangzen Alliance, disagree and still wish to fight for independence.

It is evident that respect for the Dalai Lama's religious position prevents a large-scale opposition organisation from being formed that could continue to insist upon independence (Norbu 1990). The inherent ambivalences of organisations like the Tibetan Youth Congress are seen in the way in which it operates through political information campaigns to lessen the tensions between generations and on the other hand, it challenges the Tibetan administration by following a different political goal (Roemer 2008: 110). At issue here is the Dalai Lama's dual religious and political role, which according to Ardley (2002), constitutes one of the most profound obstacles to the Tibetan independence movement. While religion does not have the potential to be as divisive in the Tibetan community given that there is only one major religion, the placing of political events in religious contexts is a hindrance for the Tibetans. The crucial question that Ardley raises is how far Tibetan Buddhism is appropriate for a modern independence movement and whether in fact it may be an encumbrance to the progress of that movement.

Articulating Tibetan Nationalism-in-Exile

Dibyesh Anand, in his article, '(Re)imagining Nationalism: Identity and Representation in the Tibetan Diaspora of South Asia', writes, 'The story of the creation of the Tibetan community-in-exile illustrates the successful strategies of the Dalai Lama led government to foster and maintain a distinctive national identity among disparate groups of people from various parts of greater Tibet with mix of religious, cultural and political elements. This success has not been an unmixed blessing, for the contributory factors behind it also limit the vocabularies available for expressing Tibetan political identity' (2000: 271). He further states that the spatial distribution, economic differentiation, regional and sectarian backgrounds, and generational gaps compound the category of diasporic Tibetan. Thus, a unified, homogeneous Tibetan-in-exile identity is more of a rhetorical device and imaginary construct than some verifiable reality. At the same time, it is naïve to dismiss any consideration of the identity question on this ground only, for all identities are in the last instance, products of the imagination.[55] Though Tibetanness is an imagined and contested construct, it has its own effect on those who consider themselves Tibetans (Anand 2000: 272).

Since nationalism itself is a particularised discourse of collective identity, a discursive approach may be extended to a discussion of Tibet as a nation and Tibetanness as a narrative of national identity. As Venturino (1997: 103) writes, 'A unified Tibetan nation currently exists only through the anticipated (re)construction of its parts: occupied country, dispersed communities and globally networked politico-cultural support system (Tibetan support groups)'. Prior to linking identity to refugee camps or to places Tibetan refugees dwell (which would be discussed in the forthcoming chapter on ethnography of displacement), it would be necessary to make explicit notions of belonging and power that underpin the theory of how nationalism is created. Placing the study of Tibetan national identity within wider theoretical debates over nationalism is deemed critical, as this can influence the interpretation of evidence from the site of field research. Nationalism is seen as a theory of legitimacy, 'a political principle that holds that the political and national unit could be congruent' (Gellner 1983: 1).

The most common dialectic for categorising the theories of nationalism is to divide them into 'primordialist' and 'instrumentalist' camps where the former believes that nations are extensions of previously human communities and the latter believes nations are creations of modern conditions and elites.[56] The instrumentalist scholars of nationalism are often accused of over-emphasising the capacity of nationalism as an ideology to engender nations. Dibyesh Anand (2000: 274) suggests that a 'better approach would be to retain skepticism about the primordiality of the past and situate oneself somewhere in-between the instrumentalist-primordialist debate, adopting a more diversified and inclusive understanding of nationalism which highlights rather than obscures its cross-cultural variants'.

At this stage, it would be prudent to consider the ethnic theory of nation, the one that has an illustrious history[57] and one which would aid in understanding Tibetan nationalism-in-exile. The genesis of a nation is rooted in its 'heroic past, great men, glory that provides "the social capital" upon which one bases a nation' (Bhabha 1990: 19). This social capital then supplies nationals with 'the desire to live together, the will to perpetuate the value of the heritage one has received in an undivided form' (ibid.: 19). Ethnic nationalism, according to Dawa Norbu, is 'that politicized social consciousness centred upon an ethnic identity born out of shared commonalities, seeking to achieve unity, autonomy and group interest by mobilizing ethnic based constituencies' (Norbu 1992: 181). Central to this definition, Norbu continues, is the 'notion of ethnic identity which may be defined as an aggregation of ethnic variables such as race, culture, language, society and so on by which the ethnic group differentiates itself from generalized others. Since the primary function of ethnic identity is differentiation vis-à-vis others who do not share that identity, the required differentiation may be achieved by emphasizing that ethnic variable which uniquely distinguishes a particular ethnic group from others around it' (ibid.: 181).

Historically, the political control of the Dalai Lama did not exceed beyond U-Tsang (Now the Tibetan Autonomous Region), while Kham and Amdo (now part of Chinese provinces of Qinghai, Sichuan, Gangsu and Yunan) were ruled by various small principalities with often overlapping influence. What bound the people in the regions was not an allegiance to one temporal authority but certain commonalities of culture and religion. These elements may be seen as forming the basis of Tibetan 'ethnie', the features of which include 'a collective proper name, a myth of common ancestry, a shared memory of rich ethnohistory, differentiating elements of a common culture, an association with specific homeland and lastly, a sense of solidarity for significant sectors of population' (Smith 1986: 21). The failure of Tibetans to develop nationalism prior to 1950, which has been noted by Goldstein (1989), does not mean that pre-exile Tibetans did not have any sense of themselves as belonging to a distinct country. As Dreyfus (2005) argues, 'at least in Central Tibet since the thirteenth or fourteenth century Tibetans understood themselves as belonging to a country defined in terms of the shared memories articulated by some of the more hidden treasures (*gter ma*) such as the "mani bka".... These narratives identify Tibet as an originally barbarous country civilized by Buddhism and transformed into the pure land surrounded by snow mountains' (*gang ris bskor ba'I zhing khams*) often referred to in Tibetan prayers.

The beginnings of a cultural movement such as nationalism are not easy to trace. In Tibet, perhaps the first relevant document is the thirteenth Dalai Lama's proclamation upon his return from exile in 1913. In this proclamation, one can see an awareness of Tibet as a distinct country, defined by its culture and history. The Dalai Lama starts his proclamation by explaining his claim to sovereignty on the basis of a connection with Avalokiteshvara, which goes back to the time of the religious kings (chos rgyal). He also traces the history of the relations between China and Tibet from the Yuan dynasty to the present, concluding that Tibet is a separate country. He then moves to issue five prescriptions, several of them bearing little direct connection with nationalism: Buddhism should be preserved; its schools should live in good harmony; and officials should be honest. The Dalai Lama also makes two points that are more directly related to nationalism: Tibet should strengthen its defence; and expand its economical basis by allowing people to cultivate vacant land (Goldstein 1989: 60). Dreyfus identifies and narrates two significant events that came to define the idea of the Tibetan nation; one, 'The 1913 proclamation is significant for it indicates the recognition of Tibet as a distinct country that is to be defended and developed. Another significant step was the formation in 1954 of People's Committees (*mi dmang tshogs 'du*) among low ranking officials and traders. This movement of protest against the Chinese occupation was in part motivated by the realisation that the ruling elites had failed to confront the Chinese and by the desire to oppose Chinese occupation directly. A second more significant step in the formation of Tibetan nationalism was the creation of the "Four Rivers, Six Ranges" (*chubzhi gang drug*) movement against the Chinese occupation organised by some of the rebel leaders from Khams. Shaken by events taking place in Khams and the bad omen reported throughout Tibet, a group of traders from Khams living in Lhasa decided to collect funds from all over Tibet to offer a golden throne to the Dalai Lama. On 4 July 1957, the ceremony took place in the Norbulingka in Lhasa where a large number of people came together to express their allegiance to their leader and their defence of the Chinese. Offering a golden throne to the Dalai Lama was seen as a way to express and strengthen the bond between the Tibetans and their leader. It was an attempt to reaffirm the power of the Dalai Lama over the land of Tibet. This date can be seen as retrospectively as marking the birth of Tibetan nationalism, the awareness that Tibetans have of belonging to a single country' (Dreyfus 2005: 11–12; Shakya 1999).

The particularity of the nationalism that emerged in Tibet in the 1950s is that it deploys traditional religious themes to define the nation. Instead of adopting the secular lingua usually associated with modern nationalism, this nationalism defines the Tibetan nation using traditional Buddhist values such as compassion, karma and the bond between Tibetans and Avalokiteshvara. In Dreyfus's words, 'The nation thus defined is not, however, traditional Tibet with its diversity of local cultural, social and political communities but a modern country united by its opposition to Chinese oppression' (2005: 12). The religious nature of this nationalism is well captured by the anthems sung by Tibetans in exile to express their national aspirations such as the 'Prayer of Truthful Words' (*bden tshig smon lam*) and the National Anthem (Klieger 1992: 61). The particularity of both these songs, which are still used nowadays by Tibetans in exile for celebrations such as 10 March, is that they are modelled after traditional religious prayers. They contain traditional Buddhist motives such as the prayer for the continuation of the Buddhist teaching and the request to the Buddhas and bodhisattavas to help beings who are tormented by the unbearable suffering of karma (Michael 1982).

'One way to understand Tibetan religious nationalism is to relate it to the ideological and practical organisation of Tibetan political life. The religious themes contained in the "Prayer of Truthful Words" reflect the arrangements of Tibetan political life over several centuries. During this time, one of the dominant features of Tibetan politics has been the political role of Buddhism and the monastic order' (Dreyfus 2005). Such arrangements have been solidified in the ideology described as 'the union of the religious and the political' (*chos srid zung 'brel*) (Shakya 1999; Dreyfus 2005). Historically, this ideology is the result of a complex situation created by the fall of the empire, the inability of non-monastic groups to establish lasting kingdoms and the increasing political role of monastic groups. The nature of nationalism was further inflected by the experiences undergone by the Tibetan people both inside and outside Tibet after 1959 (Dreyfus 2005). In particular, the experience of the exile and the encounter with Indian democracy were important in developing the commitment to human rights and democratic values expressed in the constitution promulgated by the Dalai Lama in 1963. This constitution in turn inspired activists within Tibet, particularly the young monks and nuns who demonstrated against the Chinese rule in 1987–88. As Ronald Schwartz (1994) has shown, these young people saw the Dalai Lama's stance as reflecting a progressive political position through his articulation of key Buddhist concepts such as compassion and the prohibition of killing. These young activists based their democratic principles on Buddhism, which is depicted as a set of undogmatic religious and moral principles compatible with human rights and democracy. 'Within the Tibetan exile community, Tibetans contest the notion of Tibetanness in various ways. Religion comprise the main idiom of Tibetan identity; the source of unity between all Tibetans. Religion as source of identity seems to be especially important to the uneducated, the elderly and the recent arrivals from Tibet. On the other hand, the secular concept of Tibet is now being established as a primary idiom of identity, as an elite project' (Kolas 1996: 64).

As Melvyn Goldstein puts it, 'As a classic nationalistic dispute, the Tibet question pits the right of a people, Tibetans, to self-determination and independence against the right of a multiethnic state, the People's Republic of China, to maintain what it sees as its historical territorial integrity. Such disputes are difficult to resolve because there is no clear international consensus about the respective rights of nationalities and states.... In the case of Tibet, both sides have selectively patched bits and pieces of the historical record together to support their viewpoints, the ensuing avalanche of charges and counter-charges is difficult to assess, even for specialists' (1998: 83). The key to resolving the dispute is crafting a compromise that will ensure the preservation of a Tibetan homeland where ethnic Tibetans predominate and Tibetan language, culture and religion flourish. Goldstein notes, 'To win the above concessions from China, the Dalai Lama would have to return to China and Tibet, publicly accept Chinese sovereignty over Tibet.... There is no consensus in the exile community about the advantages of such a political compromise, let alone about the exclusion of the ethnic Tibetan areas outside the Tibetan Autonomous Region, so the Dalai Lama would very likely have to decide to pursue this course without the unified support of his government-in-exile. It would not be an easy decision and his tendency will be to resist compromise' (ibid.: 96).

Notes

1. After the Dalai Lama's flight, the first report of an uprising in Lhasa was broadcast by *Voice of America* on 22 March 1959; see Sen 1960: 26.

2. With its invention of the word and world of 'Shangri-la', it quickly became both a bestseller and a Hollywood success.

3. The word 'epiphany' refers to a manifestation of the divine; to a moment of sudden intuitive understanding. In the late eighteenth and nineteenth centuries, this notion of a flash of comprehension, while deeply connected to Christian notions of salvation and revelation, gained wide currency in Britain.

4. Notwithstanding the debates around the extent of penetration of Western constructs into the Tibetan world, Donald Lopez (1998) likens the Western representation of Tibet to that of a 'prison' in which Tibetan lamas and their students, in their attempt at counter-appropriation, continually get caught up in the representative frames offered by the West.

5. The term 'sacred territory' is standard in China's discussions of its territoriality. For more on this, see Norbu 2001.

6. The exile government in 1986 commissioned a brief on Tibet's legal status, which formed the basis of Michael van Walt van Praag's 1987 book *The Status of Tibet* and provided much of the legal rationale for the Strasbourg Proposal; it discusses the role of human rights briefly but significantly in its conclusion. Tsering Shakya and other observers have noted that this internationalisation initiative coincided with an increase in political tension between India and China.

7. There is a long history of Tibetan political perceptions of their state as unique. The Tibetan National Assembly issued a communiqué addressed to Chiang Kaishek in 1946 copied to the British mission in Lhasa, which relies on this theme: 'There are many great nations on this earth who have achieved unprecedented wealth and might but there is only one nation which is dedicated to the well-being of humanity in the world and that is the religious land of Tibet which cherishes a joint spiritual and temporal system' (Goldstein 1989: 542).

8. For a collection of the Dalai Lama's speeches, see *Political Philosophy of His Holiness The Dalai Lama*, Tibetan Parliamentary and Policy Research Centre, New Delhi, 1998.

9. Here, marriage is a metaphor for China's civilising mission towards backward peoples; it is thus similar to the Chinese view of their modernisation project in Tibet in contemporary times.

10. Hu's phrase about civilising Tibet is still one of the most frequently-used slogans of the local government in Tibet.

11. 'For the last 47 years, the Tibetan people have maintained a peaceful, non-violent resistance to the Chinese government's policy of cultural genocide; but time is running out for the Tibetans and the power to stop this is in our hands' ('Boycott all Chinese Products', Press Statement, Milarepa Fund (San Francisco), 30 April 1996).

12. For example, three monks were murdered in Dharamsala on 4 February 1997 by Tibetan followers of the banned Shugden sect, according to the Indian police (see Clifton 1997). For more on the Tibetan resistance, see McGranahan 2005: 570–600.

13. Efforts at bringing to light the 'ecological deterioration in Tibet had begun through the activism of Petra Kelly and the Green party in Germany by the early 1990s' (Barnett 2001: 276).

14. The fourth item in the Dalai Lama's Five Point Peace Plan 1987 was 'restoration and protection of Tibet's natural environment'.

15. Chinese official discourse refers frequently to the uniqueness of Tibetan culture as well, but focuses on what are seen as its non-religious aspects, such as the medieval system or the Gesar epics.

16. See the 'Statement of the Dalai Lama on the 38th Anniversary of Tibetan National Uprising Day on 10 March 1997 Dharamsala'.

17. In 1995, media reports sought to link the Dalai Lama with the Asahara cult in Japan in order to demean his image. For more on this, see http://www.larouchepub.com/eiw/public/1995/eirv22n43-19951027/eirv22n43-19951027_052-dalai_lamas_ties_to_aum_sect_exp.pdf (downloaded on 16 September 2012).

18. In fact, the Dalai Lama and his advisors had strategically encouraged Tibetan youth movements to express diverse opinions but generally the Tibetan Youth Congress has its objectives clearly marked out, that is, the independence of Tibet, which is at variance with the policy of the exile administration and the Dalai Lama (personal informant in the Tibetan Youth Congress).

19. Increasingly in the Western political perception, the Sino–Tibetan conflict had come to revolve around the interpretation of the Dalai Lama as an individual. The exile administration and the Dalai Lama had expressly sought to avoid such an outcome during and after the talks with Beijing collapsed in 1985.

20. For more on the institution of the Dalai Lama, see Goldstein 1968.

21. Nowak treats the figure of the Dalai Lama as the 'summarizing symbol', a term which she borrows from Ortner's article on key symbols (1973) which distinguishes between 'summarizing symbols' and 'elaborating symbols', the latter category being further divided into 'root metaphors' (cognitive) and 'key scenarios' (behavioural elements).

22. Boundaries between Tibet and China were first established by treaty in the eighth century AD when the forces of the Tibetan Empire dominated the Silk Road lands and challenged the Chinese Tang rulers (Kolas 1996: 52).

23. For a discussion of Buddhist kingship, see Tambiah 1976.

24. Samuel (1993) makes a distinction between clerical Buddhism and Shamanic Tantric Buddhism.

25. Till date, there is no study which compares the works of these contemporary Tibetan and Chinese authors. These may be because of the obviously polemical and hyperbolic rhetoric used in most English works on Tibet by Tibetans and the Chinese cause many readers to dismiss as propaganda those with which they do not agree.

26. This is in keeping with how 'Imperial China understood itself as the cultural center of the world and its culture as the culture of all humanity' (Herberer 2001: 113).

27. Much of this is strikingly reminiscent of Western colonial discourses that justified invasion and colonisation on the basis of the purported cultural benefits that colonial rule brought to the natives.

28. The overall thrust of Goldstein's analysis is that the weakness and isolation of Old Tibet coupled with the bungling and corruption of its leaders created a situation in which the Chinese takeover was inevitable.

29. The Tibetan term for 'history' is *lo rgyus*, a translation of the Sanskrit *itihasa*. The term encompasses both historical and mythological sources as well as chronicles and hagiographies. There is no clear distinction between factual accounts of events and mythological narratives and beliefs about the past that have been passed down from generation to generation.

30. For an insight into the origin of Tibetan civilisation, see Snellgrove and Richardson 1968.

31. According to the story, Avalokiteshvara consciously chose to take the form of a monkey to begin the process of creating a Buddhist country on the Tibetan plateau and as the Tibetan civilisation developed, he continued to intervene to prepare the people for the introduction of Buddhism. He nurtured the spiritual inclinations of the Tibetan people, helping them to suppress their negative tendencies and develop their culture. The first stage of this process culminated in the initiation of the 'first dissemination' of Buddhism during the reign of King

Songsten Gampo who is characterised by several traditional Tibetan histories as an incarnation of Avalokiteshvara.

32. See Wang Furen and Suo Wenqing 1984: 10–12. This book attempts to impose a Marxist paradigm onto Tibetan history, which requires that the authors sometimes have to invent historical events in order to fit the model.

33. While Tibetan histories unanimously assert that the Tibetan army defeated the Chinese, the Tang annals contend that the Tibetans were defeated and that after a period of several years, Tibet apologised and again begged the Tang emperor to consider a marriage alliance. See Bushell 1880: 444.

34. In Chinese imperial statecraft, giving royal princesses in marriage was the one means used to pacify the barbarian tribes. This was part of the heqin policy which worked to subvert the barbarians by giving them gifts from China's superior civilisation and flattering them with grandiose titles; see Rossabi 1975: 19.

35. See Bushell 1880: 457; Wang and Wenqing 1984: 19. These authors believe that Wencheng has become a culture hero for Tibetans, who celebrate her life and her importation of Chinese culture to Tibet.

36. According to Hashang Mahayana, buddhahood is a sudden flash of realisation in which one awakens to one's innate Buddha-nature. It results from meditative practices in which one halts the flow of thoughts and allows the Buddha-nature to manifest spontaneously. The opposition was headed by Kamasila who followed the traditional Indian Mahayana paradigm according to which sentient beings suffer because of the results of their previous actions which were motivated by ignorance, this ignorance is primordial and has been cultivated and reinforced during countless lifetimes and so it is impossible to eradicate it all at once. He likened the process of attaining buddhahood to climbing a mountain which must be done step by step.

37. For more on the life and times of Atisa, see Chattopadhyay 1994.

38. For more on the Mongol and Tibet relations, see Department of Information and International Relations, Tibetan Government in Exile, 'The Mongols and Tibet: A Historical Assessment of Relations between the Mongol Empire and Tibet', Dharamsala 1996: 9.

39. 'The common understanding of the tribute payments is that the vassals pay a regular indemnity in exchange for protection or to avoid being invaded by a superior military power. But the Chinese system was not this sort of medieval protection racket unlike the Mongols, it involved complex economic exchanges that were connected to imperial myths about China's place in the world' (Powers 2004: 57). What this means is that in case of the Chinese, the patron–client relation did not work in the classical framework, because although the Chinese acted as patrons or clients in some contexts, they had a sense of cultural superiority over others.

40. The discourse of transformation was often appropriated by some groups that were conquered by the Han in order to establish themselves as having an equal standing.

41. For more on the rise of Gelugpa sect, see Shakabpa 1984: 103.

42. Tibet and Tibetans have historically needed a powerful ruler or third party to oversee them, protect them. Dawa Norbu (2001: 399) notes that, 'If the present Dalai Lama frequently runs to the American president which attracts so much global media attention and which outrages Communist authorities in Beijing, it is because of the Lama's instinctive need, which has been internalized for centuries to search for a "protector" the twentieth century equivalent of the all powerful Mongol Khan in the context of Communist occupation of Tibet.'

43. Dawa Norbu (2001: 88) prefers to use the term 'indirect rule' because it is devoid of Eurocentric connotations and associations. Indirect rule refers to a rule that is not based on direct political action by a reigning external power but on behind-the-scenes influence, subtly but effectively exerted through the medium of local elites so that foreign domination appears to be native rule in the eyes of the native population. This was characteristically been the Mandarin manner by which Imperial China exercised indirect rule over neighbouring or relatively distant countries outside China itself where direct domination was unacceptable or illegitimate from the Mandarin point of view.

44. The British advocates of this line of legal thinking include most of the British colonial officials dealing with Tibet.

45. The sense of territoriality was inherent in Confucian cultural practice but only at the level of family and clan. What transformed this clannish territoriality into a nation-wide consciousness about Chinese territory was the Maoists' mobilisation of Chinese peasants for the anti-Japanese war (1934–45) in China.

46. This includes Han, Mongols, Manchus, Tibetans and Turks (Hui). This was Sun Yatsen's conception of the 'five race republic'.

47. These tributes were called *lo-phyag* (annual submission). Bhutan used to pay annual tributes but Ladakh, being far away, used to pay every second year. Usually, tributes consisted of local products of the countries concerned. For example, Ladakh offered apricots and Bhutan various types of Bhutanese cloth. It appears Sikkim stopped paying tributes when it became a British protectorate in 1890.

48. Despite the ban on the entry of Europeans into Lhasa, the British did send spies to explore Tibet; for example, in 1865, Mann Singh and Mani Singh were to conduct a route survey work up to Lhasa, and Sarat Chandra Das, disguised as a Sikkimese lama, was sent to observe the political conditions of Lhasa and Shigatse in 1879.

49. For an examination of the international treaties signed on or by Tibet, see Van Walt Van Praag 1987: 70–73.

50. See Takla 1969.

51. See Mao Tse-Tung 1977: 64.

52. For a detailed account of the events surrounding the 1959 revolt, see Barber 1969.

53. Most of the protest inside Tibet against Chinese rule has been spearheaded by monks and nuns who in large numbers have taken to the streets of Lhasa several times in the past few decades. For an illustration of this, see Barnett 1994.

54. For more on this, see the two-part article by Tsering Topgyal in the March and April 2003 issues of the *Tibetan Review* which offers an analytical insight on the circumstance leading to the culmination of the 10 March 1959 Tibetan National Uprising against the Chinese takeover of their country.

55. In this sense, Tibet according to Dibyesh Anand, is an 'imagining community'. According to Anand, the term 'imagined community' used by Benedict Anderson (1991) does not fully convey the sense of continuous imagination that goes into the making and existence of a nation.

57. In the rhetoric of nationalism, what is ignored is that the need to present one's own community as a nation is a modern day phenomenon. More often than not, the proponents of nationalism take a primordialist view of nationalism. Nationalist movements in most places trace their genealogy to antiquity.

57. Renan delivered a lecture at the Sorbonne in 1882 that contained many elements of later theories.

5

Organising for Exile!*

Routes to and Roots in India

What began as a steady flow of Tibetan refugees into India since April 1959, following the flight of the Dalai Lama into exile, soon turned into a mass exodus. What requires mention is that the historical and political antecedents leading to the flight of Tibetans are part of an exceedingly tangled web of policies, politics and legal ambiguities and it would be beyond the scope of the study to delve deeply into these matters. What follows is a brief description of the prelude to the Tibetan diaspora and the motives for flight. The principal causes that led to forced migration can be traced to the differentiated Chinese policies towards Inner and Outer Tibet in the 1950s (Saklani 1984; Norbu 1979; Grunfeld 1988).[1] 'Chinese Communists formulated and pursued two radically different policies: radical communist policy measures in Inner Tibet and non-Communist liberal ones in Outer Tibet. Radical policies designed to replace core Tibetan Buddhist values and key institutions by Chinese Marxist ones was deeply resented and resisted widely in Inner Tibet' (Andrugtsang 1973). This then led to the first wave of forced migration from Inner Tibet to Outer Tibet during the mid-1950s and by 1959 into South Asia.

For those Tibetans who fled, the decision followed upon a personal conviction that life in Tibet had become unendurable. The following account of a 42-year-old farmer from southern Tibet testifies to this. The volume from which it comes, *Tibet under Chinese Communist Rule* (1976), was compiled by Tibetans associated with the government-

* Previously published as Sudeep Basu, 'Organizing for Exile! "Self-Help" among Tibetan Refugees in an Indian Town', in *Refugee Watch – A South Asian Journal on Forced Migration*, vol. 35, 2010, pp. 1–13. The article has been modified by the author for the current volume.

in-exile in Dharamsala. They have translated the statements into English and edited them slightly by omitting their concluding lines (an oath of truthfulness and accuracy) and by deleting 'unqualified personal interpretations of events and actions, expressions of hopes and prayers and emotional descriptions of the Chinese':

> We (the narrator, his wife and daughter) escaped from Tibet because life was getting more and more difficult and tension and fear of persecution was increasing every year. We had nothing that we could call our own. Everything belonged to the commune or the Chinese ... the Chinese demand labour from the people and take away most of the products from the lands for themselves. The people, are in fact, slaves of an alien conqueror. The amount of food available is barely enough to feed half the population. Heavy taxes are levied on every article of daily need.... What was most unbearable was the increasing hardship and mental torture. I was classified as a middle-class peasant and continually harassed for the crimes I had never committed. Last year, I decided to escape. The Chinese somehow came to know of it. I was blacklisted and accused of turning away from the proletarian socialist revolutionary path and following the way of the reactionary Dalai bandits. I was given the alternative of either making a frank confession of my crimes and wrong thoughts or else facing public trials, imprisonment and torture. I could not change my thoughts as the Chinese wanted and knew that the only change I was going to bring to the whole situation was escaping from Tibet. On the night of March 2, 1971, while everybody was attending the nightly study-cum-meeting session, we fled and headed towards the Nepalese border. (1976: 126–27)

Examples such as this (see Nowak 1984: 11–12), multiplied by the thousands, do serve as individual explanations for the Tibetan diaspora. In ascertaining the motives for flight, Dawa Norbu cites T. C. Palakshappa's fieldwork among the Tibetan refugees in Mundgod (south India), where he interviewed 869 families in the late 1970s. Norbu elaborates on Palakshappa's field data, showing the respondents' motives for their flight in the following order of descending importance: The first and more general reason given was the popular feeling of acute anxiety about the future of their religion and culture under the communist regime. They were afraid that they would not be allowed to practice Buddhism and maintain their way of life2. The second and more specific reason was that the numerous Tibetans had heard about the atrocities committed by the Chinese in Lhasa such as torture and humiliation in public for anyone unwilling to embrace Chinese communism. The third reason was that the Chinese authorities were obstructing endogamous marriages among the Tibetans who were forced to take a bride or a groom from among the Chinese. This measure, they explained, was aimed at destroying 'their race of which the Tibetans were so proud'. The fourth reason was the news that their leader, the Dalai Lama, had escaped to India. Saklani also writes that many Tibetans she interviewed took to flight after hearing about the Dalai Lama's escape. The fifth reason was the confiscation of property from the propertied classes. Moreover, the Chinese had planned the takeover in such a way that the communities and families were split among themselves. Children were used to spy upon their parents, the wife upon the husband. The occupation of Tibet by the Chinese created a sense of insecurity and this insecurity in their daily life was at the core of the Tibetan exodus. (Norbu 1994: 4)

Most refugees had to leave their families behind and make the treacherous journey to India. The old and the young among them perished along the way. India was an alien land, with its low altitude. The cultural shock on arrival was more telling (Phuntso 2004). Avedon (1984: 70) writes about the emergency meeting called by the Dalai Lama on 25 April 1959, with few senior Tibetan officials who had accompanied him from Tibet to discuss the situation and plan for the reconstruction in exile.[3] Soon after the meeting, the Dalai Lama re-established the Tibetan government-in-Exile in Dharamsala to meet both the immediate and long-term needs of the Tibetan people. The Dalai Lama said, 'In 1959, when I escaped with a few cabinet ministers, the Tibetan government, which has history of three hundred years also came into exile. The exiled Tibetan government is not a new creation. Wherever the Dalai Lama resides, the Tibetan people consider that as the seat of the Tibetan government'.[4]

Taking Refuge in India

The Early Years

Upon his arrival, the Dalai Lama received a telegram from Prime Minister Nehru, which read, 'My colleagues and I welcome you and send greetings on your safe arrival in India. We shall be happy to afford the necessary facilities to you, your family and entourage to reside in India. The people of India, who hold you in great veneration, will no doubt accord their traditional respect to your personage. Kind regards to you. Nehru' (Tenzin Gyatso 1983: 144). Avedon notes how Nehru stresses 'that his support of the Dalai Lama was humanitarian only, based on a "tremendous bond" growing out of centuries of spiritual and cultural exchange between India and Tibet' (1984: 166).

As the Tibetans poured into India, they stayed in two large transit camps. Phuntso notes, 'These camps were established by the Government of India in consultation with the refugee leadership. One was at Missamari, located ten miles from Tezpur in Arunachal Pradesh; the other was at Buxa Duar, a former British prisoner-of-war camp situated near the Bhutanese border in West Bengal. Within a few weeks after the setting up of the camps, 6000 refugees arrived at Missamari and 1000 at Buxa Duar' (2004: 135). Camps became overcrowded and there was risk of disease and epidemics. This apprehension was not unfounded, since many Tibetans, unaccustomed to tropical climate, fell victims to tuberculosis, cholera, skin diseases and malaria.

The transit camps closed down in July 1960. In order to make the process of rehabilitation somewhat more bearable for Tibetans, they were engaged in road building works in cooler Himalayan regions in north India that are climatically similar to Tibet. 'The first batch of 3394 people was sent for roadwork in Sikkim in September 1959 in several groups and another batch of 400 to Kalimpong and Darjeeling and some to Bhutan. Later in early 1960 more people were sent for roadwork in the North Indian states of Himachal Pradesh, Arunachal Pradesh and Jammu and Kashmir' (Phuntso 2004: 135–36).

Avedon wrote, 'As the Tibetans discovered, in common with one road group after another, contact with the local people, though necessary, was often hazardous. Whatever infectious diseases were present among the inhabitants – tuberculosis in particular passed indiscriminately to the Tibetans who lacking the proper antibodies most often died. Within a few weeks of the exile's arrival in India it became clear that the task of transition was not only more threatening than that of escape but so universally destructive, affecting virtually every family that the survival of the refugees as a coherent group was itself called into question' (1984: 78). On 29 April 1960, after a little more than a year's stay, the Dalai Lama left Mussoorie for Dharamsala, which came to be known as 'Little Lhasa'[5]. In Dharamsala, the Dalai Lama revitalised his administration-in-exile and called a special meeting of the deputies and staff members on 2 September 1960 to formulate new rules and regulations and reallocate portfolios of the Kalon.

Roadwork provided temporary employment in the initial period, although the job was hazardous. Refugees had to risk their lives, climbing up steep slopes with little formal training. Children and the elderly found this task particularly cumbersome and the unsettled nature of roadwork added to their woes. The environment was harsh and many Tibetans contracted tuberculosis and other diseases due to the lack of sanitation. Aware of the possible protracted nature of the Tibetan struggle, the Dalai Lama said, 'Some Tibetans at that time, however, put forward the idea of temporarily settling all the Tibetan refugees along the border areas of the Himalayas so that we could be ready to return to Tibet at the first opportunity. But we decided to give priority to more permanent rehabilitation with facilities to enable all the Tibetans to live in homogeneous communities and provide the young with good education, modern as well as our own traditional education so even if the struggle takes generations, new generations could replace the older ones and take on the responsibility'.[6] Thus, the Dalai Lama approached Nehru for assistance in the permanent rehabilitation of the refugees. Nehru on his part canvassed the state governments for vacant land. Mysore State immediately responded, initially offering 1,500 hectares of an uninhabited stretch of jungle in gently rolling hills at Bylakuppe, 80 km west of Mysore city, situated at the altitude of 900 m above sea level.[7] The state government initially agreed to accept 3,000 Tibetan refugees and provided a grant of Rs 3,784,800 for the rehabilitation project (Phuntso 2004: 137).

Formation of Agriculture-based Settlements

Soon after, the first Tibetan agricultural settlement was set up in December 1960 at Bylakuppe, accommodating a total of 3,217 Tibetan refugees by the end of 1965. For administrative reasons, the settlement was divided into six camps, each with 250–300 hectares of land. In the first few years, the settlers engaged in clearing jungle, digging wells and constructing houses during which they were paid daily wages and given regular rations. Phuntso writes about the early establishment, 'The settlers were divided into artificial families of five people, relatives or not, and each family was given two-and-a-half hectares of land. They were accommodated in one-room, brick-walled, tile-roofed single storey houses built on 50 sq. m., part of which also served as a kitchen garden. A cooperative society was set up in 1961 and later formally registered. The cooperatives set up in 1961 procured and advanced seeds, fertilisers and pesticides; marketed agricultural produce collectively and provided common services such as tractors, trucks and warehousing. Besides, the cooperatives played a crucial role in managing carpet-weaving centres, flour mills, poultry farms and other ventures such as retail outlets in the settlements. In the same year, a school was opened in the settlements, which was later managed by the Tibetan Schools Society (an autonomous body under the Ministry of Education of the government of India. When the Bylakuppe settlement first started, a small dispensary was set up in a tent to care for the emergency medical needs of the refugees. Later, in 1964, a special complex of concrete houses was built with assistance from foreign aid organisations to accommodate a dispensary with inpatient facilities. For the first five years, the settlers cultivated cotton, tobacco, rice, millet, paddy, lentils and oilseeds, all of which failed miserably. Farming in south India was so different from Tibet's unique high-altitude agronomy that many settlers became totally discouraged and helpless.' (2004: 137–38)[8]

The Bylakuppe settlement was the progenitor of other agriculture-based settlements to follow. 'In 1962, the second settlement was set up at Chaglang in Arunachal Pradesh, accommodating 1,503 refugees by March 1963 on 1,900 acres of densely-forested land. In February 1962, the third settlement was opened at Tezu in the Lohit district of Arunachal Pradesh, accommodating 864 Tibetan refugees. The fourth settlement, established at Mainpat in Chhattisgarh in March 1963, accommodated 1,726 Tibetans on 750 hectares of land. In May 1963, the fifth settlement was set up at Chandragiri in Odisha, accommodating 3,000 refugees. In April 1965, the sixth settlement was founded at Mundgod, nearly 495 km north of Bylakuppe, accommodating 4,000 refugees on 2,000 hectares of land. By 1969, 21 agricultural settlements for over 20,000 refugees were operating in India, Nepal and Bhutan. Later, eight more agricultural-based settlements were set up at Hunsur and Kollegal in Karnataka, Byhandara in Maharashtra, Bomdila in Arunachal Pradesh, Changtang and Leh in Ladakh, and Herbertpur in Uttaranchal' (Phuntso 2004: 138–39).

Agro-Industrial Settlements

The nomadic background of the early Tibetan settlers came in the way of their taking up farming as an occupation. Most refugees had to also look for other avenues of employment and in that direction, the Tibetan Industrial Rehabilitation Society (TIRS) was established in October 1965, with its headquarters in New Delhi. It was registered as a charitable society under the Indian Societies Registration Act of 1860. For the next three years, the TIRS launched several small industrial projects. These included a wool mill at Bir, tea estates at Bir and Chauntra, Tibetan crafts at Bajnath (all in the Kangra valley, Himachal Pradesh), a limestone quarry at Kumrao, a hydrated lime plant at Sataun, a fibre glass factory at Paonta Sahib and a handicraft centre in Puruwala (in the Simour district of Himachal Pradesh) (Phuntso 2004: 139). More than 4,000 refugees were ultimately settled in these projects. However, many of these efforts failed due to lack of technical and managerial skills. The majority of the industrial settlements gradually began to depend more on traditional carpet weaving and roadwork in summer and wool garment trade in Indian towns and cities in winter (Phuntso 2004: 140). With regard to the TIRS, Girija Saklani observed, 'The shortage of funds even for administrative purposes proved to be a formidable obstacle. Donors were reluctant to provide continuous assistance as their earlier aid had been more or less abortive. Besides, after 1971, all voluntary agencies in India were concentrating on relief to the Bangladeshi refugees. Under these circumstances, it is stated that the TIRS was advised (mostly by the donors) to wind up its activities' (1984: 232–35). The Society, however, took the bold step of carrying on but decided to reorient its policy and streamline its activities by rectifying past mistakes. It introduced some commercial discipline to prevent any financial irregularities. It decided to pool all financial assistance into a rolling fund and gave assistance to the undertakings, which cooperated with the TIRS and furnished full accounts of their working. The TIRS decided to have agricultural-cum-handicraft projects. The undertakings, which were not immediately feasible, were shelved until the required funds were forthcoming and a few others were finally closed (Saklani 1984: 234).

Handicraft-based Settlements

Pre-exilic trade flourished between India and Tibet, which resulted in the growth of many traditional crafts in Tibet. Skilled craftsmen were involved in metal work, woodcraft, clay modelling, thangka painting, handmade paper, leatherwork, weaving of wool cloth and carpets, among others. These were practised in homes and were part of local networks that enabled the sale and production of these artefacts within and outside Tibet. By the early 1960s, Tibetan craftsmen came to settle in traditional trading posts like Kalimpong in north Bengal and were self-settled refugees in Darjeeling and Sikkim. The Dalai Lama stressed that 'our performing arts, our literature, science and religion as well as those crafts from which we could earn a livelihood – painting, metalcraft, architecture, woodworking and carpetmaking – these we took special pains to safeguard. To achieve this we employed modern methods although they were altogether new to us and posed many difficulties' (Avedon 1984: 92). The first handicraft-based settlement was founded on a two-hectare estate in Darjeeling in October 1959.[9]

Encouraged by the success of the first handicraft-based settlement, other centres were set up in the following years. These included the handicraft centres in Dalhousie, Dharamsala, Kalimpong, Shimla, Clement Town, Rajpur and Dehradun. Similar settlements were also set up in Nepal. In these handicraft-based settlements, cooperatives were established to procure raw materials and market the products. While the cooperatives marketed the settlement's produce both in India and abroad, the Tibetan refugee settlers soon took up the somewhat lucrative business of selling sweaters knitted initially by them, but later bought from factories in Ludhiana. Tibetans selling sweaters during winter seasons is a familiar sight across towns and cities in India. Saklani noted, 'In the winter months almost every town in India is thronged with Tibetan refugees – men, women and even children who have almost established a strong hold on the woolen knitwears is that these are supposed to be knit from pure Tibetan wool' (1984: 208). By the latter half of the 1960s, sweater-selling became the supplementary trade of the majority of Tibetan refugees.

Some General Comments on the Tibetan Refugee Settlements

At present, there are 46 Tibetan settlements in India, Nepal and Bhutan, home to most of the 100,451 Tibetan refugees in South Asia (Planning Council, Central Tibetan Administration 2000).[10] Within a span of a few years, the refugees from Tibet became self-supporting and emerged as 'one of the most successful' refugee communities in the world.[11] Girija Saklani wrote that Tibetans have, on the whole, 'successfully emerged from a self-sufficient barter economy into a competitive economy and have adjusted to the new situation which is a tribute to the Tibetan community in exile' (1984: 216).

According to Dawa Norbu (2004: 193), 'By far the most fundamental features of the Tibetan success lay in the indigenous leadership and organisation that emerged out of the traditional social and political structures. Such leadership and organisation, especially during the initial and critical years were instrumental in the successful implementation of various projects. What is of concern to those analysing the Tibetan refugee crisis is the fact that the Tibetan government-in-exile in Dharamsala is not recognised as a legal entity by the international community at large. At the same time, the Tibetan government (bod gzhun) is considered a legitimate authority in relation to the refugee community as a whole, which has a bearing on the lives of refugees in the diaspora. The government of India recognises the position of the Dalai Lama and his pivotal leadership role vis-à-vis his community members. This is consistent with India's approach to Tibetan refugees, which is one of giving 'due recognition' to Tibetan refugeehood as well as giving space for them to preserve their cultural identity in exile.

Organisational Structure of the Refugee Settlements

The question of leadership and organisation within refugee communities is a crucial part of the subject matter of refugee studies. An elucidation of the role of indigenous leadership and organisation in the process of refugee rehabilitation and settlement is therefore deemed critical in the present study. Dawa Norbu states, 'The settlements are not completely identical in their organisation, but they follow a pattern, the terms for the functionaries and the levels may differ' (2003: 195). In principle, there are three layers of decision-making. At the head is the settlement officer, who belongs to the Tibetan Central Administration. The settlements comprising 1,000–8,000 people are divided into camps, also called villages. The inhabitants elect a camp leader called *chimie.* S/he is assisted by four spokespersons called *chupon,* representing 250 inhabitants. The chupon originally represented 10 households but as the population has increased, this number is no longer strictly adhered to.[12]

Some Illustrations

Bylakuppe Settlement

In Bylakuppe, where about half the Tibetan refugees in south India live, there are two settlements. Thr first of these is Lugsung Samdupling founded in 1961, therefore also called the 'old settlement'. It has a population of 7,631 (Tibetan Demographic Survey 1998). The second, Dekyi Larsoe, founded in 1969, with 3,096 people, is the 'new settlement'. In addition to these, there about 7,000 inhabitants of the monasteries: monks, novices and staff. The four sects in Tibetan Buddhism have rebuilt their famous monasteries, namely Sera, Tashilhunpo, Kargye and Namdrolling next to the settlements. These monasteries and their monk population follow their own organisation and have to find their own funding; they are not part of the settlement administration. Bylakuppe settlements are organised along hierarchical lines. Dawa Norbu describes them as such: 'the chupon or "head of ten" [is] at the base. The chupon's duty is to organise labour for community projects, call for meetings, organise festivals and hear grievances. Such deputies, numbering four in each camp, are annually elected. The most important functionary is the chimie or 'general leader' nowadays called camp leader. Above these democratically-elected positions are the appointees of Dharamsala and chief among them is the Settlement Officer (*sku-tsab*). He heads a fully-staffed office and is accountable to the Department of Home of the CTA. The settlement officers and their staff plan the policies for the settlement as a whole with respect not only to economic matters but also to socio-cultural ones. Such policies and projects are implemented through the useful offices of the chupon after consultation with the chimie. Internally, the settlement officer seeks to integrate diverse sub-cultural units by articulating pan-Tibetan identity. The settlement officer uses the prestige of his office to mediate disputes but only if efforts at the lower levels fail. Externally, the settlement officer often acts on behalf of his settlers in their dealings with Indian legal and political officials.' (2004: 196).[13]

Mundgod Settlement

The Tibetan refugee organisation at the Mundgod settlement that Palakshappa (1978) describes seems slightly different. We cannot fail to observe the centrality of the Dharamsala-appointed settlement officer and the organising principle of the social organisation. The economic and political nerve-centre of the Mundgod Tibetan settlement as in other settlements is the Tibetan cooperative society whose membership is open to all the male heads of all the households in the camp. In the Mundgod settlement, we see the overwhelming presence of the Dharamsala-appointed settlement officer overseeing operations. The Tibetan cooperative society is the central organising principle whose membership is open to all male heads of households in the camp. The secretary appointed by the Dharamsala administration is the head of the cooperative society. He mediates between the Dharamsala administration and the Mundgod settlement. (1978: 43).

Dawa Norbu elaborates on the structure and process of the Mundgod settlement, which has built-in checks to prevent any autocracy to emerge from within, 'It consists of nine villages and each village elects a leader called Gambo meaning "the elder" (corresponding to the chimie at Bylakuppe). The village leader acts as a link between the village and the cooperative society's secretary. The secretary delegates authority to the village leader and the latter transmits messages and policies from the cooperative society; he tries to solve his villagers' problems such as getting loans from the bank, meditating in civil disputes, getting fertiliser from the cooperative and above all, he gets tasks and projects ordered by the secretary done by the villagers. The village leader is assisted by group leaders (chupon). The group leaders are subordinate to the village leader and are in constant touch with him. They report to the village leader about the needs and problems of families whom they represent and who have elected them. Communication and command flows through hierarchy: from the secretary to the village leaders from the village leaders to group leaders and from group leaders to individual households" (2004: 197–98).

On Dharamsala: Little Lhasa

Before undertaking an ethnographic analysis of the Darjeeling Tibetans, it is important to interrogate the role played by Dharamsala[14] (which is at the centre of the Tibetan diaspora) in circulating particularised meanings of Tibetanness, especially those connected to the theme of preservation of traditional culture and return to homeland and the desire to project a sense of continuity in a changing external environment. This would enable an understanding later on of the mode and reasons Tibetan refugees at Darjeeling live both inside and outside their ethnic community, of how Darjeeling becomes another space at once central and marginal to the Tibetan diaspora, where Tibetans 'mediate between cultures' and groups, in James Clifford's sense of diasporas as 'mediating cultures' (1994: 311), as they become more localised and more cosmopolitan over time.

Kiela Diehl describes Dharamsala as '[b]oth a place of rest or refuge and a place to pass through, both a destination and a place one must leave to fulfill the very promise of pilgrimage' (2002: 32). This focus on Dharamsala as a 'place of rest' can be complemented by a play with the root word dharamsala.[15] Dibyesh Anand's contention is that the 'symbolic geography of the place along with a particular implication of the word dharmshala supports the dominant story preferred by the exile elite and their non-Tibetan supporters (the "salvage mentality" or "Shangri-La paradigm" as they are often termed)' (2002: 13). In consequence, Dharamsala is only seen as a static stage for theatrics of Tibetan diasporic culture and politics. This notion of fixity hides the fact that the geography of Dharamsala has had a changing symbolic role for Tibetan diaspora. As Dibyesh Anand notes, 'A movement from a poor refugee settlement to one of the most popular tourist destination, a change from a small, dilapidated village to a cosmopolitan small town – all these are indicative as well as constitutive of changes within Tibetan exile community' (2002: 15).

The physical location of Dharamsala in the hills of Himachal Pradesh has facilitated its projection and promotion as 'Little Lhasa'. For those white Westerners to whom Lhasa is a 'forbidden city' that is inaccessible, lying on the 'roof of the world', Dharamsala, in some senses, appears close by. The hilly terrain of Dharamsala replicates Lhasa's aura and grandeur, albeit in a truncated form.[16] The mountainous terrain of McLeod Ganj and its distance from any big city contributes to the symbolic geography of Dharamsala. There are logistical and practical problems because of such a location and the government-in-exile recognises it. However, there is reason to believe that it would be slightly more difficult for Tibetans to pursue a strategy of limited acculturation had Dharamsala been near some big city (Anand 2002: 17). The location of Tibetan settlements has been decided entirely by Indian central and state governments.

Drawing upon the usage of the word dharamshala, Dibyesh Anand in his essay (2000) attempts to theorise Tibetan identity discourse in broadly two ways. 'Dharamshala', in popular Hindi usage, refers to a 'temporary home'. The first way, which has a wide currency among the Tibetan government and non-Tibetan supporters of the Tibetan cause, looks at the experience of diaspora as a temporary phenomenon. It is not therefore surprising that Dharamsala is projected as Little Lhasa in India and several dynamics go on to support such a projection. The institutionalised expression of the theme of preservation of culture is best found at the Norbulingka Institute, which is dedicated explicitly to the preservation of Tibet in both its literary and artistic forms.

The idea that Tibetan culture in diaspora is more authentic than one prevalent in Chinese-controlled Tibet is supported by a few factors. One of them is the passing down of cultural authority through the practice of reincarnation. A significant part of Tibetan culture and religion had been embodied within reincarnate lamas, the most important being the Dalai Lama himself. The idea of true cultural authority in exile rather than within Tibet is also supported by the presence of some great mastercraftsmen[17] who had been trained in their arts in Old Tibet and then moved to exile.

Tibetan Refugees vis-à-vis the Law in India

The dominant paradigm of 'Little Lhasa' as a temporary station where Tibetan culture is being preserved is rendered most problematical by the experiences of Tibetans living as urban refugees[18] in Darjeeling. It would be prudent to focus at a general level on the diverse and complicated concerns of India's as yet incomplete refugee law and practice that would have a bearing on the lives of Tibetan refugees leading an increasingly diasporised existence.

India's policy towards the UNHCR and joining the Refugee Convention of 1951 has been ambivalent due to a succession of historical reasons. At first, India's perception was that the Convention was too Eurocentric. That changed with the Cold War raging between Russia and America and others. The focus of refugee policy and practice was overtly on those who had fled from communist regimes. India handled the Tibet and Bangladesh crises with some help from foreign agencies, including the UNHCR.[19] Within India, there has been some social and political resistance to joining the Convention of 1951 and to altering India's foreigner's law to provide specific recognition to refugees to write in protections towards refugees as a matter of legal entitlement. Historic notice is taken of the range of migrations, conquests and refugee absorption, which is now characteristically a part of India's past and present. Behind this is the social assumption that care and concern are always available for foreigners in India. A general attitude seems to have emerged that India can deal with refugees in a convincing and humane way without invoking a cumbersome refugee-specific regime. Rajeev Dhavan (2004: 12) notes an irony that emerges in the policy of both the Indian government and the UNHCR. UNHCR profiles India as a nation in which 'local integration' is preeminently possible. Local integration acquires a priority over other durable solutions[20] including in particular 'resettlement'. This provokes anguish and protest by refugees who feel that 'local integration' in India is exaggerated and incomplete and that there is a lack of proper and non-discriminatory approach towards evolving just solutions.[21]

The legal framework concerning refugees in India has been in a state of undefined and unsettled evolution. India has a liberal constitutional framework that guarantees certain fundamental human rights even to foreigners. However, the Indian statutory regime dealing with foreigners refuses even to acknowledge refugees as a special class of people deserving its consideration. It is here that the determination of citizenship becomes important to the operation of a refugee regime. The basic provision for determination of citizenship in 1950 was Article 5 of the Constitution which states that 'At the commencement of this Constitution, every person who has his domicile in the territory of

India and who was born in the territory of India; or either of whose parents was born in the territory of India; or who has been ordinarily resident in the territory of India for not less than five years immediately preceding such commencement shall be a citizen of India'. In the Constitutional Amendment in 1986, every person born in India after the commencement of the Citizenship (Amendment) Act, 1986 had to show that one of the parents was a citizen of India before his or her claim to Indian citizenship was accepted. Thus, if a person was born in India after 1 July 1987 to non-Indian parents, that person would not be an Indian citizen. The Citizenship (Amendment) Act, 2004 adds a further qualification, whereby a person born in India can become an Indian citizen only if both his/her parents are Indian or if one of his/her parents is Indian and the other is not an illegal migrant. This immediately begs the question as to the status of a child born out of wedlock between an illegal migrant and an Indian. This Act does not allow such a person to become a citizen of India merely by birth in India. Such provisions do increase the possibilities of statelessness.

Even though the general law on foreigners in India is silent on treating refugees as a distinct class of foreigners needing protection, there have been special legislative measures reflecting India's refugee policy to address particular problems. Most of these measures have been either compensatory or rehabilitative, as in the case of partition refugees or giving exemptions from the general law applicable to foreigners as in the case of Tibetan refugees. The Registration of Foreigners (Exemption) Order 1957 made several exemptions for certain foreigners from the stringent registration requirements generally applicable to all. Children under the age of 16 were entirely exempted. Rule 3 of the said order also relaxed certain regulations for, inter alia, 'indigenous inhabitants of Tibet region of China'. The Order Regulating Entry of Tibetan Nationals into India, 1950 stipulates that a Tibetan national 'at the time of his entry into India obtain from the officer-in-charge of the Police post the Indo-Tibetan frontier, a permit in the form specified'. The permit allows such a person to stay and travel in India for the prescribed period, which is extendable on application.

The absence of an identifiable legal regime to deal with refugees is reflected in the manner and extent to which refugees are protected in India. At a formal level, the Indian government has no specific mechanism or machinery or even normative principles designated for the determination of refugee status and protection. If such a procedure is opened as a formal process, any decision on the determination of refugee status would be a decision of the government of India and instantly amenable to judicial review by the High Court and Supreme Court. Nevertheless, in exercise of the powers conferred by Section 3 of the Registration of Foreigners Act 1939 and Section 3 of the Foreigners Act 1946, the central government issued S.R.O. 1108, dated 26 December 1950, regulating the entry of Tibetan nationals into India. The order states:

> Any foreigner of Tibetan nationality who enters into India hereafter shall
> 1. At the time of his entry into India, obtain from the officer in-charge of the police post at the Indo-Tibetan frontier, a permit in the form specified in the annexed schedule;
> 2. Comply with such instructions as may be prescribed in the said permit;
> 3. Get himself registered as a foreigner and obtain a certificate of registration.

Tibetans, like other people who flee persecution in their own land, are handled legally under India's Foreigners Act[22] from 1946 and the Registration of Foreigners Act, 1939.[23] Every foreigner who arrives in India must furnish true particulars of oneself, the place of stay in India and the purpose of visit. Rule 6 requires a foreigner to inform the registration officer of one's presence in India and obtain a certificate of registration from the officer. Thus the government is free to expel refugees as it would any other foreigners.[24] Kevin Garratt writes, 'In the absence of specific treaty obligations, India's international protection of "refugees" is based essentially on sufferance' (1997: 32). The RC, issued under the Foreigners Registration Act, must be renewed on an annual basis. It serves as an important marker of refugee status in India. Refugees in Darjeeling testified to the fact that the process of the renewal of the RC every year was cumbersome and indicative of the precarious nature of life in exile.

When discussing Tibetans' status in India, it is important to distinguish between two different groups. The first are those who fled to India around the same time as the Dalai Lama in 1959 and through the early 1960s. These people and their children are 'born refugees', the majority of whom remain stateless are nonetheless slightly more advantaged than 'newcomers', or those who came from Tibet after the end of the Cultural Revolution from the mid-1980s to the present.[25] Since the UNHCR opened an office in Kathmandu and began counting Tibetan refugees in 1991, there has been a steady flow of about 2,500 arrivals in Nepal each year. In 2001, the UNHCR number was 1,381, down by 1,000 from the previous year, and roughly half of the annual average. (Report on Dangerous Crossing Conditions Impacting the Flight of Tibetan Refugees in 2001 © 2002 by the International Campaign for Tibet: 5) Since 1994, the policy of the Tibetan government-in-exile is to encourage newcomers to return to Tibet after receiving an education (Garratt 1997). The government-in-exile's justification is that 'new arrivals settling permanently in India to increase in number means that through our own efforts we are assisting the long-term evil Chinese policy of transferring large numbers of Chinese into Tibet. It is unnecessary for new arrivals to stay permanently in foreign parts for all the time. It has become vital that returning in whatever number to our own land of Tibet will maintain the policy of being able to hold on to what is our own' (Garratt 1997: 47).

The Indian government has followed a fairly liberal policy of granting refuge to various refugees. Past experience indicates that entry into India for most refugee groups is somewhat in line with the international principles of protection and non-refoulement. Refugees are generally not allowed to work in India. Some do find employment in the informal sector without facing any objection from the administration. There are similarities in the situation between refugees in general and foreigners in that the restrictions in place with regard to employment and work apply to both. Tibetan refugees are granted loans and other facilities for self-employment. However, refugees who enter India illegally or overstay the permitted period have strict restrictions on their movement in accordance with the legislation relating to foreigners, such as the Foreigners Act, 1946, the Foreigners Order, 1948 and the Passport Act, 1967.[26]

As residents of India, they move around freely from place to place unlike foreign visitors to the country. Yet they are expected to comply by the same terms and report to the same office as foreigners do. However, this RC document does not entitle them to travel abroad. In fact, this was another reason why some Tibetan refugees decided to apply for Indian citizenship, although this choice is far from unambiguous. In recent years, the Ministry of External Affairs has issued an Identity Certificate (IC) to RC holders. The IC is a small yellow book in lieu of a national passport issued for a period of 10 years to allow RC holders to travel abroad. If an RC holder takes up Indian citizenship, then the person must relinquish his IC at the nearest passport office. However, the overall ambiguity of the refugee status and laxity in enforcing rules has given RC holders sufficient leeway to create several identity papers and therefore negotiate between several contextually-determined identities.

Darjeeling as Our Place(s) of Rest/refuge!

To be in exile is to have been deprived of a land and the temporal rhythms of life appropriate to it. To live in exile is to live as an alien and perhaps in a state of 'elend' or misery, the English word 'alien' and the German word 'elend' do, in fact, share the same root (Tabori 1972: 31). At the same time, in an increasingly transnational world of diaspora cultures and communities, one is obliged to take account of how the place or places one is supposed to return to are constantly changing and evolving. The 'myth' in myth of return increasingly denotes not only the greater or lesser likelihood of a person eventually returning, that is the 'when' of return but also the 'where' of return and the very possibility that one cannot return home[27] either because home no longer exists or because it has moved elsewhere. Diversity of lives that Tibetan refugees lead owing to their dispersion and the size and span of the Tibetan diaspora prompts us not to ascribe any singular orientation to enforced existence outside Tibet. On 12 June 1998, the exile Tibetan population reached 122,078 from the initial estimated population of 80,000 in 1959, out of which 85,147 live in India and 13,720 in Nepal. The next largest group of exile Tibetans in Asia lives in Bhutan with 1,584 people and 109 in the Russian Federation and Japan together. The United States of America and Canada has the largest share of Tibetans in the West with 7,000 in total followed by 2,243 in Europe of which 68.6 per cent are distributed in Switzerland alone (Tibetan Demographic Survey 1998: 7). While there is no confusion among Tibetan refugees regarding the whereabouts of their homeland, after more than 40 years in exile, Tibetan refugees have developed relationships to multiple homes. James Clifford notes that even a specific longing for 'home' may be focused on more than one place, particularly in the case of people living in a multiply-centred diaspora network (1994: 305). Clifford has, however, been criticised for overemphasising the multilocal or global nature of diasporas at the expense of people, like Tibetans, who remain sharply focused on a literal territorial centre (Venturino 1997: 107). While home for the Tibetans lies without a doubt over the Himalayas, Darjeeling has emerged as the community's home in exile among other settlements throughout South Asia, Europe, Australia, the USA and Canada. The 'place' Darjeeling is, however, not strictly speaking a home to the generation of Tibetans who escaped into exile. Protracted exile however has produced a new generation of India-born Tibetan refugees who oscillate between the need to keep the notion of the homeland alive on the one hand and of the different kinds of material investments and emotional or social ties with host populations as a creative result of being the heirs of the displaced.

The most widely accepted meaning of the name Darjeeling is 'the place of dorje' – Dorje, among the Tibetans and to those who speak languages akin to Tibetan, could just be the name of a person, a thunderbolt or even a reference to a Buddha.[28] Consequently, 'the place of Dorje' has been translated as 'the Place of the Thunderbolt' (Waddell 1978: 299) where ling means a place in Tibetan.[29] Some are of the opinion that it was named after a lama who once lived there and constructed a monastery on the Observatory Hill. E. C. Dozey records that there was a monastery atop the hill as far back as 1765, which was a branch of the Phodang Monastery of Sikkim (Dozey 1989: 79).

Today, except for a makeshift arrangement, the monastery does not exist on account of the historic structure being removed by the Gorkhas in order to accommodate a temple to house the Hindu Shiva-linga in 1775. The monastery, or what was left of it, was later shifted to a sight near the Gymkhana Club but it was removed once again, this time to Bhutay Basti (also called Bhutia Busti) where it still stands today, to allow the St Andrews Church to be built. Despite the shifting of the monastery twice, first by the Hindus and then by the Christians, there is an exceptional religious tolerance and the Hindus and Buddhists worship together at the Observatory Hill without any apparent trace of enmity. The early Nepali settlers called Darjeeling 'Gundribazar' and perhaps this name survives in the truncated 'Bazaar', which is what the population of the surrounding locality call Darjeeling. Despite the suburban population adopting the abbreviated name, it is still possible to hear the name Gundribazar amongst the old folks living in the neighbourhood.

The Tibetan refugee/diasporic segment of Darjeeling's ever-shifting population cannot be understood without taking cognisance of the changing politico-ethnic boundaries of the place with its ebb and flow of administrators, nomads, traders, tourists, pilgrims and groups of varied ethnicities. The ways in which Tibetan residents of Darjeeling understand 'where they are' depends on the physical, historical and personal resonances for them between Darjeeling and other places and more specifically on what their route to Darjeeling has been. Tibetans came from all parts of Tibet as they embarked upon a trek over the Himalayas into exile in 1959. Those older generations came mainly from regions in Tibet which were proximate to India. Tibetans from far away provinces like Amdo and Kham were unfortunate. Tibet's wilderness and hugeness made the journey to India through eastern Nepal, Bhutan, Sikkim and the north-east more traumatic.[30]

The winter out-migration of Tibetan refugee sweater sellers and traders to the plains of India and their return to the mountains to celebrate Tibetan New Year (Losar) in February is an important reminder of the refugee community's continuing dependence on their hosts and of the need to reconsider the tentative relationships that most Tibetan refugees have with their co-ethnics, that is the Bhutias

(Tibetans who came to Darjeeling prior to 1959) and other ethnic groups such as the Nepalis (comprising Khambus, Murmis, Limbus, Chettri, Gurungs, Tamangs, Yolmos); and then the Lepchas; Sherpas; Rajbansi residing in Darjeeling Town. Focusing on the problematic, which Tanka Subba spells out with respect to the history of Darjeeling, would be crucial in order not only to apprehend the Tibetan refugee–host relation ('local integration' in refugee law) in Darjeeling, but also to understand the import of the shifting nature of territorialised or deterritorialised (in Appadurai's sense) identities in the refugee/diasporic context. Tanka Subba states, 'It may be further said that the history of a region should not be mixed up with the history of a people. The former is often space bound but the latter is seldom so. The lack of such an understanding among pro-establishment scholars have given rise to an unnecessary debate over what length of time a people requires in order to be eligible to claim a region it inhabits. If the Nepalis had more than three centuries' association with Darjeeling would they be considered eligible for claiming it? It is indeed unfortunate that such questions have to be raised, the answers to which lead us nowhere, they neither solve our problems nor enlighten us in any way. Yet we have to live with them?' (1992: 29). Such claims and counter claims of different ethnic groups over a region and its relation to time has had profound implications towards forging refugee identities of Tibetans and in determining the nature of their integration (the concept of integration will be elaborated upon later; see Harrell-Bond 1986 and Bulcha 1988) in the host society since 1959.

A brief outline of the history of Darjeeling at this stage would aid in understanding the more literal or geographically-based notions of ethnic identity and displacement. The territories of Darjeeling district were acquired by the British from two neighbouring states, Sikkim and Bhutan, in 1835.[31] The whole tract of Darjeeling comprising one, the Hilly region; two, the Terai; and three, the Dooars, belonged to the Raja of Sikkim. Between 1780 and 1810, Nepal annexed a portion of the Terai and Hilly regions of Darjeeling. In the Anglo–Nepal war in 1817, the East India Company wrested away the territory from Nepal and restored it to Sikkim. As a mark of respect, the Raja of Sikkim gifted the territory, scarcely populated by Lepchas, to the Company in

1835. Prior to the Passage of Councils Act, 1861, Darjeeling remained under a non-regulation scheme. In the Councils Act of 1861, distinction between regulated and non-regulated provinces ceased to exist. Act no. XV of 1874 declared Darjeeling as a Scheduled District granting it a special status along with other four districts of Bengal. These districts were kept outside the ambit of general laws in operation throughout the rest of India. The Government of India Act, 1919 replaced the term Scheduled District with a new terminology, 'backward tract'. The Government of India Act 1935 brought in its wake significant changes in the administrative system and substituted the 'backward tract' with 'excluded' area or 'partially excluded area' with the intent to provide special status to certain areas including the district of Darjeeling. The policy of 'excluded' and 'partially excluded areas' was designed to alienate the tribes from the general population and divide the country by playing on ethnic distinctions. The colonial concept of exclusion found expression in the Indian Constitution in the form of the Fifth and Sixth Schedules wherein certain mechanisms were evolved for the administration of tribal areas. The tribal policy initiated by the British and subsequently adopted by the government of India facilitated the process of ethnic consolidation among groups. Not all groups could translate ethnic identity into political gains (Sarkar and Bhaumik 2000: 15–16).

Among Our Pre-exilic Tibetan Hosts!

Although literature does exist on the post-1959 Tibetans and their trials and tribulations under Chinese rule and in the diaspora, there is scarcely any literature on the old Tibetans who were residing in Darjeeling prior to 1959. Ethnographic encounter with these early Tibetans known as the Bhutias reveals how they not only aided in the adaptation of Tibetan refugees in Darjeeling (Subba 1990) but also helped in shaping their identity in exile. O'Malley (2001: 188) writes that the Bhutias are of 'Tibetan stock, the name meaning the people of Bhot, the sanskritic name for Tibet (which is a corruption of the Mongoloid Thubot)'. A large number of Tibetans began settling in Sikkim from the middle of the seventeenth century and got mixed up with the local people, particularly the Lepchas. The early history of the Bhutias in Sikkim is shrouded in myth and legend but a common belief is that they came from eastern Tibet. Some theories suggest that they may have been exiles from the great Tangut (Tibetan) Buddhist kingdom of Minyak, which flourished at the eastern end of the Central Asian Silk Road between the tenth and thirteenth centuries.[32] The legendary ancestor of the Sikkim Bhutias, Guru Tashi, was apparently a younger prince from the royal house of Minyak who lived in the twelfth and thirteenth centuries. Since he had no prospect of inheriting the throne of Minyak, he travelled with his family to seek his fortune and arrived at Sakya monastery in Tibet. There his eldest son performed what was then considered the miraculous feat of erecting the pillars of the new monastery that was being built and he became known as Khye-bum-sar (Rhodes and Rhodes 2006: 5). Thereafter, the family settled in the Chumbi valley from where they made contact with a Lepcha chieftain living near Gangtok. The descendants of Khye-bum-sar's three sons who settled in Sikkim and in the Chumbi valley formed 12 clans one of which was called the Nam-tsang-khopa and it was from this clan that Laden La, a highly influential figure in Darjeeling and Tibet during the first three decades of the twentieth century, was descended. Although little is known of their early years, these Bhutia clans brought Buddhism with them and established Nyimapa temples and monasteries throughout the region.

In 1907, the first ever demand for a 'separate administrative set-up' for the district of Darjeeling was placed before the government by the leaders of the hill people.[33] The three communities comprising the hill people had already developed various sorts of interdependence, agrarian and trade being the two most important sectors in this regard. A common forum for interaction between the three main hill communities of Darjeeling was non-existent until the establishment of the Hillmen's Association. It is evident that an informal association of these three communities had already come into existence in 1907 itself (Subba 1992: 78). According to Bagadi and Danda, the Hillmen's Association came into being in 1921 to 'safeguard and advocate the legitimate interests of the hill people in the sphere of politics' and under the leadership of 'Bahadur Rai, Hari Prasad Pradhan and Laden La' (1982: 342).

The influence of the Tibetan émigré community in the region is amply demonstrated through the life and works of Sonam Wangfel Laden La. He was born in 1876 in Darjeeling, possibly in Bhutia Busty or in Ging and into a Sikkim Bhutia Lama family, who were small landowners in the region. He was the first local boy to be given a 'European' education in Darjeeling, as well as a comprehensive education in his own Sikkimese Tibetan culture. After successfully completing his education, he was the first local hill boy to be appointed to the Imperial Police Force in Darjeeling at officer rank. As regards the relationship with Tibet, after the Younghusband military expedition of 1904, Laden La did play an important role in establishing a good rapport between British India and the Dalai Lama. When the thirteenth Dalai Lama sought refuge in India in 1910, Laden La was assigned to his party on a full-time basis and from then until 1914, he was continually involved with Tibetan affairs.[34]

His interest in local politics continued and he advanced the view that Darjeeling be separated from the rest of Bengal and became the President of the Hillmen's Association twice. As Tanka Subba writes, 'a cursory glance at the various memoranda…indicated a tremendous strain that Laden La the key figure in the region until the mid 1930's had taken to keep the Hillmen's Association true to its name. It was his status as "Sardar Bahadur" and the respect he wielded among the Nepalis that enabled him to stop this Association from turning into a Gorkha Association' (1992: 80–81). In December 1934, he organised a meeting in Darjeeling with the express intention of resolving the internal disputes of the three hill communities. After that meeting, Parasmani Pradhan proposed the establishment of the Hill Peoples Social Union and in February 1935 they published a magazine called *Nebula* (short for Nepali-Bhutia-Lapche). The petition submitted by the Hillmen's Association in 1934 had recommended that Darjeeling should not be incorporated as part of Bengal but should have a separate status. However, the Government of India Act, 1935 ignored these petitions and Darjeeling was integrated into Bengal as a 'partially excluded area' and at the same time it was decided that a representative from Darjeeling should sit in the Bengal Legislative Assembly.

Ruling elites of pre-exilic Tibet who had fled from Tibet before 1959 had already secured a comfortable niche in the socio-economic environment of the region. Some of them had come along with their cattle and others with enough riches, gold and precious stones to be soon counted among the richest in the region. It was also these refugees and the Bhutias who extended financial and other forms of assistance to those less fortunate refugees coming after 1959. The cultural affinity between the Bhutias and the Tibetan refugees would have had a role in creating a temporary home for Tibetans in exile. However, the proposition put forward by Tanka Subba that proper adaptation of groups is a function of cultural affinity requires further examination. Subba (1990: 68) notes that the 'Bhutias like their Tibetan refugee co-ethnics are Buddhists and have been successful throughout in staying away from the influence of Christianity'.

With regard to the linguistic connection, the Bhutias are familiar with the Tibetan language, although the Bhutias of the region call their language 'Sikkimese'. Some of the kin terms like 'pala' or father, 'amala' or mother, and 'achala' or sister were well known and understood by the local communities in Darjeeling. As the number of Indian Tibetan Bhutia began to grow, they felt it necessary to remain organised. At the initial stages, some associations were formed but they began to affiliate themselves under one banner appropriately named '*Kidu Chu*' – an umbrella organisation of 10 Bhutia associations. The office of *Kidu-Chu* is located at N. B. Singh Road below Laden La Road car park, Darjeeling. As one Bhutia respondent said, 'All Tibetan Bhutias are Buddhists and regard Dalai Lama as their spiritual head. We celebrate Tibetan New Year. Other important festivals include *Saka Dawa* (Buddha Sakyamuni's Birth, Enlightenment and Parinirvana); *Zam ling Chisang* (Universal Prayer Day); *Choekhor Due Chen* (Buddha Sakyamuni's first preaching at Sarnath). We speak Tibetan and our script is known as *Umay* and *Uchen*'.[35] Bhutias also observe the occasion of Phupati with members of other ethnic groups. The president of *Kidu-Chu,* on the occasion of Phupati, said, 'We are here to promote communal harmony and national integration. Anyway, it said Buddhism evolved from Hinduism and this is why we are taking part in these celebrations'. The general secretary of *Kidu-Chu* added, 'We also celebrate Laxmi puja and

Bhai tika during Diwali. Dussehra and Diwali have evolved more as social festivals in the hills and we have always been part of these events'.[36]

Notes

1. As Dawa Norbu notes elsewhere, 'By "Inner Tibet" the British officials referred to what Tibetans call Amdo and Kham most of parts of which were already incorporated into the neighbouring Chinese provinces of Sichuan, Yunnan, Gansu and Qinghai before 1951. And "Outer Tibet" included Central, Southern and Western Tibet and some parts of Kham, which were under the effective control of the Tibetan government in Lhasa at the time of the Chinese takeover' (1996: 79).

2. This motive was supported and emphasised by Christoph Von-Furer Haimendorf in *The Renaissance of Tibetan Civilization*, Oxford University Press, 1990.

3. The meeting was held in Mussoorie, which served as the Dalai Lama's initial headquarters. The discussion at the meeting was also greatly influenced by Nehru who had called on the Dalai Lama at Mussoorie the day before. His advice to the Dalai Lama was to 'rest and consider things well without being hasty'. The meeting identified a few areas of concentration: rehabilitation of the Tibetan refugees, education of Tibetan children, preservation of Tibetan culture and identity, gathering and disseminating information regarding Tibetans both inside and outside Tibet, pursuing the Tibetan question at the United Nations and preserving and promoting unity among the Tibetan refugee community.

4. See the Dalai Lama's keynote speech to the Second International Conference of Tibet Support Groups, Bonn (Germany), 14 June 1996, in the Tibetan Parliamentary and Policy Research Centre, 'The Political Philosophy of His Holiness the XIVth Dalai Lama', New Delhi 1998: 118.

5. Though 'Little Lhasa' was put on the map of global tourism mostly after the mid 1980s, the name had come to be associated with Upper McLeod Ganj from the 1960s itself (see passing reference to it in Avedon 1984: 103).

6. His Holiness the Dalai Lama's keynote address to the Second International Conference of Tibet Support Groups, Bonn (Germany), 14 June 1996.

7. The Office of H.H. the Dalai Lama, 'Tibetans in Exile: 1959–69', A Report on Ten Years of Rehabilitation in India, Dharamsala 1969: 4.

8. The agony of the repeated crop failure was solved in 1965 when a Swiss technical advisor in consultation with the Agriculture University of Bangalore conducted soil tests and also tested the yields of bullock-ploughed and tractor-

ploughed fields. This test resulted in the cultivation of maize crop instead of cotton, tobacco and other crops and also the replacement of bullock ploughs by tractor ploughs. The new crop methods proved so successful that by the end of 1966, the settlement became self-supporting (Phuntso 2003: 138).

9. The thirteenth Dalai Lama, during his exile from Tibet in 1910–11, had used this site as his temporary residence and therefore it has a special sentimental value for the Tibetans. A more detailed description of this handicraft-based settlement would follow later while taking up the ethnographic case of the Tibetan refugees in Darjeeling.

10. There is a floating population of about 6 per cent which could not be counted. The Planning Council reckons that the population increases by 2.2 per cent per year due to natural growth and influx of more refugees.

11. The Dalai Lama, 'Inaugural Speech' in Conference-cum-Workshop on 'Tibetan Refugees in India: A Report', Council for Home Affairs, Central Tibetan Secretariat, Dharamsala 1986.

12. This echoes the traditional Tibetan decimal organisation, hence the refugees had no problem accepting this system (Norbu 2003: 195). For more on the traditional Tibetan political system, see Goldstein (1971) who writes, 'The essence of the Tibetan political system was the delicate balance between centralized and decentralized political authority'.

13. For more on the Bylakuppe settlement and other Tibetan refugee settlements, see http://www.tibet.net/en/home/settlements/settle/settleindia.html, downloaded on 24 March 2014.

14. The place name is spelt either as Dharamsala or Dharamshala. But the government-in-exile, following Indian government surveys, uses the former spelling. Throughout the discussion, the spelling Dharamsala would be used in order to designate the place. Dharamsala is a common name used for Dharamsala proper (the Kotwali Bazaar area) or the Lower Dharamsala, McLeod Ganj or the Upper Dharamsala. Lower Dharamsala is a predominantly Indian area. While many Tibetan establishments are located here, there are more in the vicinity of Dharamsala (for instance the Norbulingka Insititute). Dharamsala is used as a generic name for all. Location wise, it is characterised as a hill station in Himachal Pradesh.

15. 'The place name "Dharamsala" comes from the Sanskrit word dharamshala comprising of two parts – dharma (religion) and shala (house)' (Anand 2002: 13).

16. There seems to be a difference of motive for travelling to Dharamsala between white Westerner and others. The influence of a Shangri-la paradigm is less noticeable in the case of Japanese and Korean visitors (for whom Dharamsala is often only a constituent part of Buddhist pilgrimage circuit in India) or the Indian tourists (for whom it is a replacement for crowded hill stations like

Shimla). This is not to say that all the Westerners who come here are affected by the Shangri-la myth or that all non-Western tourists are free from it. The distinction made is a result of general observation, which may be highly limited and selective.

17. The emphasis on craftsmen is deliberate in order to highlight the gendered character of traditional cultural practices and their reinforcement by preservation ethos.

18. There is a growing body of theoretically and methodologically sophisticated literature within the parameters of 'urban studies' much of which is applicable to the study of urban refugees as forced migrants. Urban studies' inquiries into displacement, social and political marginalisation and livelihood strategies all speak explicitly to established themes within refugee studies. For more on urban refugees, see 'UNHCR Policy on Refugee Protection and Solutions in Urban Areas', downloaded from http://www.forcedmigration.org/guides/fmo024/ on 25 May 2014.

19. The UNHCR returned operationally to India during the Afghan crisis and has provided some verificatory help in respect of the Sri Lankan repatriations. The status determinations by the UNHCR have been generally respected, even though the Indian government reserves the right to deport at will if necessary. Since 1994, India is a member of the Executive Committee of the UNHCR.

20. According to Goodwin-Gill, 'a durable solution entails a process of integration into society; it will be successful and lasting only if it allows the refugee to attain a degree of self-sufficiency, to participate in the social and economic life of the community and to retain what might be described, too summarily, as a degree of personal identity and integrity'. See Goodwin-Gill 1990: 38.

21. This has led to protest to the UNHCR by the Afghan refugees, who allege both discrimination and inadequacy in respect of the solutions. The UNHCR's view that the majority of Afghan refugees being Hindu and Sikh refugees are susceptible to local integration is not shared by all, still less by the 'Muslim' refugees who feel they are in limbo. The protest turned violent in the case of the Burmese refugees who in 2003 intimidated and threatened the UNHCR staff with protests outside its office in Jorbagh, New Delhi.

22. Section 2 (a) of the Foreigners Act defines a foreigner as 'a person who is not a citizen of India', thus covering all refugees within its ambit as well. Section 3 (1) of the act allows the central government to 'Make provision either generally or with respect to all foreigners or with respect to any particular foreigner or any prescribed class or description of foreigner for prohibiting, regulating or restricting the entry of foreigners into India or their departure therefrom or their presence or continued presence therein'.

23. The Act empowers the central government to make rules regarding the procedure for foreigners to report to a prescribed authority about their presence, movements, departure and proof of identity. Section 4 of this Act states that the burden of proof in determining whether a person is a foreigner or not, of a particular class or description, shall lie upon the person concerned.

24. While the principle of non-refoulement is respected, granting asylum is seen as the provenance of the nation-state.

25. Julia Hess (2006: 82) notes that this difference in status is reflected in the fact that 'newcomers' as of 1994 are not supposed to be granted registration certificates. Sources in the government-in-exile have said that this is an unofficial policy, an agreement between the government of India and the Tibetan government-in-exile. In practice, this means that a Tibetan must prove that s/he was born in India to obtain a registration certificate.

26. Provisions of the Foreigners Act apply to all – no distinction is made in law between asylum-seekers and other aliens. However, courts have been lenient with regard to the imprisonment terms and fine amounts imposed in view of the special situation of refugees.

27. There is a growing body of literature that pronounces the demise of a place called home see Massey 1991; Bammer 1992. Globalisation, the opening up of the local economy to international capital, migration flows and the impact of information technologies which transit events happening on the other side of the world live into people's homes are all implicated.

28. Dorje-den is the Tibetan for Buddha Gaya in Bihar. Translated, it would mean the diamond seat or the throne of Buddha at Gaya (H. Jaschke: A Tibetan English Dictionary) where den translates as the throne and dorje represents the Buddha himself.

29. 'Ling' as an independent word is difficult if not impossible to find in the Tibetan vocabulary. However, it is extensively used as a suffix to denote a place; for example, Namling and Phuentsholing, among others.

30. According to the Secretary of TRSHC (interviewed on 30 September 2006 at TRSHC), most of the people at the Centre have come from U-Tsang province in Tibet (about 70 per cent): about 20 per cent from Kham and 10 per cent from Amdo province.

31. For closer scrutiny of the 'deed of grant' wherein part of present Darjeeling was 'granted' away by the Raja of Sikkim to the British, see Dash 1947: 37–38.

32. The Minyak kings reputedly came from the kingdom of Urgyen, where the Lotus-born Buddha, often known as Guru Rimpoche or Padma Sambhava, was born in the eight century. All Sikkimese Buddhists including Laden La hold Guru Rimpoche in great veneration.

33. The 'Hill people' referred to here were the Lepchas, Bhutias and the Nepalis (Subba 1992: 76).

34. For more on Laden La, see Rhodes and Rhodes 2006.

35. Excerpt from an interview with a Bhutia respondent on 19 May 2005 in Bhutia Busty.

36. See Our Bureau, 'Dashain Strikes Harmony Note', *The Telegraph*, Calcutta, 21 October 2004.

6

Preservation, Integration and the Pragmatics of Diasporic Identity*

Animating the Spirit of Self-Help!

Being thrown into exile—into an alien environment, oblivious of the customs and institutions of the country of refuge—made rehabilitation and eventual resettlement for the Tibetan refugees agonisingly difficult and protracted. Unlike the rehabilitation strategy for the permanent agricultural settlements like in south India, which were built at the behest of the Tibetan government-in-exile, the TRSHC began with an altogether different approach to rehabilitation. The Department of Home, Central Tibetan Administration does not mention TRSHC in its list of Tibetan settlements in India but considers it as part of the category of 'scattered settlements' in Darjeeling. The exception is Tashiling, Sonada near Darjeeling town which is mentioned under handicraft-based settlements. The scattered settlements are relatively free from the direct administrative control of the Tibetan government-in-exile in Dharamsala (with only the welfare officer stationed in Darjeeling town). It is in such locations—marked by fluid boundaries, identity and difference and traffic of people and things—that Tibetan refugees are seen to reinvent themselves and to

* Previously published as Sudeep Basu, 'Interpreting the Tibetan Diaspora: Cultural Preservation and the Pragmatics of Identity', in *Central European University Political Science Journal*, vol. 4, no. 3, 2009, pp. 419–45; 'Interpreting the Tibetan Refugee Problem: The Pragmatics of Diasporic Identity', in *Contemporary Social Problems in India, Vol. 1*, Ruby Sain (ed.), Kolkata: Tandrita Chandra (Bhaduri) Readers Service, pp. 133–69; 2010. 'Organizing for Exile! "Self-Help" among Tibetan Refugees in an Indian Town, in *Refugee Watch – A South Asian Journal on Forced Migration*, vol. 35, 2010, pp. 1–13; and 'Of Camps and Communities-in-exile' in *International Journal of Migration and Border Studies*, vol. 2, no. 2, 2016, pp. 176–86. The article has been modified by the author for the current volume.

explore the possibilities of 'becoming' other than their being 'refugees', following their expulsion from Tibet.

A 10-member committee[1] was formed in Darjeeling to organise a rehabilitation centre which came to be known as the Tibetan Refugee Self Help Centre. The current members of the committee include Khedroop Thondup[2] —president, general secretary and treasurer— Chimay Rinchen, Mr T. Lawang, Ms N. L. Ladenla, Dr T. Wangdi, Mr Dawa Tsering, Mr Dorjee Tsetan, Mr Sonam D. Pasang, Mr Jampa Tenzing, Mr Dorjee Thokme and Mr Palden. Over time, the TRSHC has acquired a simple administrative structure consistent with its ethos of self-help, unlike the administrative structure seen in the Tibetan settlements in south India. Besides the president, there is a secretary and an assistant secretary of the centre. The workshops have managers and assistant managers. The school has a headmistress. The hospital has a doctor-in-charge. There is also an accountant. The welfare officer, who is the representative of the Central Tibetan Administration, does not look after the everyday affairs of the centre

IMAGE 6.1: PLAQUE MENTIONING TIBETAN REFUGEE CENTRE AS REHABILITATION CENTRE, TRSHC, DARJEELING

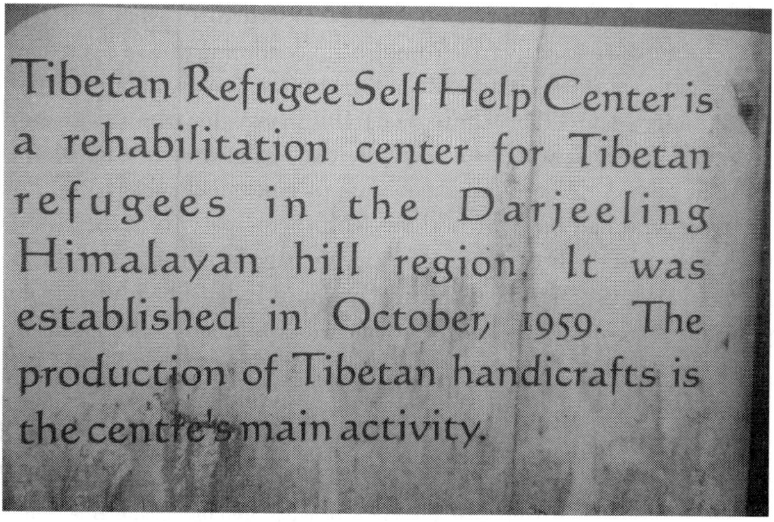

Source: Author's Fieldwork, 2005.

IMAGE 6.2: TRSHC FROM ATOP THE HILL, TRSHC, DARJEELING

Source: Author's Fieldwork, 2005.

but has under his jurisdiction the Darjeeling Municipal Area and its adjoining areas.

Situated at 'Hill-side' Lebong West in the area locally known as 'Hermitage', the TRSHC[3] in Darjeeling town became operational in 1959. It began with four workers, two males and two females. It initially provided a base for distribution of emergency relief to Tibetan refugees who had brought nothing with them apart from the clothes they wore and the little provisions they managed to bring along during their hazardous trek over the Himalayas into India. The Hill-side was a small estate under St Joseph's College. Comprising 3.44 acres, the land was taken on lease and eventually bought from the college. There was space to build and develop a small community outside the town but easily approachable by motor road. The fact that the much-revered thirteenth Dalai Lama spent his exile in India in 1910–12 following the Chinese invasion of Tibet has lent this place a symbolic significance for its inhabitants.[4]

According to the official website of the Tibetan government-in-exile (www.tibet.net), the total population of the settlement in recent times is 650. Under-enumeration in the case of Tibetan refugee populations is a problem at the local level and arises due to the floating nature of such populations. The number of absentees at the time of enumeration at the particular household level remains high. Further, it is difficult to convince the purpose of survey data to refugees. The community has to be constantly reassured of the direct and indirect benefits of survey data.[5] Such surveys are rarely taken very seriously by the members of the Tibetan refugee community in Darjeeling town. Table 6.1 has the population data of the TRSHC gathered from local sources.

TABLE 6.1: TOTAL POPULATION BY SEX

Year	Total Population	Males	Females
1959	4	2	2
1970	800	–	More in number
1986	486	210	276
1989	436	205	231
1990	414	195	219
2002–03	374	180	194
2003–04	290	127	163
2005	282	–	–

Source: Fieldwork data from local sources (May–November 2005).

In Table 6.1, the total population of the TRSHC was highest in 1970. The rise in population was due to the steady flow of Tibetan refugees into Darjeeling from Sikkim, few from Lhasa, Shigatse and Amdo

TABLE 6.2: AGE-WISE DISTRIBUTION OF POPULATION AT THE TRSHC

Age	Total Population	Males	Females
Above 85	1	–	1
60–84	83	42	41
25–59	99	23	76
14–24	48	23	25
8–13	32	18	14
Below 8	19	8	11

Source: Fieldwork data from local sources (May–November 2005).

province. There has been a steady decline in the population of the settlement through the 1980s and 1990s. In the 1990s, there was out-migration of population to Dharamsala and other settlements in India and abroad (USA). It is reported that about eight to nine families left for USA in the 1990s (Official Records, TRSHC Darjeeling). The Welfare Officer mentioned that the reasons for out-migration are for search of better economic opportunities, that is, for livelihood and business.

Again, the data on age is notoriously unreliable in the older generation of Tibetans. This is because of the Tibetan system of age reckoning. It is not a common practice for Tibetans to celebrate their birthdays.

The initial fund for setting up the TRSHC was raised locally by subscriptions, donations, charity shows and an exhibition football match. This was augmented shortly afterwards from contributions by a number of voluntary agencies through the Central Relief Committee notably CARE, Catholic Relief Services, American Emergency Committee for Tibetan Refugees, National Christian Council, the Red Cross, World Veterans Federation, American Friends Committee, Church World Service as well as several individuals. With the reception of this aid, the Tibetans who fled from Tibet back then gradually became labelled as refugees. Their ambivalent response to relief programmes in the subsequent years may be seen as a result of client–group compliance and dependency, as these led to indifference in the refugees' reactions to the relief programmes arising out of the resultant perceived loss of status and dignity of the group.

Given below is an excerpt (in the form of few articulated statements) from the report which the secretary of the TRSHC showed to me during my conversation with him which was centred around the history of the TRSHC and of Tibetans in exile. 'But right from the start, we realised that what was needed was the determination to stand on our feet and rely first and foremost on our own effort—in short, the spirit of self-help (*rang tsho*). We need assistance no doubt and there are people who are generous. But there can never be rehabilitation without self-help, which could be built only from within our community.'

This sums up in categorical terms not only the orientation of the inhabitants of the TRSHC to life in exile as a whole but also provides a glimpse of the form and the limits to the relationship which they intend to forge with their hosts; other diasporic members of their ethnic group, non-governmental organisations and the state. 'Refugee relief programmes because of their self-evident humanitarian derivation are particularly prone to the neutralizing conformity which the label conveys about refugees' status and their situation' (Zetter 1991: 45). What began as the labelling[6] of target groups—in this case the Tibetan as 'refugees' who are recipients of aid—led on the one hand to client conformity and loyalty with the institutionally-imposed stereotype and on the other to a gradual transformation of the identity expressed through the adoption of Goffman-like metaphors to describe alienating feelings like 'we are foreigners here' by asserting individuality and by not remaining acquiescent.

Self-help through Handicrafts

In 1961, the centre was fully registered as a charitable organisation under Indian law. It has also received exemption from income tax on all gifts and donations made to it. The centre has undertaken multifarious activities ranging from the production of handicrafts and training of artisans and craftsmen to homes for the elderly, care for the sick and the orphaned. The production of handicrafts continues to be the cornerstone of the centre's economy. Besides traditional items such as Tibetan carpets, wood carvings, metal and leather works, the emphasis is also on testing new production lines incorporating traditional Tibetan motifs which would find a ready market in Darjeeling and elsewhere.[7] During the financial year April 1998–March 1999, sales reached a total of Rs 53,45,538, more than half of which represented foreign exchange earnings from export sales. The centre had been exporting to 36 countries all over the world (Report TRSHC 1999).

The report brought out by the TRSHC emphasised that 'in traditional Tibet, market for fine handicrafts was limited and master craftsmen who had to undergo long periods of apprenticeship were few. Fewer managed to escape from Tibet and hence it was of the utmost importance for the future of handicrafts that skill and expert knowledge of these masters be passed to a new generation of workers'. This was conveyed by the manager of the workshop who pointed to some of the objectives for

IMAGE 6.3: WORKSHOP FOR THE OLD AND INFIRM, TRSHC, DARJEELING

Source: Author's Fieldwork, 2006.

IMAGE 6.4: AN ELDERLY TIBETAN REFUGEE MAKING SHOES, TRSHC, DARJEELING

Source: Author's Fieldwork, 2006.

the promotion of handicrafts. 'We impart useful and marketable skills to refugees who would otherwise have to earn a precarious livelihood living as coolies or unskilled workers.[8] Without skilled craftsmen, the centre would not be able to produce and sell handicrafts (*lag shes*) which

IMAGE 6.5: REFUGEE WOMEN AT THE CARPET-WEAVING WORKSHOP, TRSHC, DARJEELING

Source: Author's Fieldwork, 2006.

IMAGE 6.6: REFUGEE MAN AT THE WOOD-CARVING SECTION, TRSHC, DARJEELING

Source: Author's Fieldwork, 2006.

provide the main source of income. Training programmes ensure survival and growth of traditional Tibetan arts and crafts'.[9] As exiles who feel that their culture and very identity as Tibetans are under siege in their homeland, the replication of Tibetan 'tradition' through the promotion of art and crafts in the diaspora becomes a self-conscious and strategic undertaking. The manager of the TRSHC, aware of the threat of assimilation in the context of living in a host society, stated, 'Even in India, Tibetans face other more subtle forms of assimilation. We must preserve our culture (*rig gzhung*), our religion (*chos*), our Tibetan language (*bod skad*): otherwise we would mix into the local population'.[10]

There are 13 workshops at the centre namely, wool sorting; wool washing; wool spinning; wool dyeing; carpet weaving; old workers—ball making; carpet trimming; leather work; tailoring; wool knitting; painting; wood carving; shawl and apron making.[11] Over the past four decades, the centre has been able to train 1,600 persons in various crafts. The objective of training individuals in the various crafts is to make persons able or self-supporting. About 1,000–1,200 persons have, over the four decades, left the centre on their own discretion to set up enterprises (Report TRSHC 1999).

Work is allotted based on skill and ability. The old and the weak are given lighter work. They mainly perform simple chores such as winding thread into balls and caring for the toddlers in the centre's nursery. The familiar sight at the centre is that of elderly men gathering bundles of wool to be sent to the spinning factory. A homemade wooden ladder with crooked rungs leans against one of the buildings. On top of the building, wool is kept for drying in readiness for the next stage of production. In the spinning room, rows of elderly women feed rolls of wool into a rotating bicycle wheel. In the carpet-weaving hall, young women work in pairs creating Tibetan carpets. Thick white threads are attached vertically between horizontal wooden poles. The weavers painstakingly tie multi-coloured threads around each white strand to produce colourful knots and these are then packed tightly together using a heavy bronze comb. The centre's handicraft shop has a large range of items such as placemats, silk wall-hangings and woodcarvings. Handmade carpets are the shop's most popular item and are exported overseas. The waiting period to obtain one of these labour-intensive works of art is six months.

IMAGE 6.7: ELDERLY TIBETANS IN CONVERSATION AT BHUTIA BUSTY MONASTERY, ADJACENT TO TRSHC, DARJEELING

Source: Author's Fieldwork, 2006.

The wage rate is fixed at Rs 300 per month regardless of whether an individual is in a position to actually do the work. This provision provides relief to those who are unable to work and battered due to the long years of toil and the mental anguish caused by the conflicting demands of exile life. The day's work begins at 7 am and ends at 5 pm punctuated by lunch and a tea break (for an hour from 11 am to 12 pm followed by a tea break at 2 pm). This work schedule is ritualistically followed by the inhabitants of the centre. The community bell can be heard ringing from even the remotest corner of the centre which serves to remind the inhabitants of the time to resume and close work.

HOUSING AND THE REFUGEE LABEL

For the Tibetans, their designation as refugees was instrumental in gaining access to important resources. In this process, their aspirations were filtered into the housing programme at the TRSHC which they accepted with gratitude. The initial responses of the refugees to housing in the self-help project was one which seemed to indicate settlement in the host society but retaining at the same time a strong belief in 'return' ('repatriation' in legal terminology) to Tibet as a paramount and still achievable objective. With more than five decades into exile, there are few indicators of such temporariness with respect to their attitude towards settlement and resettlement in host societies.

The form and the location of housing at the TRSHC set within the context of rehabilitation have given a distinctive physical identity to the label 'refugee'. This has accentuated the development of a 'refugee consciousness' among the inhabitants of the TRSHC. The refugees who fled the invasion of Tibet could not come to Darjeeling in groups but came as individuals leaving their family members, spouses, children, fathers and mothers behind. It was difficult for them to retain their pre-exilic identities drawn upon past norms—community, village, notions of extended family in the housing programme. Exile for the Tibetans has prevented village re-formation. The architectural style of the houses at the TRSHC has faint resemblance to the houses in Old Tibet.[12] In 1970, there were wooden sheet houses. By 1990, four buildings with 200 rooms made of brick came up in the area. Tibetans show great interest in indoor decoration. Most families have auspicious patterns on the indoor walls. In the sitting room, the inner wall is painted with blue, green and red stripes representing the sky, the earth and fire respectively. There are also houses which have altars for worshipping Buddha or images of the Great Kings of Tibet or pictures of the Dalai Lama, the Potala Palace or the Norbulingka. Doors and windows are highlighted with red, blue and white cloth screens, with a canopy (consisting of red, white, blue, yellow and green cloth pieces) around the parapet of the roof and its corners. While the appearance of houses from the outside is unostentatious and reminiscent of dwellings found in Old Tibet (in regions such as southern Tibet and around Lhasa and Shigatse), the furnishings inside some houses (particularly the interior of the house of one of my respondents who worked in the woodcarving section to which I had access) are strikingly modern with television sets, high-tech radio cassette recorders, digital cameras and piles of expensive-looking

Western clothes that are either gifted to them by their patrons in foreign countries or sent to them by their kinfolk in the diaspora.

Housing, which becomes the obviously recognisable symbol of their refugee status, creates a distinction between refugees and non-refugees, between 'the Tibetan refugee' and their 'categorical other'. The label becomes, through institutional processes, a potent tool of differentiation far removed from the initial premise that refugees need shelter. That the type of housing as seen from the outside clearly does not serve as a clear-cut objective indicator of the levels of prosperity or deprivation of the Tibetan residents of the TRSHC, is revealed by two Nepali youths in their late 20s belonging to the Brahmin caste, Chhetris, who live in the neighbouring hermitage area. On having made a point to the Nepali youths in a deliberately provocative manner in the form of 'how poor the Tibetans appear from the look of the houses in which they live', they immediately replied with the intention to correct, in their judgement, my somewhat touristic perception or lack of knowledge about the actual status of the Tibetans living in the TRSHC. 'What others (they were referring to the tourists) see in the refugee camp is eyewash. *Yeh sab dikhava hai* (this is only a show). *Woh bare amir hai* (Most of them are well off) and are in government (*gzhung*) jobs, have with them ration cards, doing good business (*tshong las byas*) in town area. This is how it is'.[13] This sense of relative deprivation of the Nepalis is something which they have learnt to live with now. The older Nepalis are reconciled to the fact that the Tibetans are characteristically more hardworking than themselves, which is the reason for their economic success in the Darjeeling area. Numerically, in an absolute majority, Nepalis know, albeit to their cost, that they can afford not to be hardworking, indolent and yet survive, an option unavailable for Tibetans. The Nepali unemployed or under-employed youths, who are in large numbers, are of the opinion that it is the external assistance from foreigners in the form of donations and gifts that have given the Tibetans an edge over their neighbours in the competition over resources. The claim by Nepali youths that the refugees at the centre are not poor (a kind of perceptual data) had to be corroborated by collecting further data in the form of statements made by other ethnic hosts in the area. Till then, the perception of the Nepali youths had to be taken on face value but it did serve as an important pointer to the unfolding refugee–host dynamic in the Darjeeling Municipal Area.

WE ARE ALSO A WELFARE INSTITUTION!

Since its inception, the centre has undertaken the task of helping orphans, the aged, the infirm and the needy among the refugees. The centre has 89 old and infirm persons as well as 42 orphans[14] who have no means of their own. It provides free housing, food, medical care, education and pocket money for children, uniforms and stationeries. The provision of these services consists of the bulk of the centre's expenses.

'Although the production of handicrafts forms the main activity and is the primary source of income, the Centre was not planned to be and has never been solely a business concern' (Report TRSHC 1999). This statement is echoed by my key informant, a resident of the centre and

IMAGE 6.8: HOME FOR THE ORPHANS, TRSHC, DARJEELING

Source: Author's Fieldwork, 2006.

who works for a travel agency in Darjeeling town. He emphatically said, 'The Refugee Centre is like a cooperative (*mnyam las*). Anyone wanting to join is welcome. We know that we are good in doing business. See how we attract customers. It is seen in the display of the items in our shop. If I enjoy with the money earned, what about my brothers and sisters in Tibet? Running after money will not give us anything. One life as a beggar is not bad, if it is led sincerely and honestly'.[15] The question, 'If I enjoy with the money earned, what about my brothers and sisters in Tibet?' is consistent with 'the currently emergent consensus that diasporans are deeply implicated both ideologically and materially in the nationalist projects of their homelands' (Werbner 2002: 120). Something more is at work than merely the nationalist agenda served by Tibetan diasporic groups. What is evident is the moral trajectory of Tibetan exile subjects and the projection of an 'ideal Tibetan refugee' to 'significant others'. It is indicative of the development of a Tibetan cultural self-consciousness in exile which according to Ekvall (1960: 376) focuses on the concept of oneness which has religion as its most important attribute among others such as Folkways, Race and Land, that gives assurance of belonging, provides guidance for mutual recognition and differentiates and excludes those who do not belong. In ethics, it sets up compassion and the creation of merit as the ultimate ideal governing motivation consistent with the Tibetan notion of 'karma'. It also conditions the Tibetan's intellectual life by furnishing a purpose of existence.

Medical Care and School

The medical centre came up as a crucial welfare activity of the centre. Starting as a small infirmary, the medical programme catered not only to the refugees, but also non-refugees, a means by which they could gain greater moral respect and acceptance among locals. A hospital was established in 1961 through foreign aid such as the American Relief Services. It eventually grew into a 20-bedded hospital staffed by a qualified doctor, two nurses and some helpers. The medical unit routinely carries out blood tests, screening for tuberculosis, vaccinations, pre- and post-natal care. The majority of the clients are poor. A further extension of the medical services offered by the centre's hospital is the establishment of an X-Ray Clinic and a Pathological Laboratory in Darjeeling town. The X-Ray Clinic, consisting of a small unit along with the requisite generator, was set up by a grant given by the government of West Bengal through the Hill Affairs Branch Secretariat, Darjeeling. The clinic is entirely staffed by trained boys and girls of the Refugee Centre.

Beginning with a nursery in June 1960, educational facilities expanded to form a full-fledged primary school.[16] The primary school, following the syllabus of the Central Tibetan School Administration, caters to children from other Tibetan settlements as well. There are instances of junior and senior students attending different schools and colleges in and out of Darjeeling town. The children are not only provided with free education up to class XII, but also free clothing, meals and textbooks. However, those students who continue to receive financial assistance from the TRSHC for their college education are required to work for the TRSHC for three to five years (for which they are given remuneration) once they complete their education. If they get a better employment offer during this period, they have to pay back the amount received for their college education to the TRSHC.

The government of India brought the issue of education of Tibetan refugees under its ambit and the Central Tibetan Schools Administration was established as an autonomous organisation under the Ministry of Education, government of India, in 1961 and registered under the Societies Registration Act, XXI of 1860. The Central School for Tibetans, Darjeeling was set up in 1961 and affiliated to CBSE. Initially housed in the NBMR building which belonged to the Ministry of Defence and other rented buildings ('Digpatia', 'Ray Villa' and 'Kailash'), it was taken over by the Tibetan School Society which was also set up in 1961. By 1966, the NBMR had been demolished and the new block with 10 classrooms and a multipurpose hall was constructed. Later, the administration constructed a three-storied building which today houses a girls' dormitory, dispensary, senior classrooms, science laboratory, dispensary, and a room for music and dance. Later, next to the 10 classrooms, another building came up, which was meant for primary classrooms and classes VIII and IX. The first principal, Lhawang Paljor, started the school with 30 students and five teachers in 1961. Affiliated to the CBSE, the school offers courses in the humanities and commerce. Special emphasis is laid on the preservation and promotion of Tibetan culture, protection of the environment and inculcation of human values. Career counselling receives equal importance with trained staff with frequent visits of the department of education, Dharamsala counsellor.[17]

Our Early Period of Exile!

As in the case of most refugee groups world over, the early years in exile for the Tibetans was one of extreme hardships arising out of 'lack'. Much of what was recounted by refugees living was that there was widespread poverty, hunger, disease, lack of adequate shelter and work. The Tibetan youths (the new generation) relayed the early exile experiences of their preceding generation. They talked about the difficulties or struggle (due to their lack of knowledge of the local language) the latter had to go through in their attempts to forge meaningful relations with 'locals' or 'citizens'. Cooperation from unexpected quarters, conflicts, fears and insults were the stuff of what constituted refugee life for Tibetans in the early years in an alien host land, as told and retold by the older generation to the new. These framed the nature of the Tibetan refugee–host relationship as it unfolded in the Darjeeling region in the subsequent decades.

The refugees who chose to stay in the refugee centre and other settlements were those who were not in a capacity to establish themselves privately, mainly due to the lack of capital. Others resorted to collecting alms.[18] Like other Nepali residents of Darjeeling, Tanka Subba, a well-known scholar, states from his recollections as a young boy, 'I saw at least 2 to 3 Tibetan alms collectors come to my house everyday. Most of them came singly with a sling bag and a rosary chanting *Om Mani Peme Hung*. The alms collectors lived in sheds in the town areas. There used to be little communication between them and the local people but the latter readily offered pulses, rice and coins. The non-Tibetan respondents, specially the Bhutias, spoke of their eagerness to know about the future of Tibetan refugees in the region' (1990: 55).

The following excerpt of an interview with a Tibetan youth, who was studying in Loyola College in Chennai at the time of the interview, summarises aspects of refugee life brought up by many informants in their chronicles of early hardship faced by their preceding generation who first arrived from Tibet: 'My father and grandfather are there to give advice. They told me how they suffered, when they came here, they had no financial assistance[19]. Gradually my grandfather did small business. He always tells me to do your education well only then you would not suffer like them. Without education (*shes yon slob sbyong*) you cannot do anything, he says. The duty of our elders was to motivate us. From what they told us, it seems that our identity as refugee was very marked then. Now we can pay to go to school (*slob grwa*)'.[20]

The following passage shows that the early years were associated with social and economic hardships. It acknowledges that 'suffering' is attached to poverty, to the fact that 'financial assistance' was not forthcoming in the beginning. The whole figure of the refugee appeared thus to be constructed from the stigma of being impoverished. It also suggested that the identity as refugees made them a special kind of people but which caused them to 'feel bad'. The importance of imparting education in the early stages of one's life as a remedy to the various ills of poverty and indolence arising out of exile was acknowledged by the leadership and elders of the community. The passage ends with a reference to how their lives have improved since the beginning. By improvement, the respondent meant not the augmentation of their political worth as refugees but the betterment of the economic conditions of individual lives reflected in their greater access to quality education. It suggests that it is possible to improve despite the refugee label.

For instance, a respondent talked about the improvement in his socio-economic status as compared to his father. He said, 'We had nothing when we came here. My father had a coolie's job. We had to take help from the refugee camp then. I did many things. I had a tailoring job in Delhi, Mumbai. I learnt tailoring from Tungsung. I did think of doing a garment's business then. I got a trekking job for four to five years. Left that and now I have a garment's business in town. Now I do not take help from the camp. Things are alright now'.[21] What is avoided by the respondent in the conversation is any reference to the involvement of locals in Tibetan refugee life in the early years. The role of locals in Tibetan refugee life is an issue that is not voluntarily taken up for discussion by Tibetan refugees, especially when conversations with them were struck in the Darjeeling town context. They remain guarded in this respect for the sake of what many Tibetans in the course of conversation have stated as 'communal harmony or peace'. For instance, a Tibetan in his 20s stated, 'They know we are refugees. We do not discuss communal things you know. We do not talk about Tibet and all with the locals (*sa gnas*)'.[22] On being asked why he frequents the refugee centre, he stated that he has friends there and likes to hang around in the evening after work. His visit to the centre serves the unstated purpose at an individual level as well, by allowing one to reassert or reproduce one's Tibetan identity which has struck deep roots within the TRSHC in the last four decades. The Tibetans who do visit the centre frequently are not unaware of the goodwill that they acquire among the settlement residents. In a general way, however, while most Tibetans mentioned that early exile was characterised by great hardships, they hastened to add that they did not face any overt or real threat to physical security; locals, in fact, donated without any qualms. They however unanimously attested to the fact that the feeling of helplessness was palpable stemming due to their unfamiliarity with the topography and language of the region and their perceived lower status attached to their identity as refugees.

There are no Refugees in this Area!

Darjeeling town and its environs have served as a heterogeneous and cosmopolitan crossroads of human and other traffic. The town's resident population comprised many different, interspersed categories of people having different ethnic identities sharing neighbourhoods and continual streams of visitors, travellers and other less permanent inhabitants. This plurality meant that it was difficult to fix or classify a person in the street by virtue of his or her locale. Further, it becomes impossible to discern who among the residents might be a refugee from Tibet, owing to the racial and religious affinity between Tibetans refugees and other communities residing in Darjeeling town. 'Any person with a preliminary knowledge of the Himalayas is aware of the fact that the entire Himalayas, not to talk of merely Darjeeling, Sikkim are inhabited principally by the Mongoloid people. Be it Nepal, Tibet, Bhutan or the Himalayan border areas of India from east to the west, the people by and large bear Mongoloid features' (Subba 1990: 59). Shakabpa wrote, 'The majority of the people in the U-Tsang region of Tibet are of short stature, round-headed and high-cheek boned, therefore slightly different from those of other two regions, the people of Dote (Kham) and Dome (Amdo) are tall, longheaded and long-limbed' (1984: 6). The Nepalis have a large number of groups like the Tamangs, Yolmus, Sherpas, Gurungs who are Buddhists or their culture is to some extent Tibetanised. However, some neighbourhoods in Darjeeling town are generally known to be more populated by Tibetans than others and they are just as mobile as other residents in the township. The distribution of the Tibetan populace in West Bengal is given below in Table 6.3.

TABLE 6.3: DISTRIBUTION OF TIBETANS IN WEST BENGAL

Region—West Bengal	Total Population	Absentees as on 12 June 1998
Calcutta	50	7
Darjeeling	2,411	44
Ghoom, Darjeeling	442	4
Jalpaiguri, Jaigaon	45	0
Kalimpong	2,023	118
Kurseong	447	1
Oodlabari	139	0
Salugara	108	2
Siliguri	22	0
Sonada, Tashiling	641	8
Total	6,328	184

Source: Compiled from the Tibetan Demographic Survey, 1998.

The 'Bhutia' Label: Problematic of Assimilation

What marked the socio-cultural landscape that provided the initial and subsequent help and assistance to the Tibetan town refugees was the presence of the Bhutias. It provided the Tibetan refugees an anonymity which was like a shelter, a fortuitous situation put to effective use. Tibetans could thereby conceal their refugee status before strangers. Their frequent use of the Bhutia label to designate themselves was often seen in the town at the time of initiating a conversation in places like the Mahakal market (the most trendy and fashionable market selling garments and other accessories) on Ladenla road. A respondent who owned one of the shops in Mahakal market refused to talk despite the presence of my key informant (a Bhutia) who knew him well. He needed reassurance and continuously claimed to be a Bhutia himself, and by that token, an Indian.[23] He said that he had lived in Japan for four years but then came back to Darjeeling to take up business. He insisted that there is similarity between Bhutias and Tibetans in terms of religion and place. 'We are Buddhists, we are one', he said. On being asked why he decided to remain in Darjeeling, he explained his situation in the following words: 'I know this place better than any other place.[24] I do not want to go and stay in any other part of India. It is convenient to do business in India but given the chance I would like to go to America (*a mi ri ka*) you know, there is opportunity (*go skabs*) there'.[25]

On further probing, which became possible after some degree of trust was established, what came to light was the fact that the respondent was socialised into becoming aware of the connection between his identity as a Tibetan refugee and the place Darjeeling (he had many Bhutia friends, like my key informant who was a Bhutia). His knowledge that the Bhutias are Tibetans and diasporics of an earlier era like the Tibetan refugees themselves initiated the process of 'emplacement', by creating a sense of belonging to the place (Darjeeling) which in the imaginative sense formed part of what he, echoing my key informant called, 'the Great land of Tibet'.[26] This similarity of sentiment generally held by Tibetan refugees and Bhutias echoes the British colonial perception that the Bhutias and Lepchas were unlikely to shift their loyalty from Tibet as they were strongly integrated by a common heritage, religion, language and culture. They all belonged to the Tibeto-Burman group and adhered to a pan-Buddhist religion of 'Lamaist Buddhism' from where they derived their ethnic identity. The British policy of encouraging Nepali migrants to Darjeeling throughout the second half of the nineteenth century and in the subsequent period originated from the colonial design to outbalance the original ethnic domination of the Lepchas and Bhutias in the region (Dasgupta 1999). The British found in the Nepali immigrants, a group of loyal subjects whose allegiance would lie with the British and not with the Dalai Lama of Tibet.[27] The overwhelming predominance of the Nepalis, which became a paramount reality towards the end of the nineteenth century, contributed to the acceptability of the Nepali language as the lingua franca of Darjeeling region. The Nepali language gradually forged an ethnic link between the various groups who had migrated from Nepal. Even the Lepchas and the Bhutias, despite their religious and cultural differences with the Nepalis, slowly accepted Nepali as the lingua franca.

A sample of a conversation between two Tibetans (a Tibetan refugee and a Bhutia or a Tibetan refugee and a fellow Tibetan refugee) when they meet for first time typically starts with the exchange '*Tashi Delek*' followed by the question: 'Are you a Tibetan?' and the other answers with a certain sense of pride: 'Yes I am a Tibetan' (*la yin nga bod pa yin*). This commonality of identity generates a feeling of warmth between them. But even as they become conscious of their mutual identity as Tibetans, most of the time the Tibetan refugee becomes acutely conscious of the limited grasp that a Bhutia or a fellow Tibetan refugee has over the Tibetan language and expectedly so. This uneasy scenario is more common among Tibetans of Nepal, Darjeeling, Kurseong and Kalimpong. However, since they are extremely eager to know more about each other, the conversation lapses into Nepali or English or even Hindi.[28] This explains why the interest starts with the question 'Are you a Tibetan?' for it begs the question 'Is it sufficient merely to look like a Tibetan?' 'Who is more Tibetan and who is less Tibetan?'—to questions of authenticity. To be a Tibetan, Tibetans must surely be able to speak their mother tongue but the facts show that not all Tibetans in the diaspora can speak Tibetan. Fewer can read and write in face of the pervasive influence of the Nepali language speakers which includes the Bhutias of the Darjeeling region. The effective literacy rate of the Tibetan exile population stood at 74.5 per cent in 1998 while the general literacy rate was 69.3 per cent (Tibetan Demographic Survey 1998). Table 6.4 demonstrates the Tibetan language ability by place of birth.

TABLE 6.4: TIBETAN LANGUAGE ABILITY BY PLACE OF BIRTH

(Birth) Region	Total Population	Tibetan Language (Read, Write, Speak)—Total Population	Tibetan Language (Speak Only)—Total Population
India	40,382	31,077	9,305
Central India	8,934	6,378	2,556
East India	16,659	10,273	6,386
North India	24,629	17,841	6,788
South India	25,576	19,384	6,192
West India	1,159	766	393

Source: Compiled from the Tibetan Demographic Survey, 1998.

While the entry of Nepali language into the private conversations among Tibetans is unproblematic for the Bhutias, it is of major concern among Tibetan refugee families living in Darjeeling town. A Tibetan refugee (a shop owner) in Dragon Market expressed his concern thus: 'My niece is going to a good English medium school now. I am seeing that she is forgetting Tibetan language. Her mother has arranged for a private tutor to teach Tibetan to her. But I try to speak in Tibetan to her at home'.[29]

Understandably, what is generally held is that speaking, talking and writing in Nepali by Tibetan refugees amounts to assimilation that has to be resisted. The term 'assimilation' is used here with some reservations. It does not suggest that the social world into which the refugees were trying to insert themselves was itself a stable, fixed point of reference to which newcomers had to 'adapt'. On the contrary, the 'locals' of Darjeeling town were for long caught up in the same fluid, contingent social field as the refugees, albeit having different trajectories, predicaments and concerns. The problem of the Nepali migrant subjectivity is not different from those of the refugees. 'His subjectivity was bitterly torn between the calling of the home and the hard reality of never returning to see it again. There was optimism and hope when he said, "Darjeeling will take care of me". But there was also a fear of the uncertain'.[30]

The town refugees' assessment of their actual relations with Bhutia immigrants and vice-versa vary considerably. Some informants say that Tibetan refugees and Bhutias have got on very well together and a good deal of cooperation exists between them. My respondent (a Bhutia) spoke about his childhood friend (a Tibetan refugee who lived in the TRSHC): 'He did not hesitate to mix with others in the town. He was like this from young years. We played football at the local club—Viva sporting club—and in Darjeeling Government College and Himalayan sporting club. It is his sporting spirit that has helped. He is like a non-playing captain. Now he works like a liaison man. He even knows some police personnel in town. Any trouble in TRSHC everybody goes to him for help. In the centre, the people are orthodox type. They think that young generation if they mix with local guys, they will get adulterated. My friend (*grogs po*) is different. But I see that the centre's members can choose to have less and remain with their limits. A very good quality, very few Tibetans are like that. My friend did not choose to go abroad'.

My Bhutia respondent hastened to add that there is mutual support between Tibetan refugees and the Bhutias. His remarks testified to this: 'Last year wool that was being imported to Darjeeling was seized at Dalkhola by commercial tax check post. I called up commercial tax office and got them (Tibetan refugees) out of the problem. They need us for the day to day problems and interactions with local authorities. We need them also. In my marriage (*chang sa*), I was not getting a groom hat. The self help centre has a cultural section. They lend hats to other Buddhists. I got the groom hat from them. In schools too when some Buddhist functions are to be held, we approach the refugees for assistance. Anybody can come of help later that is why I help others'.[31]

Other informants believe that the Bhutias desired first and foremost to distance themselves from the Tibetan refugees when they first arrived, even when support was extended to them. Conversation with an elderly

Bhutia, a former councillor of the Bhutia Busty ward, revealed this aspect: 'Tibetan refugees who came with precious stones and gold did not go to the centre. They settled in different parts of Darjeeling town, even in Bhutia Busty area. The refugees used to stink. They coughed all the time. We avoided contact with them. Refugees would not stay in queue for collecting water. Khampas were brute people. They carried the habits of Tibetan highlands with them to India. They did not take bath when they came here. Many had TB. In schools the Tibetan refugee students used to vomit. In Bhutia Busty some Bhutia families gave them shelter. My family had given rented accommodation to a Tibetan refugee when he came here. We had even given him permission to enter our kitchen. He told me about stories of Chinese atrocities. He told of the times in Tibet when the Tibetans never trusted their own brothers who could be spies. They did not sleep all day long. Such a grave situation was not there when they came to live with the locals of Darjeeling'.[32]

Many other residents interviewed at Bhutia Busty spoke of their unwillingness to associate too conspicuously with the Tibetan refugees. 'We Bhutias do not take part in any political activity that is for the cause of Tibetan independence',[33] said a few respondents. The disjuncture that exists in the refugee–Bhutia relationship is further revealed in the subsequent discussion with the Bhutias about the Bhutia encounter with the refugees. One Bhutia respondent echoed the sentiment of the youth members of his community. 'The Tibetan refugees used the term "*Ghyagar Khampas*" to denote Indian citizens. They see Bhutias at a lower stage than them. They do not express it openly. Their reason may be that our Tibetan language is not good. We do not have foundation about that. We are comfortable here since we are interacting with Indian Nepalis and India is where we belong. So we do not mind if the Tibetan refugees feel this way about us. But sometimes we have to talk in Nepali in order to put them down'.[34] Nepali language here is deliberately used as an instrument of domination by the Bhutias to keep the Tibetan refugees at bay. The use of Nepali is a constant reminder not only of the minority status of the Tibetan refugees but also of the threat of assimilation. However, speaking fluent Nepali is the easiest method adopted by Tibetan refugees to fend off outsiders' suspicions.

The other is by negating the refugee label in front of outsiders by passing[35] themselves off as Bhutias.

For an outside observer, it becomes well-nigh impossible to distinguish a Tibetan refugee from his Bhutia counterpart or even Nepalis based on physical or cultural traits. Locals in Darjeeling town insist emphatically that they can immediately recognise a Tibetan refugee when they see one. For them, recognising a Tibetan as refugee becomes an intuitive exercise, a 'feeling', a combination of physical appearance, mannerisms and behaviour ranging from 'ways of walking' to 'ways of speaking a language' among others. Using the 'adoptive label' of a Bhutia therefore does not conceal the actual identity of a Tibetan as refugee in contexts where the traffic existed between Tibetan refugees and locals. The strategy of concealing their refugee identity and to become invisible did not emerge out of a real threat of deportation or repression from the Indian state. Their involvement with strangers was minimised so as to avoid embarrassing situations while revealing their real status as refugees. Their deployment of identities in shifting contexts opened up avenues whereby they could become self-employed or join the competitive market, take up education, obtain licenses for trade and spend leisure time in town. The use of the Bhutia identity by Tibetan refugees shaped by the nexus of relations in gaining success in business and employment did not go unnoticed by Bhutias and Nepalis. One Bhutia respondent living near the Tibetan-dominated Dragon and Mahakal markets spoke about the Bhutia–Tibetan refugee relationship in the following words: 'Human beings have the tendency to settle down in the place where they come to stay. This was true for the Nepalese in Darjeeling. Tibetans came as migrants before 1959. They came as refugee after 1959. Earlier Bhutia people were not literate, so they allowed refugees to take advantage of the name of "Bhutia". After some time, when literacy among Bhutias grew, competition among Bhutias and other Scheduled Tribes[36] to get government jobs intensified. If an outsider comes, then it creates problems for us. Bhutia Welfare Association did raise protest against Tibetan refugees taking up government jobs under the Scheduled Tribes certificate'.[37]

Success in charting out a career in exile had its underside. Their achievements created fear and apprehension in their minds, for they would often say that the locals would look upon them with feelings of 'jealousy, envy and deprivation' (Subba 1990). They exercised caution in their conduct with 'significant Others'. As Tanka Subba notes (1992: 206–07),

> [T]he racial similarity between different ethnic groups could also be a point of disadvantage. The Lepchas, Bhutias, Tibetans and Indo-Mongoloid Nepalis belong to the same racial stock and look alike. As a result, the CRPF personnels chasing the GNLF activists, who were mostly Nepalis could not distinguish between these various groups. They arrested them indiscriminately, beat up before locking them up in the cells and even shot at them. So many Lepchas, Bhutias and Tibetans suffered from police torture and offensive though they had practically nothing to do with the Movement. Even where no such thing happened they suffered from as much tension and anxiety as the Nepalis did.

In recent times, the All Gorkha Student's Union (AGSU) has on few occasions vociferously expressed its resentment towards the emerging domination of Tibetan refugees in the region and their alleged or surreptitious use of voters' identity cards for gaining employment or for commerce. Four Tibetan youths interpreting the relation between Tibetans and Nepalis hastened to add that 'Nepalis think good about Tibetans, they want to make friends with us; Nepali girls nowadays want to get friendly with Tibetan boys because they think we have a lot of money (*dngul*). They are in a majority, there is no point avoiding them'.[38] For Tibetan refugees, sensitivity to potentially hostile feelings of locals is deemed crucial in order to maintain peace and order. It enables them to gain self-confidence and avoid potential conflict by invoking an ideal image of a 'non-violent Tibetan refugee'.[39]

Tibetan Aloofness and Citizenship

The desire for anonymity arose out of the need to circumvent excess bureaucratic entanglement. By virtue of not remaining spatially isolated as in a camp, refugees in Darjeeling town could translate this desire into a workable reality in the form of obtaining ration cards, entering their names in the voters' list and procuring Scheduled Tribes certificates by using the surname 'Bhutia'. The passage to obtaining Indian citizenship was thus clear but had to be arranged discreetly.[40] The need to buy nationality was deemed more necessary for those refugees who had become wealthy on account of owning houses, restaurants, hotels, shops or valuable items like taxis and cars. Wealth made them visible in town areas which necessitated the procurement of citizenship documents to deal with 'exposure'. Identity documents, on the one hand, signalled permanent residence in Darjeeling town but it did not have a fixed one-to-one correspondence with particular degrees of commitment to place among the refugees-turned-Indian citizens. Citizenship documents were only a technique of invisibility or means for commerce. It was something more than a simple matter of have or have-not for Tibetans at the TRSHC. In a situation of protracted exile, the citizenship question is a controversial one confronting Tibetans in the diaspora. Other problems or complications were raised in its wake and had its distinctive resonance in Darjeeling town in particular. These were the perspectives on the problem of 'return'; to questions of identity as an effect of diasporic (multiple) attachments to several places at one time; in the framework of the CTA's policy which officially discourages Tibetans from taking up Indian citizenship consistent with the cultural preservation thesis which it espouses.

Tibetan youths working in the wood-carving section at the centre interpreted the problem of citizenship. They said, '*Black se to hum Indian citizen ho sakte hain* (We can become Indian citizens illegally). They were times when Nepalis would come along to our houses and ask us to make ration cards and voter-identity cards. But Darjeeling people know that there is a refugee centre here and we have our address of this place. They can easily make out. They would recognise us. Getting Indian citizenship would not help. But we should not forget our culture'.[41] Successfully claiming to be a Bhutia, producing the ration cards at food ration shops, voters' identity card at the time of Municipal elections provided sufficient proof of naturalisation for many town refugees. Although it was possible for Tibetans to garner Indian citizenship through use of these identity signs, they could not hide their identity as refugees from locals. The effectiveness of these identity signs depended upon the general acceptance of and tacit support from sections of the local population. The immigrant agents and officers at the Foreigner's Registration Office (who were recruited from the local Bhutia and Nepali Buddhist community) were reluctant to disclose information about the size and spread of the Tibetan refugee population in Darjeeling town to an outsider. This is indicative of a tacit approval from sections of the local community of the workings of this 'naturalisation' or de facto citizenship of town refugees. Yet nearly all Tibetan refugees in Darjeeling town fulfilled the requirements of the Foreigners Registration Act by obtaining the RC.[42] Several Tibetans reiterated that the procedure for renewing the RC every year was problematic, cumbersome and indicative of their changeable and precarious status. Further, it is incumbent upon Tibetan refugees having the RC to report his/her presence to the district registration officer within seven days of his/her arrival, every time one moves out of the district of registration and residential address for more than seven days. In practice, few Tibetan refugees in Darjeeling who are RC holders take the trouble to report. As residents of India, they move around freely from place to place unlike foreign visitors to the country. The RC document does not entitle them to travel abroad. In fact, this was another reason why some Tibetan refugees decided to apply for Indian citizenship.

Citizenship versus Tibetan Patriotism

Closely connected with the situation of protracted exile besetting the Tibetan community in India are the controversies regarding citizenship and patriotism. The paradox can be summed up thus—are citizenship and patriotism two sides of the same coin or two different coins altogether? A Tibetan respondent made clear the paradox in the following words, 'Becoming an Indian becomes important, we get opportunity. With Holiness there, we feel proud we are Tibetans. I do not mind becoming an Indian but I want to keep my status as refugee. It is important that we believe that we will get our freedom. We can always convert to Tibetan, when Tibet is free. I am a Tibetan but since

I am born in India I am an Indian'.[43] The need to seek opportunity is acutely felt among Tibetan refugee students who are deprived of both higher education and government jobs. The exile government runs a few institutions and training centres but these are inadequate to accommodate the hundreds of high school graduates. Hence their only option is to apply to an Indian college or centre. However, admission to a state college or institution requires a domicile certificate that confirms that the applicant is a legal resident of the state. The inability of Tibetan refugees to provide the necessary documentation makes it next to impossible to get admission. To be eligible for the domicile certificate, one must be an Indian citizen. The use of an adoptive label by Tibetan exiles—that of Indian citizenship—does not suggest that they seek assimilation into Darjeeling society or have assumed 'deterritorialized' cosmopolitan identity. Some of the Tibetan refugees in Darjeeling town who have assumed adoptive labels are the ones who have taken active interest in organising demonstrations and protests and in expressing their loyalty to the Tibetan freedom struggle by paying the 'patriotic fund' to the exile government. Popularly called 'Green Book', this is a receipt book of the monetary pledge to support the expenses of the exile government. The book reads:

> As per article no. 7 of the resolution passed in a meeting convened by the committee for the movement of freedom of Tibet, held on 30th July 1972, it has been pledged voluntarily that each Tibetan would pay one rupee a month and extra if possible and the salaried person shall pay 2% of one's salary with effect from August 1972 to the Tibetan government in exile for it was felt that the government in exile needed to be strengthened mainly by supporting the expenses of the government for both short-term and long-term benefits of the Tibetan people. This book is a receipt of the acknowledgment of the monetary pledge.

A Tibetan refugee having garment business in town said, 'Any special occasion, we shut down all our business. We go for the procession march, whatever it is like. I stick to my business, if it is not like this. We are brought up this way. We have to respect the community leader. There are some who do not go. That particular person is not pointed at. Our religion does not allow this'.[44]

Dharamsala's pressure and expectations regarding patriotism and citizenship is nuanced. The chairperson of the Tibetan Cabinet, Samdhong Rinpoche's statement conveys the sentiment of the exile administration. 'Tibetans living in the diaspora are free to go where they want. We do not try to control them. Rather, we try to facilitate whatever they want to do. I am not in favour of sending Tibetans on a large scale to emigrate from India, Nepal or Bhutan. Therefore, the Tibetan government-in-exile does not look for, nor does it try to have large emigration programs. If governments offer, we do not turn them down. Tibetans living in the Diaspora are making travel documents. We don't stop that. On the contrary, we try to make it easy for them because it is their right. But our government does not encourage them to emigrate. The reason is very simple. Once Tibetans emigrate to the West, they cannot preserve the Tibetan identity for the second generation'.[45] From the above statement, it is clear that the exile administration sees these Tibetans in the West as their ambassadors. The fact that they cannot be depended upon to preserve Tibetan culture is equally conveyed.[46]

While 'preserving Tibetan culture' in exile includes inheriting and reproducing the marginal political status of the older generation in India (Diehl 2002: 117), acquiring citizenship in the West serves an explicit political agenda for those Tibetans in the West who have close affinity with the cause and Dharamsala. Geographical differences produced by displacement therefore have a strong impact on life-chances and access to resources of refugees which can be utilised for dealing with protracted refugee situations. This position is conveyed by a Tibetan refugee youth now living in America over the Internet:

> Although the Tibetans have adapted very well with American society but it is too early to say if we would be able to preserve our culture in this big country where many minorities have lost their identities. For us right now, His Holiness the Dalai Lama is one of the biggest reasons most of the Tibetans have maintained unification and are thriving well. The Tibetans who have migrated to the United States from India and Nepal are helping their relatives and family back home in India and Nepal. Many Tibetans have very strong ties with the people in India. Since most of the young Tibetans grew up in India and Nepal. I especially go to India twice a year for the last eighteen years. Also I as a photographer regularly

> document our diaspora and ever changing situation of the Tibetans inside and outside of Tibet. Every year, many Tibetans visit India and Nepal to see their families and relatives. Some of them send their children to Tibetan schools in India and also in some private Indian schools. The Tibetans in the States get most of the latest news from Internet such as phayul.com and other Tibetan sites. Also many Tibetans regularly talk with their friends and families in India on regular basis. Thus far, I think the Tibetans have done very well in spite of all the distractions and hard working schedules. In New York, the Tibetans regularly get together at various functions, concerts, cultural events, demonstrations and religious events. So I think the Tibetans have not melted into the melting pot.[47]

The underlying assumption at work here is that a refugee who has been away for considerable time and has continued to interact with individuals still living in the home country or country of first asylum do relate to the world in a substantially different way from those who have never migrated.

Resettlement has a life-altering effect on refugees who are part of established social networks in the diaspora. The above passage suggests that Tibetan exile youth now living in the United States who have links with co-ethnics in India have a strong sense of national identity that is not linked to physical occupation of their homeland (their emphasis is on the ever-changing situation inside Tibet rather than an image of an unchanging Tibet). Rather it is linked to a patriotic desire to someday regain their independence (which remains the avowed goal of the Tibetan Youth Congress also operating in the United States) or autonomy for Tibet. Since only small minorities of refugees are actually resettled, the resettlement process does split up refugees' social networks; even those who are resettled may end up in different locations or even on different continents. The last sentence of the above passage—'So I think the Tibetans have not melted into the melting pot'—points to how the dominant importance of separation in the construction of meanings, identity, family and community influences the relationships refugees finally create and develop with their societies of residence.[48] This was conveyed by a Tibetan refugee living in the United States on being asked whether they take the help of lamas in the United States for performing various rituals or if there is a lack of these functionaries, 'There are Tibetan Associations in almost all the cities in the US, Canada, Europe and so on. In most cases here, it is the case of one organisation serving all functions, be it cultural, social, political, religious and so on. Regarding your question about monks and pujas, on account of the relatively more hectic lifestyle here in the West compared to India and Nepal, and also largely due to the virtually nonexistent members of the sangha (in our communities here), many of them give up their vows once they are in the West. Most pujas are ordered to be done in India and Nepal where our families and relatives are still residing and have the time and resources to host these day-long and week-long pujas. Interesting, isn't it?'[49]

Home and Place is Where You Make It!

What is foremost in the minds of refugees when they arrive in the resettlement country is the overwhelming transnational obligation that they have to cater to from the moment of their arrival in the resettlement country. Recently-arrived refugees who are not in a position to meet transnational obligations have feelings of guilt and rationalise about this newly-acquired status in a new society of residence. One Tibetan refugee made clear his stand on the issue of extending help to his co-ethnics in India: 'Since I came to the US as a student, I have not been able to send remittances home to my parents in India as often and as much as I would have liked to. However, every Tibetan in the US I would venture to state has relatives in India and Nepal and Tibet in some cases to whom they send money understanding that it is their responsibility now that they are in the West to help out those back home'.[50]

For recent refugees who find themselves in the 'country of second asylum', living life trans-nationally begins with acts of diasporic giving, occurring intermittently. Once they establish themselves in the host society, they are obliged to assist members of the refugee community cope with exile life. A Tibetan refugee who works as an administrative assistant to the athletic director of a private school on the east side of Manhattan wrote about the predicament of a Tibetan refugee child when they arrive in the United States and the steps taken by them to alleviate their lot:

'Once the children come here it is overwhelming for them, because in India they're used to living within Tibetan communities and settlements, and they're always in touch with other Tibetan families. Suddenly when they arrive in New York City it's very difficult, because there are not that many Tibetan families. Then when they go and attend the public schools, there are cases where some of them are the only Tibetans in their school. So of course they pick up a lot of things from other cultures, and at the same time they're not able to speak or read or write in Tibetan—and it becomes a problem. I feel it's very important within the family for the parents to try and keep this in mind as much as possible, when the kids are at home, and to try to give them as much exposure to the Tibetan culture and the Tibetan religion as possible—also to speak in Tibetan and try to teach them the language'.[51] Here India enters the imaginative map of the Tibetan exile in the United States, the expression of the need to replicate the diasporic practices of these India-born Tibetans contributes to the creation of settlement that occurs within a context that simultaneously connects refugees to multiple nation-states.

The evolving complexity of networks and transnational practices increasingly challenge the idea of a society firmly perched upon the nation-state. It opens up new ways of conceptualising 'home', of territorial identities and the notion of 'return' to one's homeland or to one's 'country of first asylum'.[52] As one Tibetan exile ruminated upon the shaping of his identity in the diaspora over the Internet, 'As a Tibetan who has lived in India and now living in the US, I believe I have assimilated influences consciously and unconsciously that have shaped my current identity as a stateless person in another country. In today's globalisation era where few are immune to outside influences leading to a homogenised kind of identity, I believe Tibetans are no exception and I personally feel that the fact that we are refugees and somewhat rootless and nowhere to call home, we are more apt to adopt outside influences. In addition, our Indian experience allows us in the West and specifically in the US to relate well and blend in with our Indian friends—we find we have enough in common and make many Indian friends in college and at work. Personally, when I was in school, I had many international student friends from India and regaled them with Hindi songs and my knowledge of Bollywood and so on'.[53]

On each Sunday, the Tibetan Association of New York and New Jersey takes over the building where the Office of Tibet, the Tibet Fund, and the US-Tibet Committee are housed, and turns it into a Sunday school. There is a staff of volunteer teachers who devote that one day of the week to teaching the children of the local Tibetan families to read and write Tibetan. They also teach them to perform traditional Tibetan music and dance while speaking, as much as possible, in Tibetan. The emergence of transnational activities of refugees and refugee groups is affected by conditions within both the host and the sending country and does vary over time and space depending on the attitudes of home states, differences in current status and differences in conditions in home society. Here the traditional naming and meaning of diasporas can be expanded to include several communities that express new identities and practices as a result of displacement and transnationality.[54]

Creating a Home in Exile

A Tibetan refugee, an inhabitant of the TRSHC, expressed how he related to the hostland—Darjeeling—while recounting his childhood: 'This is their land (*sa thog*). It is not ours. This is all that we are getting. We have tolerance as a Tibetan refugee. If someone says no you are not supposed to play in this ground, we won't fight. Otherwise we have the right to fight. The local people will not say you are a refugee. If they say let them have it, then we will have it. We cannot say this is mine. My land is there'.[55] Thinking and feeling about one's country of first asylum through socialisation does not always translate into a wish to return 'home' to Tibet. Leaving Darjeeling does not automatically involve returning. It can mean the possibility of moving to another country in order to escape the drudgeries of localised existence.

This possibility is conveyed by Tibetans who are firmly entrenched in Darjeeling arising as a result of inter-marriage. Inter-marriages, although not an everyday occurrence, are not uncommon. Recent trend is that more number of Tibetan women are getting married outside their community, that is, into the Bhutia and Nepali communities and even to foreigners, whereas Tibetan men more often get married within their community.[56] A Tibetan refugee woman married to a Bhutia described how her life changed with marriage: 'In the refugee centre, it is not liked if we speak in Nepali or have friends from the Nepali community. There was a lot of strictness. I can now enjoy some freedom. In my in-laws family, they do respect me for teaching them Tibetan customs and culture. I do remember Tibet but I have strong feelings for India which is my home now. I do not want to go back to Tibet, if Tibet gets free. I am keener to go to United States where my sister is living'. She hastened to add that 'in America, Tibetans are expected to show that they are Tibetan. In India you need not show that'.[57]

Home is usually seen in terms of a 'boundary'—it encloses people. It also represents a place where one can live more or less unselfconsciously. As the above passage suggests, there is also the comparison made by individuals of life in other places or sites (which was once one's home, especially in the case of Tibetan refugee women), which evokes different sentiments. It goes to show that the refugees in the TRSHC had some of their family members among the town refugees and vice-versa. It is also not unreasonable to assume that symbiotic and reciprocal economic and social interactions exist between the two groups. According to a refugee living in Darjeeling town, 'TRSHC is part of everyone. It is a home (*nang*). It is about looking after others. Camp (*sgar*) should be there to take care'.[58]

Creating a home in exile can be experienced by some as reconstructing a culture in a host-land that is truer to the 'original' than the culture that now dominates in the homeland itself. In the case of refugee women, triumph lies in spreading Tibetan culture among affines who are in this case 'hosts' to Tibetan refugees. The presence of Tibet in prints, music, television programmes, Tibet sites, the arts and crafts which dominate home decoration, clothing and food[59] does not signify an alienation from the present problems or concerns nor does it indicate a straightforward longing to 'return'. This is reflected in the way a Tibetan refugee perceives the problem of creating a home in exile inter-generationally. In one instance, a Tibetan refugee reflected upon this problem stating that 'My son would not be so patriotic (*rgyal gces*) because the environment is different now. Young ones have a deep feeling for the Dalai Lama but their knowledge about Tibet is less. It is only through books. Because of hectic school schedules, parents do not get time to interact and talk about Tibet like before. Children are sent to different schools'.[60]

A tension between the self-conscious honour/burden of being bearers of their heritage and the seemingly unlimited opportunities for innovation and interaction in exile informs the socialisation of Tibetan refugee youths from the moment they are born and have been institutionalised in the structure of their schools. Most Tibetan youths spoke of the marked difference in the level of exposure while studying in Convent schools like Mount Hermon or Loreto Convent than in the Central School for Tibetans in Darjeeling or in Tibetan Children's Village in Dehradun. 'Ask me where I'm from and I won't have an answer. I feel I never really belonged anywhere never really had a home. I was born in Manali but my parents live in Karnataka. My sisters are in Varanasi but my brothers are in Dharamsala. My Registration Certificate states that I am a foreigner residing in India and my citizenship is Tibetan. I like to speak in Tibetan but prefer to write in English, I like to sing in Hindi but my tune and accent are all wrong.'[61] This suggests that the major problems confronting the Tibetans is the threat of alienation from self and other Tibetans; disillusionment over hopes and expectations; and confused ethnic identity.

Despite a well-articulated academic curriculum, what is taught is not passed on unchanged, since Tibetan refugee youth are living culturally hybrid lives. The self-consciousness of forging viable links between tradition and modernity is exhibited by a young Tibetan writer who recognises the importance of speaking Tibetan with youngsters. He states, 'As a Tibetan of the diaspora, I can attest to the fact that most young Tibetans at some point develop a strong desire to connect with their cultural heritage. One of the most precious gifts my parents have given my sister, brother, and me is the language. Through our native tongue, we have been empowered to choose how and when to explore Tibetan culture. Certainly, much can be understood through other languages.[62] But much more of the culture can be felt by speaking face to face with knowledge bearers. Thus, the challenge lies ahead for current and future parents to somehow ensure that the future generations speak this ancient word'.[63]

Our Bond with Darjeeling and India!

New-generation Tibetan refugees are those for whom the Tibetan government's policies, the refugee community's concern about the future of Tibetan culture and the identity-challenging realities of life in the host society come together most complexly. What is observable is the emergence of concrete images of Tibetan refugees in Darjeeling of 'having made it', of having achieved material success in exile over the decades. As one Tibetan refugee having a garment business in Darjeeling town stated, 'It is convenient to do business in India. But I know about Darjeeling best. It is difficult to go elsewhere when you have a child'. Most of the success stories deal in some measure with wealth that was not inherited but made in the course of one's lifetime. Darjeeling became a productive place for Tibetans by providing a context for using their hybrid status as refugee/diasporics and citizens towards productive ends.

In talking about one's own work prospects and business growth in the present place, the starting point was the arrival in Darjeeling and not the reference to the 'past', that is, pre-occupation Tibet. The early exile was remembered as the period that had been overcome and lived through by the older generation. In narrating their struggle in exile, it emerged that the new generation expressed their indebtedness to their preceding generation (mostly their grandparents from whom they hear inspirational stories) who faced the hazards of early exile life in Darjeeling and not the people they had left behind in Tibet as a result of the Chinese occupation.

Yet those Tibetans studying in college or simply vagabonding ruminated about Tibet in their own characteristic way. One Tibetan refugee studying in Loyola College in Chennai and having a home in the TRSHC said, 'I would live like a refugee. This is better for me. My parents suffered a lot. I would like to do something. We have a dream of a free Tibet. In everyday life, the dream sometimes vanishes. But it is in there. It cannot be erased or something. It is in there. Anytime it can come up. Even if it does not come up, it is in there'.[64]

The significance of 'dreaming' about a place is brought out by Woeser in her essay, 'Tibet does not Exist, Tibet does Exist' where she writes about the conversation she had with her friend (a Tibetan born in the diaspora) via the Internet about the film 'Dreaming Lhasa' by Tenzing Sonam and Ritu Sarin, released in 2005. Her friend wrote to her, 'Everybody has their version of Lhasa. In particular, although most Tibetans in exile have not been to Lhasa, they have always talked about Lhasa from when they were little. But how can they know what kind of a place Lhasa is? So, it is just like a dream…though this movie is about Tibet, Tibet does not appear in it even once. There is no Tibet!' Woeser continues, 'Tibet does not exist! But everybody knows that Tibet does exist. It is precisely because we feel that Tibet does not exist or that it does exist that we have become kindred spirits. We still have our dream' (Woeser 2008).

These refugees also talk about Darjeeling as a place which serves as a signpost to know more about other places; to compare life in Darjeeling and in the diaspora, India and abroad. Tibetan youths remarked, 'Darjeeling being cold climate, makes it different from Bylakuppe. The way we dress up or diets are different. In South, Tibetans have sambar, dosas. Out here in Darjeeling we are into music, mostly rock music. In South they are more into Hindi film songs. In Delhi, they are more prosperous than we are. They mainly speak Hindi. We have become more Nepali'.[65]

A Tibetan refugee in Darjeeling town spoke about the place, Darjeeling, in the following manner: 'Darjeeling is there till we are here. It is not our country. It is our birthplace. Till we are here in India, it is our home'.[66] Darjeeling becomes a place of rest, a place to return to for students and sweater-sellers who go to other parts of India for their education and business respectively. It also becomes a place that produces monotony and drudgery in the lives of Tibetan exiles, who mention that they 'get fed up of living in Darjeeling and so move to other places for short and long retreats, like Gangtok, Kalimpong, Dharamsala, Gaya, Dehradun, Bylakuppe, New York or San Francisco among other places in order to refresh and gain knowledge'.[67] Darjeeling stands, using Stuart Hall's (1990) words, 'for the endless ways in which the Tibetan people have been destined to "migrate"; it is the signifier of migration itself—of traveling, voyaging and return as fate, destiny'.

Having achieved success, the point of consideration for the new generation in Darjeeling town was the prospect, desirability and extent of participation in the affairs of the homeland, besides pursuing business and work-related ventures. Through public acts of mobilisation, Tibetan diasporic communities are seen to come to terms with their invisibility in the everyday. Reaching out to the 'Other' is a means to prove their identification with their homelands and diasporic causes that are close to them. However, a Tibetan refugee in the garment business expressed the dilemma of refugee identity that emerges while engaging in commercial and other worldly pursuits which necessitates naturalisation and the adoption of the identity of an Indian citizen: 'There is a risk of joining any organisation for Tibetans, especially when you are in business and you have a Bhutia name. Others can point fingers at you. I have been part of U-Tsang association. I see that many of the young are interested in associations, movement and processions. Through associations (*tshogs pa*), we make them learn about the Tibetan movement for independence (*rang bstan*)'.[67]

People pointed to the expenditure of time and resources that would be swallowed up by the process of transforming oneself into a legally documented citizen. Those refugees who became very wealthy and began to own immovable property like houses or restaurants or valuable items like cars, taxis and lorries acknowledged the need to purchase nationality. It was considered that wealth made them more visible and liable to be questioned by immigration agents or strangers. So it suffices to call oneself a Bhutia or in other words, an Indian citizen. Legal naturalisation of this sort was a pragmatic expediency for some and according to others it meant a better option for securing work and cash and utilising that resource for use in free Tibet in the future. Those who think of the possibility and desirability of return to Tibet also recognise the trouble that could break out when the repatriation occurs. They assert that they 'do not want to go back to pre-1959 Tibet' which would appear, according to them, like *Gaon*—meaning village in the Hindi language.

The above statement indicates that what matters to the Tibetan refugees is living without difficulties, of the importance of taking a far-sighted view, similar to what Malkki writes about the manner in which 'town refugees tended to structure their lives and conversations in such a way as to leave both their immediate and more distantly perceived options open' (1995a: 194). The long-term plan in having Indian citizenship could not make life unproblematic for the Tibetan refugees. Interviews with some non-Tibetan shop owners next to the Tibetan-dominated Dragon market revealed the misgivings of Tibetan refugees about their relationships with non-Tibetans. Some of their comments are: '*Tibetans bus naam ke hi refugees hai*' (Tibetans are refugees only in name); '*Sarkar unke liye suvidha kar diya hai*' (Government has made it easy for the Tibetan refugees); '*Nara dene mai kiya hai*' (There is nothing in shouting slogans for Tibet); '*Tibet free ho jata hai to bhi koyi vapas nahi jayga*' (Even if Tibet gets freedom, nobody will go back to Tibet).[68]

One Tibetan doing business in Darjeeling town said, 'Inside the refugee settlement you have to go by rules of the settlement. Once outside you have to pay from your pocket. We do exactly like other Indian businessmen but we are yet to get social recognition for our efforts. We pay sales tax, income tax and rent but it is not recognised'.[69] For the Tibetan refugees intending to put down roots in Darjeeling, this social recognition remains elusive and rather hard to come by.

Notes

1. The founding president of the TRSHC was the late Mrs Deky Dolkar Thondup, who was the wife of Mr Gyalo Thondup, the elder brother of The Dalai Lama. The other members of the founding committee included Mr T. Lawang, Mr G. Tesur, Mr Tenzing Norgay, Mr and Mrs Joksari, Mr T. Tethong, Monsignor Benjamin, Mr Chumbay Tsering and Ms Tesur.

2. Khedroop Thondup is the nephew of the fourteenth Dalai Lama. He was born in Calcutta in 1952 and educated at the Jesuit school in Darjeeling, India, and later at the University of San Francisco. After returning to India, he served as special assistant to the Dalai Lama and travelled with him extensively. In 1986, he was appointed to run the TRSHC in Darjeeling.

3. The address of the registered office of the Tibetan Refugee Self Help Centre is: 65, Gandhi Road, Darjeeling—734101, West Bengal, India. TRSHC is situated in Ward number 25 of the Darjeeling Municipal Area.

4. The reference to thirteenth Dalai Lama's association with Hill-side Darjeeling by some of the inhabitants of TRSHC in their introductory remarks about their current place of residence in the host society is suggestive

of the symbolism that is consequential in enabling them to live the present in historical terms.

5. However, the extent of net under-enumeration was lower in the Tibetan Demographic Survey 1998 exercise due to two reasons: i. the field enumerators went from house-to-house and recorded the data; ii. a fair presence and excellent participation by the 'immobile' population of the enumeration day (Tibetan Demographic Survey 1998, Planning Council, Central Tibetan Administration 2000: 40).

6. In the context of refugee studies, 'labeling is a process of stereotyping which involves disaggregation, standardization and the formulation of clear cut categories. In the institutional setting these characteristics assume considerable power for labeling simultaneously defines a client group and prescribes an assumed set of needs (food, shelter and protection) together with appropriate distributional apparatus' (Zetter 1991: 44).

7. Among the successful items is footwear and coats which while keeping the traditional Tibetan styles are modified for suitable wear with European clothes. 'The immense popularity of these items as well as the several letters that TRSHC receives from all over the world have proved the success of this venture' (Report TRSHC 1999).

8. The coolies or unskilled workers who form the backbone of the Darjeeling economy belong to the Nepali community of Darjeeling. Contrasting the occupations and occupational skills which Tibetans can develop and preserve vis-à-vis the 'hazardous occupations' of the Nepalis signifies for the Tibetans a certain self-attestation of a perceived sign of progress; of creativity and continuity in exile. It does not, however, point to the making of categorical or essentialising judgements about the 'locals-Nepalis' or 'citizens'.

9. Excerpt from an interview with the manager, TRSHC held on 18 May 2005 at the TRSHC. 'Our wool is from 100 per cent Tibetan sheep from Ladakh', says the manager of the TRSHC, where the threatened culture is proving to be resilient (in 'Spirit of Tibet' by Carleton Cole, published in World Tibet Network News, Canada Tibet Committee, downloaded on 24 May 2007). The centre had been able to train 1,600 persons in various crafts, of which 1,000 to 1,200 persons have left the centre to set up their own enterprises (Report TRSHC 1999).

10. Excerpt from the interview with the manager on 18 May 2005 at the TRSHC. The extent of 'mixing' with the local population which the manager pointed out would be discussed while taking up the case of Tibetans living in the main town. It is important to recognise that the threat of assimilation is particularly acute for the refugees since if the assimilation were to be successful, the label 'refugee' would be blurred and the pressure for repatriation would be lost.

11. As told by the manager of workshops at the TRSHC on 20 May 2005.

12. Houses in the TRSHC have small windows like the blockhouses which were the most common type of civilian housing in Old Tibet. Blockhouses had flat roofs and small windows. These houses were usually of two storeys—the wall base is laid with stone and the upper part is earth-piled solid.

13. Interview of two Nepali youths at the hermitage on 22 May 2005

14. 'Most of the orphans have been sent to various schools across India and several have been sponsored for study abroad. These orphans have no known relatives or any to care for them and thus are entirely dependent on the Centre. With the generous help of several individuals scattered all over the world, the Centre has been …able to lay the foundation for their future' (Report TRSHC 1999).

15. Excerpt from a conversation with my key informant, a Tibetan man of 40 years at the TRSHC, on 20 May 2005. He introduced me to his father who arrived in Darjeeling from the Amdo province of Tibet after the Chinese invasion of Tibet. He had visited India on pilgrimage several times before 1959.

16. The teaching and curriculum in Tibetan schools is similar to schools of the host country, India. One major difference is that Tibetan language and culture is an integral part of the curriculum of most Tibetan schools. In the secondary schools, Tibetan children follow the syllabus established by India's Central Board of Secondary Education and take their national examination to be eligible to enter higher education. It is only at the primary level that an intensive Tibetan culture and language curriculum is implemented.

17. For more on the Central School for Tibetans in Darjeeling, see http://www.cstdalumni.org/ (downloaded on 24 July 2015). Again, special emphasis in this school is understandably laid on preservation and promotion of Tibetan culture, protection of environment and inculcation of human values. Career counselling is also an important activity.

18. It is difficult to assess what percentage of those refugees resorted to collecting alms. Even those who were once engaged in it are unable to give any tentative figure. It is generally agreed that they constituted a large number and were conspicuous in the town area.

19. The term 'financial assistance' used by the respondent is a pointer to the acute awareness that refugees have of the presence or absence of aid organisations in their lives or the support that is extended to them by individual donors.

20. Interview with Tibetan youth aged 19 years at the TRSHC on 29 May 2005. It is important to note that for the new-generation, India-born Tibetans, their identity as refugee was something which had to be cognitively learnt. Tenzin Tsundue, in his essay 'My Kind of Exile', emphasises this point, 'When we were children in a Tibetan school in Himachal Pradesh. Our teachers used to regale us with tales of Tibetans suffering in Tibet. We were often told that we were

refugees and that we all bore a big "R" on our foreheads' (downloaded from www.friendsoftibet.org on 15 June 2007).

21. Excerpt from an interview with a Tibetan at his garments shop in Darjeeling town on 26 May 2005.

22. Excerpt from an interview with a Tibetan youth at the TRSHC on 26 May 2005. His resides in Darjeeling town. The word 'communal' to the Tibetan had a specific usage which referred to the 'local community' (*mi sde*) of host groups in Darjeeling town. The usage of the word 'communal' indicated, in the context of the interview, an awareness of the need to prevent the possible rise of communal feelings that would disturb the prevailing social order in the area.

23. Laying claim to Bhutia identity is a common strategy adopted by most Tibetan refugees doing lucrative business in Darjeeling town area. It serves a strategic end of securing ties to Indian citizenship and providing business opportunities in a condition of anonymity and security.

24. For the respondent, 'knowing this place' meant a certain degree of identification with the place Darjeeling, its history and geography.

25. Excerpt from an interview with a Tibetan shop owner at Mahakal market, Darjeeling town, on 19 May 2005. The source of the respondent's knowledge of the places he mentions (Darjeeling, India and America) is both experiential and imaginative. Here we see the process of diasporic identifications at play. While the feeling of belonging to Darjeeling is the greatest, the place is evaluated in relation or opposition to India. America is there in the distant horizon, for him an abode of prosperity, a projection into the future. Tibet as a place is not mentioned by him in the initial phase of the interview.

26. My key informant, a Bhutia, in the numerous conversations with him, once interjected and told about the historical fact that the king of Sikkim used to traditionally give tributes periodically to the Dalai Lama of Tibet at Lhasa, as demonstration of his allegiance to the Lamaist State. He said that he had read it somewhere but could not recollect the source.

27. In order to understand the ethnic domain in the context of Darjeeling spelt out here, it is particularly relevant to recall Michael Fischer's (1986: 230–31) essay, 'Ethnicity and the Arts of Memory', in which he states, 'The different ethnicities constitute a "family of resemblance": similar, not identical; each enriching because of its inter-references, not reducible to mechanical functions of solidarity, mutual aid, political mobilization or socialization. It is the inter-references, the interweaving of cultural threads from different arenas that give ethnicity its phoenix-like capacities for reinvigoration and reinspiration'.

28. Other set of differences between Tibetan refugees and Bhutias were articulated by these two groups. 'There is a feeling in the Tibetan refugees that they are a bit different than us. They think that we are not as patriotic like them'

(excerpt from an interview with the Bhutia respondent on 24 September 2006 at Bhutia busty). In the course of conversation, many Tibetan refugees have commonly expressed their view that in order to live peacefully with the majority community—the Nepalis and Indian Buddhists such as the Bhutias—it is best to make 'friends'. Friendship therefore becomes a strategy for social integration at the local level.

29. Excerpt from an interview with a Tibetan refugee at Darjeeling town on 24 May 2005.

30. For more on the nature of Nepali identity, see Golay 2006.

31. Excerpt from an interview with a Bhutia respondent who worked in a government office in his mid-40s at Bhutia Busty on 24 September 2006.

32. Excerpt from the interview with the former councilor of Bhutia Busty on 29 September 2006. Both conjunction and disjunction are seen to characterise the Bhutia–refugee relationship. The Tibet that is portrayed by the refugee in the excerpt is a picture of Tibet which assumes an un Shangri-la-like appearance, which violates Western sensibilities of a pristine Tibet. Exile is, therefore, a 'place of refuge' where normal social relations are restored at the intimate level of the family.

33. Interview with few Bhutia respondents in Bhutia busty on 24 September 2006. This is not to suggest that the Bhutias are indifferent to the Tibetan cause. On the contrary, Bhaichung Bhutia, the Indian football captain who has his home in Sikkim, took the decision to drop out of the team that would carry the Olympic torch on its Indian leg in New Delhi. 'I sympathise with the Tibetans and their cause. I have sent a letter to the IOA (Indian Olympic Association) refusing to carry the torch', Bhaichung Bhutia told The Telegraph (The Telegraph, Calcutta, Tuesday, 1 April 2008; downloaded from https://www.telegraphindia.com/1080401/jsp/frontpage/story_9081674.jsp on 25 September 2009). Bhutia's decision points to how Sikkim and Darjeeling as 'places' continue to be implicated in the ongoing debate on Tibet's historical and geopolitical status.

34. Interview with a Bhutia respondent in Bhutia Busty on 25 September 2006

35. In traditional usage, 'passing' refers to the practice of assuming the identity of another type, class or groups of persons in order to be recognised as a member of that group, for social, economic or political reasons (Yeh 2002: 237).

36. The total population of Scheduled Tribes in the Darjeeling Municipality is 12,747, of which 6,448 are male and 6,299 are female (Census of India 2001).

37. The Bhutia respondent was an elderly man. His family members were helping him narrate. Excerpt from an interview with a Bhutia resident in Darjeeling town on 29 September 2006.

38. Elderly Nepalis living in the neighbouring hermitage area who have witnessed the progress of Darjeeling refugees spoke of their 'hardworking spirit' as the singular reason for their success.

39. Being a refugee demanded certain kinds of social conduct, while closing off others. It was not merely a label or legality; it was a moral condition bearing its own consequences. The two Tibetan youths interviewed in a restaurant in Darjeeling town on 4 October 2006 were well aware of the violent incident that had erupted in Dharamsala between Tibetan refugees and Gaddis in 1994. For more on the Dharamsala incident, see Penny-Dimri 1994: 280–93.

40. Obtaining Indian citizenship has never been an easy decision for a Tibetan in exile; the reasons for this will be elaborated later.

41. Excerpt from an interview with several Tibetan youths working in the wood-carving section at the TRSHC on 25 September 2006.

42. Both Tibetan refugees and Tibetan-turned Indian citizens possessed the RC. RC was an emphatic proof of their Tibetan nationality; their adherence to the movement for the independence of Tibet and an affirmation of their ethnic identity as Tibetan.

43. Excerpt from interview with a Tibetan respondent who does garment business at Mahakal market, Darjeeling town on 24 May 2005.

44. Excerpt from an interview with a Tibetan respondent who does garment business at Mahakal market, Darjeeling town on 24 May 2005. The marginality of Tibetan refugees, as de Voe (1987: 57) states, also gives 'leeway to forge their own community around their leader and religion, with little diversion from the original purpose of flight—to defend the faith and in the end, to rescue the people left behind in Tibet'.

45. Excerpt from the interview with Samdhong Rinpoche on World Tibet Network News, 12 February 2004.

46. This is contrary to the general opinion among Tibetan refugees in India that the exile administration is partial towards Tibetans in the West, especially with regard to the citizenship issue. It also becomes difficult to ignore the fact that the Tibetan refugee-turned-Indian citizens do not make a case of this partiality since they do not want to jeopardise their new-found citizenship status.

47. In the Tibetan case, though it is difficult to get an exact estimate of the number of Internet users, the use of the Internet is fairly widespread among young people of all backgrounds as it is cheap and readily available in most areas both in India (including Darjeeling) and abroad. A Darjeeling-based journalist who owns an Internet café near Mahakal market assessed this aspect, 'my cyber café remains full for most part of the day. Many Tibetans come over to the café and write to their sponsors for financial and non-monetary assistance. I sometimes do help them out with the correspondence' (interviewed on 28 September 2006 at the Internet café).

48. A Tibetan refugees' relationship with the society of resettlement in the United States is aptly brought out in the poem 'A Song from a Distance' by

Bhuchung D Sonam, August 2007, tibetwrites.org (downloaded from http://tibetwrites.in/index.html%3FA-Song-from-a-Distance.html on 26 April 2012).

49. Excerpt from the conversation over the Internet with a Tibetan exile in the United States on 15 June 2007. The desire and ability to engage in transnational practices ebb and flow at different phases of the lifecycle and in different contexts.

50. Excerpt from a conversation over the Internet with a Tibetan exile in the United States on 14 June 2007.

51. For more on Tibetan exiles in New York, see www.newstrolls.com/news/dev/wmeyers/index.html (downloaded on 26 March 2016).

52. The notion of 'return' here denotes not only the greater or lesser likelihood of a person eventually returning, that is, the 'when' of return but also the 'where' of return and the very real possibility that one cannot return home either.

53. Excerpt from a conversation over the Internet with a Tibetan exile in the United States on 10 June 2007.

54. The distinction between diaspora and transnational is not always clear in social science literature. While recognising that diasporas can eventually evolve into powerful transnational communities, it is sufficient to say that multiple and simultaneous ways of belonging and multiple ways of incorporation in the host societies is the one key theme that is common to both.

55. Excerpt from a conversation with Tibetan refugees at the TRSHC on 27 September 2006.

56. Reliable statistical information on the frequency of mixed marriages among the town refugees was unavailable. However, it is possible to say that neither town refugee nor the Welfare Officer with whom the scope for intermarriage was discussed expressed moral or political criticisms about those who had intermarried.

57. Excerpt from a conversation with a Tibetan woman at the Mall, Darjeeling town on 24 May 2005.

58. Excerpt from a conversation with a Tibetan refugee in Darjeeling town on 25 May 2005.

59. With regard to clothing of children and the youths in Darjeeling, there is no difference between the Tibetan refugees and the local people. The common styles of clothing, hairdo and mannerisms are, as far as possible, faithful reproductions of the latest trend prevailing among film stars of Bollywood, if not Hollywood. With regard to food, many Tibetans now eat rice. Meat, like before, is always there in the daily menu.

60. Excerpt from an interview with a Tibetan refugee at the TRSHC on 22 May 2005.

61. Tsundue Tenzin, 'My Kind of Exile', http://www.friendsoftibet.org/tenzin/essays/my_kind_of_exile.html (downloaded on 25 April 2015).

62. 'The exile mix of Tibetan, Hindi, and English is something I like to call "*Thinglish*" untraditional, but it works. This is a key to Tibetan survival beyond the land of snows—we approach what is around us and combine it with what we need and know to define a space uniquely ours' (Rabgey 2002).

63. Tibetan Muslims in India who are Indian citizens have been more successful in preserving the Tibetan language than Tibetans embracing Tibetan Buddhism. Their steadfastness in speaking the language is brought out in an interview with a Tibetan Muslim (on 4 October 2006 at Darjeeling town) who said, 'In a place like Darjeeling, Tibetans are losing their linguistic capacity because of the mix with locals. If you start speaking the local language, your children will forget the Tibetan language. So you must speak Tibetan yourself at home. Our mother tongue is Tibetan. We must teach Tibetan at home'.

64. Excerpt from an interview with a Tibetan refugee at the TRSHC on 24 May 2005.

65. Excerpt from an interview with a Tibetan youth in Darjeeling town on 26 May 2005.

66. This statement is similar to the manner in which Nepalis think of Darjeeling when they say, 'Darjeeling will take care of me' (Golay 2006: 40).

67. Excerpt from an interview with Tibetan youths in Darjeeling town on 27 May 2005.

67. Excerpt from an interview with a Tibetan refugee at the Dragon market in Darjeeling town on 28 September 2006.

68. Excerpt from a conversation with non-Tibetan shop owners on 28 September 2006 in Darjeeling town.

69. Excerpt from a conversation with Tibetan shop owners on 28 September 2006 in Darjeeling town.

7

Dwelling and Movement in Exile*

The principal challenge of studying Tibetan refugees in the diaspora has been to understand the relationship between place, identity in a state of becoming, movement and culture. The exploration of the lived and experiential circumstances of the Tibetan refugees in a specific host context (Darjeeling town) reinforced the idea that the Tibetan refugees and Tibetans (Bhutias) have always been mobile or 'on the move' under very different conditions and predicaments. This view cautions us against perceiving refugee groups like the Tibetans as inhabiting a bounded territory; of viewing cultures in spatial terms. The corollary of this perspective is that people, regardless of their territorial origin, have become, or are in the process of becoming, deterritorialised, resulting in generalised 'homelessness' (Said 1979: 18) or 'refugeeness'.

This conception of displacement implies that since the relation between people and places is of a tenuous kind, the idea of a 'return' home or 'repatriation' as a durable solution to protracted refugee problems is without basis. On the other hand, the transnational practices of Tibetan refugee groups as a result of their dispersion have paved the way for the creation of a complex niche in the 'hostlands'. The existence of this complex niche that directs attention to the processes, practices, actors and relations in the specific local context of Darjeeling town is seen to provide meaning to the diasporic world that the Tibetan refugees inhabit. It further reframes the category 'refugee' as simultaneously embedded within both the country of origin and the several host societies and helps us consider the ways in which Tibetans have formulated and reformulated their refugee identities in diasporic

* Previously published as Sudeep Basu, 'Interpreting the Tibetan Diaspora: Cultural Preservation and the Pragmatics of Identity', in *Central European University Political Science Journal*, vol. 4, no. 3, 2009, pp. 419–45. The article has been modified by the author for the current volume.

terms both within Darjeeling town and in the broader transnational social field associated with this place.

The concern throughout the study has been to conceptualise 'refugeeness' that is 'rooted' and 'routed' (Clifford 1997) not only in the flight and displacement of Tibetan refugee groups and individuals but also in the daily practices of living, forming relationships and constructing identities that such individuals and groups experience and take part in as they live in Darjeeling town and move to several other host settings. That the Tibetan refugee has always 'been on the move' prompts recognition that the imagination of the diaspora is constituted by a compelling sense of moral co-responsibility (Werbner 2002) embodied in performances which are extended through and across space. Refugees are seen as part of transnational family households whose members make joint decisions and partake in collective efforts to help secure livelihood for family members as they live and move in different nation-states.

What this occurrence captures is the impact of deterritorialisation on the imaginative resources of lived, local experiences of 'resettled' Tibetan refugees, given the overwhelming moral expectations placed on them in the country of second asylum and the possible lives that they are able to envision. It echoes James Clifford's statement on 'how diasporic cultural forms are deployed in transnational networks built from multiple attachments and how they encode practices of accommodation with, as well as resistance to host countries and their norms'. (1997: 251) Besides, members of the Tibetan diaspora mobilise politically to defend or protest against injustices and human rights abuses suffered by co-diasporics elsewhere. This implies that refugee groups do not have an affiliation with a single place of origin; instead, they foster multiple attachments to and stakes in several locales. It is further a pointer to the fact that, given the change in the global conditions of life-worlds, which Appadurai talks of, 'habitus now has to be painstakingly reinforced in the face of life-worlds that are frequently in flux' (1996: 56).

In a generalised way, for Tibetan refugees living in Darjeeling, the other focal places that constitute the diasporic circuit which are invested with high value are Tibet and Lhasa (north) and Dharamsala, Bylakuppe in India (west and south), China (east) and the 'West'. Their relationship to these other places are differently constituted and has framed the everyday life and identity of refugees placed in Darjeeling, thereby creating new realities 'on the ground' for their neighbours. The empowering paradox of diaspora, which Clifford talks about, is brought out in full relief, in that 'dwelling here assumes a solidarity and connection there. But the there is not a single place or an exclusivist nation' (Clifford 1994: 332). The 'place' of Tibetan diaspora reflected upon here is the whole world, with the exception of the point of origin (Tibet); an intricate network of places marked by cultural variability; a place of many heterogeneous traditions; with Darjeeling as one such place or territory that figures in the Tibetan diasporic consciousness.

The presence of pre-exilic Tibetan hosts, the Bhutias, in Darjeeling town and recognition of the fact that the current situation of Tibetan refugees is a result of past (pre-1950) migrations and eventual settlement of Tibetans in the region directs attention away from viewing the Tibetans in terms of the presumed isomorphism of people, culture and territory. The spontaneous settlement of refugees has been facilitated by the long-standing relation between Bhutias and the Nepalese in Darjeeling town. The ethnic similarities have been particularly important in the sense that a large part of the refugees have, through tribal relations (claiming Scheduled Tribes status of the Bhutias) or by echoing pan-Buddhist sentiments expressed in statements such as 'We are Buddhists, we are one', been able to lay claim upon available resources. The movement of Tibetans as refugees into the region previously occupied by the ethnic Bhutias and their use of the adoptive label 'Bhutia' for functional purposes spawned new local groups and new relationships both of cooperation and conflict with neighbouring groups.

The Bhutias were for long caught up in the same contingent social situation as the refugees, except that they have all acquired Indian citizenship. The growing competition between Scheduled Tribes created a rift between Bhutias and the refugees but there were also conscious attempts by refugees to reduce feelings of hostility among neighbours. This attitude is reflected in the following statement by the welfare officer of the Darjeeling refugee settlement who said, 'We are neither a burden nor an asset to Darjeeling local economy. As refugees we have to work that is all'.[1] Living in urban residential areas among nationals meant that the Tibetan refugees have had to fend for themselves in an otherwise economically depleted and congested urban space. Neighbourhoods where Tibetans live with non-Tibetans therefore require and produce contexts (Appadurai 1996: 184); they have to be carved out from 'some sort of hostile or recalcitrant environment' which may include other neighbourhoods. Thus, the making and remaking of ethnic communities in a place became intertwined with acts of surviving and gaining resources. Yet the construction of Tibetan identities in the diaspora remains linked to the experiences of flight from the homeland and seeking asylum, which results in differentiation of the Tibetan community dispersed across spaces on the basis of their affiliations or identity groups back home.

The dispersal of Tibetan refugee groups involves a strong sense of the danger of forgetting the location of origin (as is the fate of the Bhutias of Darjeeling, which the Tibetan refugees living there are well aware of). Even though the Tibetan refugees are in a 'Stateless' situation (Samuel 1982), the very prospect that they may never return home creates a more intensified yearning for the homeland. Thus diasporic consciousness, as Clifford states, 'lives loss and hope as a defining tension'. A Tibetan refugee's ruminations about Tibet, 'We have a dream of a free Tibet. In everyday life, the dream sometimes vanishes. But it is in there. It cannot be erased or something. It is in there. Anytime it can come up. Even if it does not come up, it is in there'[2], shows how this yearning becomes a major preoccupation and, in a sense, replaces the real possibility of returning home. Diasporic consciousness of the exiled Tibetans here reinforces the central importance of place as an organising principle and as a creative key to imagination.

Structure and pattern of housing at the refugee centre resemble those that were found in Old Tibet. Woolen rugs and various handicraft items have slowly begun to reflect the yearning for the homeland. Weavers at the TRSHC are seen to incorporate motifs of geography and architecture, and religious and national symbols into their designs. The fact that 'place' as a signifier here is expressed in and through material culture suggests a somewhat conservative attitude towards change in that it attempts to keep Tibetan refugees focused on the past. Yet the very idea of having to keep the notion of place alive is a creative result of being displaced.

When seen as not just movement but as a relational network associated with particular places, diaspora becomes a way of creating a rift between places of belonging and places of residence. The following statement made by a Tibetan refugee engaged in the garment business in Darjeeling town, 'I know this place better than any other place. I do not want to go and stay in any other part of India. It is convenient to do business in India but given the chance I would like to go to America (a mi ri ka) you know, there is opportunity (go skabs) there', points to how diasporic cultures mediate, as James Clifford argues, 'the experiences of living here and remembering/desiring or not desiring another place' (1997: 255). The notion of movement thought of here is seen as a process that entails a lot more than a basis for legal identifications of people. These people include Tibetans living in Darjeeling having legal or illegal status and refugees who have become citizens of the host society.

Though numerically in a minority, the refugees from Tibet living in Darjeeling town have charted out a successful career in exile, self-employed in various business ventures. They are the ones who do not live in the TRSHC. The presence of the refugee centre as viewed and perceived by refugees living in the town aids in reconciling material success with symbolic–cultural ends such as the need to maintain their identities not only as Tibetans but also as refugees in a changing host society—the multi-ethnic Darjeeling. The self-settlement of refugees is inevitable for two reasons. First, all refugees could not possibly be accommodated in the TRSHC because of insufficient funds and lack of space. Second, organised settlements have largely failed to achieve the objective of economic self-sufficiency. The prevalence of self-settlement of Tibetan refugees in Darjeeling town has called for a conceptualisation of 'integration' among refugee groups and different members of the host society. 'Integration' as sought by Tibetan refugees in the specific host context of Darjeeling is shown as a consequence of multi-faceted layers of participation and acceptance that the refugees and their family members seek as they live not only in Darjeeling town, but also in other host contexts.

At Home in the Diaspora!

Darjeeling has had a history of serving as a zone of contact between different ethnic communities over time. With the exception of the autochthonous Lepchas of the region, the Nepalese and the Tibetans moved to Darjeeling from Nepal and Tibet respectively. Darjeeling and Kalimpong town, for instance, served as a trading centre but its economic basis expanded to cover activities in the handicraft, transport and service sectors. Right until the late 1950s, caravans of Tibetan mules used to ply back and forth between Kalimpong and Tibetan towns through the place known as Chumbi Valley, connecting India and Tibet. In this sense, Tibetans historically neither had a boundary nor were they fixed in a territory but had a 'place' and were 'on the move'. Past migrations of Tibetans (before 1950) into the region had to be taken into cognisance. It was difficult to doubt the historicity of their move, even though it had happened long enough ago to be embellished in myth and legend.

As members of the pioneering group of Tibetans became more and more 'emplaced' in an area, they acquired a name—Bhutia—that had no reference to their place of settlement (Darjeeling) but was identified with the place that they had left—'Bhot' or 'Tibet'. When the Tibetan refugees moved into Darjeeling town from 1959 onwards, they began to settle or work in areas where their predecessors (the Bhutias) had their presence (Bhutia Busty) or in places (Ladenla road) or shops bearing Tibetan names. The refugees were aware that the etymology of the word 'Darjeeling' had roots in Tibetan culture. They began to adopt the name 'Bhutia' in their everyday life in order to conceal their refugee identity in certain contexts. This can be seen as a consequence of their need to gain shelter by presenting a veneer that they seek assimilation in a host society and their commitment to either a theoretically unending process of movement into new places or a deferred 'return' to their homeland. Their attempts to forge meaningful ties with the Bhutias and the dominant Nepalis in the town became integral to the process of rehabilitation in the early years of exile.

Notwithstanding the apparent assimilative tendencies that the refugees exhibited in their use of the Bhutia label or in their speaking of Nepali, the gradual differentiation between Tibetan refugees and the Bhutias had set in based primarily on the political commitment of the former to the idea of 'return' expressed in spatial and cultural terms. The unfolding Tibetan–host relationship characterised by conjunction and disjunction relative to local[2] circumstances makes it possible to appreciate the significance that the Tibetans attribute to their refugee identity and the 'spatial practices' by means of which the Tibetans produce and maintain a sense of 'place' in a contested environment. On examining this canvas, one can assert, following Turton (1979), that it is the 'journey or movement that had made the Tibetans'.

However, the movement of Tibetan refugees, unlike their Bhutia co-ethnics, is seen as incomplete for two reasons: first, since the refugee community's relationship to the place, Darjeeling, is seen as tentative and precarious. This makes continued vigilance of the boundaries of that community (Barth 1969) seen in the not so apparent regulation of inter-marriages between refugees and locals and the periodic performance of 'spatialising' rituals (celebration of Losar, 10 March Tibetan Uprising; Saka Dawa celebrations) in the refugee centre and in the town necessary for survival and preservation. The host context (Darjeeling) that is acknowledged or grappled with in the numerous conversations with refugees is seen either to recede into the background, providing a standard with which to ascribe meaning to their economic successes or failures or is foregrounded in order to confront the zones of overlap and difference between groups that have similar religious identities and geographical origins—Tibet. Second, while the sense of an eventual return to the place of origin seemed imminent to those who had escaped from Tibet in the initial years of exile, their heirs born in Darjeeling have instead begun to look forward to another place of arrival—the West or some other place of settlement—in order to give meaning to their present localised existence. The 'return' to Darjeeling by some refugees from the West or places in the diaspora during Losar provides additional information about the predicaments of exile life in a different host context.

Becoming legally secure through obtaining a refugee status (the RC and the identity certificate) or acquiring citizenship rights while planning to move to other host societies is perceived by many refugees as the one kind of life they can lead in Darjeeling for the present. Some Tibetan refugees in India are aware of other family members and friends who have acquired citizenship rights in the West but have found meaningful integration into their host societies unattainable. For some Tibetans, Darjeeling appears to continually refer beyond itself to other places—United States, Canada and recently, Australia. So while living in Darjeeling and India is an attractive option during certain periods of one's life, for example, when acquiring school and college education or some skill, other places of residence, such as the United States, are regarded as the best places for work or reunifying the family and kin group. As these different places become increasingly familiar, whether through direct experience, word of mouth or other communication channels (phayul.com) that allow Tibetans to monitor current events, it becomes difficult to see them as separate places. Home in the diaspora then is not bounded by the borders of one province or country but simultaneously exists across the borders of Darjeeling, India and the Western countries. Home, in the sense of kith and kin, is thus periodically reconstituted in places that are mutually agreed upon by members living in different host societies. The Tibetan diaspora encompasses all of them but is not reducible to any one of them.

In spite of expressing an interest in obtaining Indian citizenship, a Tibetan respondent in Darjeeling town confirmed having more than one identity by stating that, 'Becoming an Indian becomes important, we get opportunity. With Holiness there, we feel proud we are Tibetans. I do not mind becoming an Indian but I want to keep my status as refugee. It is important that we believe that we will get our freedom. We can always convert to Tibetan, when Tibet is free. I am a Tibetan but since I am born in India I am an Indian'[4]. Integration into the host society, Darjeeling or India, here is imagined as becoming an Indian citizen while still maintaining Tibetan identity and culture. The networks across political borders created by Tibetans in their quest for economic advancement and political recognition have afforded the possibility of having hybrid identities. People's choices of dwelling and movement in different host contexts are often influenced by the prevailing national, legal and economic conditions prevalent in hostlands.

Tibetan refugees in Darjeeling are seen as either bilingual or multilingual (knowing Tibetan, Hindi, English and Nepali), frequently maintaining homes in two or more places and pursuing economic, political and cultural interests that require their real or imaginary presence in both. Some of the self-settled Tibetans in Darjeeling town have become Indian citizens, given the perceived benefits which accompany that status, such as freedom in terms of physical movement, exercise of the right to own businesses, property and increased educational opportunities. However, in the context of Darjeeling town, acquiring citizenship documents did not tantamount to a declaration that a Tibetan has given up the belief that Tibet will eventually be free. Embracing Indian citizenship has had an instrumental dimension in that it exists alongside the desire and the practice of remaining a refugee while interacting with co-refugees or constitutive others within a refugee settlement context or becoming a diasporic in the context of the town.

As Gaim Kibreab (1999: 387) points out, 'The exponents of deterritorialization of identity may argue that one of the reasons why refugees and immigrants are in a deplorable state is because of the assumption that there are 'natural' places from which people derive their identity'. He continues, 'The "right to remain" or belonging to a territory with strong associations through long-term occupation, does not make sense unless it means the right to stay in that territory in safety and that right is exercised by the right holders themselves free from external pressure' (1999: 387).

The way Tibetans prior to 1959 and after have experienced movement into and settlement in a new place, Darjeeling, is determined by whether and how much they viewed themselves as being displaced against their will and whether their notions of territorial attachments can be retained and even extended to areas not necessarily adjacent to each other. The telling and retelling of stories told by older-generation exiles to the new-generation, Darjeeling-born Tibetans about Tibet and the early years of struggle in a new place; the re-creation of familiar features from the lost environment as recaptured in the architectural design of houses built in and around the refugee settlement; rituals of naming houses and streets with their spatial and temporal symbolism; inner decoration of refugee homes and the transportation of familiar objects and personal mementoes constitute the set of 'place-making' activities meant to re-establish continuity with the place of origin. The refugees were also able to see themselves as repeating a pattern of pioneering movements into and self-settlement in the urban areas of the Darjeeling region by the pre-exilic Tibetan groups like the Bhutias, which became part of their self-identity as Tibetans.

Further, the landscape of Darjeeling into which they moved was relatively close by and topographically not entirely dissimilar to Tibet. For the refugees, there was no obvious rupture of continuity with the place (Tibet) from which they moved. What was also at work in these forms of social action was the process of 're-territorialisation' as Tibetan refugee groups faced with a protracted exile condition have attempted to delimit and influence relationships with 'others' over a geographic area (Darjeeling town). This process assumes significance in places like Darjeeling where, drawing from Kibreab, 'the rights of access to and use of sources of livelihood are apportioned on the basis of territorially anchored identity'. (1999: 407). To be outside that physical context often entails loss of rights to belong to an ethnic or national group which is physically grounded. What is at issue are the relations, 'sociations' and stakes that refugees develop in the course of everyday life in the midst of others. Their mechanics or strategies of living without feeling the constraints of otherness are vital to leading a dignified life.

In a multi-ethnic place like Darjeeling which has been host to migrant groups in the past, Tibetan refugee groups and individuals have, over time, developed a repertoire of strategies of managing assimilative tendencies towards productive ends on the one hand and forging meaningful social relations that link several localities in more than one 'host' place. The use of adoptive labels (Bhutia label) or Nepali language by the self-settled refugees was not prompted by fear of repatriation or deportation to refugee camps. Using identity signs or documents that suggested assimilation into the host society has been a strategy of invisibility adopted by Tibetans to avoid the prospect of embarrassment or harassment because of their identity as refugees. Obtaining Indian citizenship by use of identity signs was sufficient proof of legitimate residency for many of the town refugees, particularly in the case where the host government led by the Gorkha National Liberation Front (GNLF) were favourably disposed towards the refugees. The refugees had the advantage that no serious attempt was made to exercise administrative control over them.

Confinement of some of the Tibetans in the spatially-segregated site (TRSHC) did not amount to their incarceration. Camp refugees and the refugees in Darjeeling town came as forced migrants and reciprocal economic and social interaction did exist between the two groups. These factors prevented them from developing marked differences in identity between the two groups so as to appear antagonistically opposed. These two groups have not been treated as mutually exclusive entities, although difference in physical location of the members of the two groups has resulted in differences in terms of wealth (town refugees have become more prosperous than their counterparts in the refugee settlement). These differences have not led to insidious comparisons by members of the two groups.

In general, the refugees have, as far as possible, maintained a safe distance from the agents of the state. Possessing documents proving Indian citizenship did not, however, guarantee immunity against hostility from neighbours and from being identified as refugees, particularly by locals. Tibetans living in the refugee settlement were aware of the fact that the strategy of invisibility carried with it an element of vulnerability. When the Tibetan refugees in Darjeeling town related with strangers or other ethnic groups, they tended to use the term 'Bhutia', which in consequence implied their identification with an Indian identity. Assuming an Indian identity such as Bhutia did not mean that they had lost their Tibetan identity. While referring to themselves as Bhutia, the Tibetan refugees in Darjeeling town could collectively view themselves as part of ongoing movements from the place of origin (Tibet), of long-term displacement, dispersal and resettlement in new societies of residence.

Nearly all Tibetan refugees in Darjeeling town under the Foreigners Registration Act have also obtained the RC as emphatic proof of their Tibetanness. The RC remains one of the most powerful unifying symbols for the Tibetan exiles. In such a situation, it becomes difficult to distinguish between a façade and a reality, since refugees are unwilling to disclose how they identify themselves. Identifying themselves or being identified by others as Indian citizens has the intended or unintended consequence of giving off the image that refugees 'imagine' themselves as being part of the host society or producing real or fictitious forms of cosmopolitan identity. The Tibetans as refugees and as diasporics in Darjeeling town have therefore formed understandings of their individual goals and collective projects ('preservation of Tibetan culture' and 'rangzen') by leaving the link between place and personhood ambivalent which simultaneously hint at their tentative or sometimes nebulous attachment to Darjeeling as a place of permanent residence in certain contexts and their attachment to two or more host societies as places of temporary refuge in others.

Even in more deterritorialised times and settings where the very notion of 'home' as a durably fixed place is in doubt, displaced peoples like the Tibetans who have clustered around the imagination of homelands or places from a distance are seen to be the ones who have become 'emplaced', that is, developed attachment to a 'place' or 'places' and have tried to establish firm territorialised anchors in their new place of residence. Tibetans are compelled to conceive of their communities as potential or actual 'territories' with special economic problems and peculiar interests and resources rather than simply as a culture of routine folkways and a repository of collective memories and symbols.

Tibetan refugees who have a homeland stand in a position to exploit ethnic competition in the long run and move their fragmented communities along the road to the widely-desired goal of the nation, even if present political or economic circumstances throw up successive barriers. While there is an obscuring of places and localities, there is simultaneously a greater sense that people have of continually 'placing' oneself and one's identity in everyday interactions, even in a situation of apparent 'placelessness'. Deterritorialisation has not, thereby, as Akhil Gupta and James Ferguson note, 'created subjects who are "free-floating monads", despite what is sometimes implied by those eager to celebrate freedom and playfulness of the postmodern condition' (1992: 19). Greater interconnectedness across space and time with the use of information technology allows us to rethink conventional ideas about distance and association.

What is existentially more relevant in present times is to account for the fact that the 'distance' between the Tibetans in the United States and the Tibetans in Darjeeling may be much shorter than that between ethnic groups and classes (between Tibetan refugee groups and Bhutias, for instance) in the same city. In times of utter distress, Tibetan refugees are seen to develop greater kinship and affiliation with ethnic groups proximate to their own, such as the Bhutias, and are consequential for them rather than a Tibetan living in faraway 'places of resettlement'. We need to account sociologically for the fact that the 'distance' between the Tibetans in the United States and the Tibetans in Darjeeling may be much shorter than that between ethnic groups and classes (between Tibetan refugee groups and Bhutias for instance) in 'the same' city.

In contexts where refugee and non-refugee identities and movements are deeply territorialised, host conditions are, at times, not propitious in conjuring up cosmopolitan affects and anchors which impact refugee lives. In this context, Ulf Hannerz's assertion is relevant: 'The exile, also shifted directly from one territorial culture to another, is often no real cosmopolitan either, for his involvement with a culture away from his homeland is something that has been forced on him. At best, life in another country is home plus safety or home plus freedom, but often it is just not home at all. He is surrounded by the foreign culture but does not often immerse himself in it. Sometimes his imperfections as a cosmopolitan may be the opposite of those of the tourist: he may reluctantly build up a competence, but he does not enjoy it' (Hannerz 1990: 242).

The key variable which determines how people give meaning to 'displacement' and return to places or countries of origin is dependent on the conditions under which they leave their places of origin and on the other, on the treatment they receive and opportunities existing at the destination. However, such statements, according to Kibreab (1999), have become commonplace in the debate on place, location, displacement, community and identity. Such movements have always been an integral part of the history of people inhabiting Tibet and the Darjeeling Himalayan regions. Since the Tibetans who moved to a territorialised place like Darjeeling as refugees could not claim entitlement based on past physical occupation or membership of a co-ethnic group such as the Bhutias, the desire to return to one's place of origin became an overriding preoccupation bordering obsession. The heirs to the displaced Tibetans have, however, tended to identify strongly with their society of residence by virtue of being born in Darjeeling town. As one Tibetan respondent stated, 'Darjeeling is there till we are here. It is not our country. It is our birthplace. Till we are here in India, it is our home'[5], and the opportunity this offers regarding rights of access to resources and protection that is due to citizens of a territory. They have also been the ones who have maintained multiple connections with co-ethnics living in other host societies in ways that aim at supporting a distant homeland, Tibet, and enabling opportunities by virtue of being spatially anchored.

Identities of Tibetans that operate in the context of the town are shown as being fictional, adoptive, hidden or lost, depending on the interpretive context. They do not suggest an oversimplified opposition between territorialised and deterritorialised identities or statements such as 'that people are not free to go wherever they want'. Rather, 'refugee diaspora' identities are seen as historically and culturally constituted, and are born out of the constant and shifting movements and homing practices of refugee groups in varied local settings. It is striking how Tibetans respond once the option of moving within the diaspora presents itself, regardless of whether the option is ever exercised. It is the movement of individuals and groups from place to place within the diaspora as being in the realm of the possible and not that of becoming rooted in a particular place which becomes important for Tibetans. In such a case, the meaning of home evolves with time and is far more complex than just a simplistic association of an 'individual with a group and with a particular place'. For the new generation of Tibetans born in India and Darjeeling, the original homeland of Tibet no longer represents home which meets all of a person's social, cultural and economic needs. Instead it becomes a place of nostalgia. Darjeeling represents home in the sense of place to bring up children; there is also home in the sense of a preferred destination to another place of residence.

Through the course of our excursion into Tibetan refugee life, it became evident that the attempt has not been to arrive at a holistic description of a 'total way of life' of Tibetan exiles. This ethnography of the displaced tries to gain insight into the lived meanings that displacement and refugeehood can have for specific people, in this case the Tibetan refugees in Darjeeling who see themselves and are seen by others as part of the wider Tibetan diaspora. The attempt has been to bring to bear the specific histories of groups operating in a region and their traditions of movement; their practices of 'dwelling in a place and their dwelling-in-displacement' (Clifford 1997) in order to understand how identities become allied to places.

Notes

1. Excerpt from an interview with the manager of workshops at the TRSHC on 20 May 2005.

2. Excerpt from an interview with a Tibetan refugee at Dragon market, Darjeeling town on 6 November 2006.

3. Local or locality in the study is viewed, borrowing from Appadurai, in a strictly relational and contextual sense. The refugee–host dynamic is captured in specific neighbourhoods, whether it is in the social form of the refugee centre or the marketplace in Darjeeling town.

4. Excerpt from an interview with a Tibetan refugee at Bhutia Busty, Darjeeling town on 16 November 2006.

5. Excerpt from an interview with a Tibetan refugee in Bhutia Busty, Darjeeling town on 24 November 2006.

Postscript

A Mediatising Tibetan Diaspora and Beyond*

Any writing concerning the Tibetan predicament should necessarily take into account two separate yet interlocking narratives, one that concerns the politics of development in Tibet (Fischer 2014; Yeh 2014), and the other which captures the cathectic, cognitive ramifications of diasporic living. What we see in this book is how forced migration and the seeming impossibility of return to one's home country have produced feelings of longing, despair and idealisations concerning Tibet and Tibetanness among diasporic Tibetans over time. The condition of protracted exile has also produced a 'virtual Tibet' through the proliferation of a vibrant social media communications among lay Tibetans in Tibet and in the diaspora as well as the Tibetan government-in-exile. This is supplemented by the 'new arrivals' from Tibet who have a more embodied vision of Tibet. As Heidi Swank (2011: 51) says, 'In the context where migration has continued for decades, it would seem that the homeland would be continually renewed in community discourses and imaginations through the new immigrants'. This scenario affords us an opportunity to connect the two narratives in ways that enable us to make sense of the material and symbolic stakes of the Tibetan refugee diasporas in the twenty-first century.

In pre-exilic Tibet, information and news remained inaccessible, remote and held sacred. It remained buried only to be discovered later by persons known as 'tertons' (Samphel 2004: 169). With exile, this relation between the Tibetans and information changed altogether. The

* Previously published as Sudeep Basu, 'Media, Tibet and the Tibetan Diaspora: Some Reflections', in *Forced Migration & Media Mirrors*, Sibaji Pratim Basu (ed.), Kolkata: Frontpage, 2014, pp. 123–34. The article has been modified by the author for the current volume.

profanity of Tibetan attitude to information is nowhere better seen than in the Tibetan refugees' successful efforts at creating a viable media for dissemination of information in which lies the root of Tibetan exiles' nascent democracy. Much water has flown since 1959 and we see the growth of an exile press. The interlocking network of websites, newspapers, magazines and radio services has influenced not only exilic thinking on various issues confronting Tibetans in Tibet, but also on the issues of people in the diaspora, such as the candidate for the post of kalon tripa, views on partisan politics, role of Tibetan Muslims in their polity, and the Dalai Lama's efforts at the democratisation of exile polity. Tracking the emergence of a mediatised Tibet and the role of the exilic media in constituting a 'virtual Tibet' have transformed the way Tibetan refugees think and act towards their rehabilitation and settlement in conditions of protracted exile.

The origins of the Tibetan media, especially the print media, started not in Tibet but in India as 'a result of Tibetan isolationism through much of the 19th and early 20th centuries' (Samphel 2004: 170). The first modern Tibetan language newspaper was *Ladakh Kyi Akbar* or *Ladakh News* brought out by a German and Moravarian missionary August Hermann Francke in 1904. The story of the year was the British invasion of Tibet or the Younghusband's expedition to Lhasa. *Ladakh News* met with little success and closed shop in 1908. The true origins of Tibet's print media lie in the birth of *Tibet Mirror*, a monthly Tibetan-language newspaper started by Gergan Tharchin or Tharchin Babu. He took special care to send some copies of the first issue of *Tibet Mirror* to the thirteenth Dalai Lama in 1925 apprising him about the situation in China and Britain. The impact of *Tibet Mirror*, though confined to a small circle of Tibetan aristocrats in Tibet, was enormous. 'It was the only medium through which the Tibetans in Lhasa learnt something of the fast changing world outside—revolution in China, World War II, India's independence' (Samphel 2004: 173). Avid readers of *Tibet Mirror* like Baba Phuntsog Wangyal, who served as an interpreter between Mao and the Dalai Lama when the Tibetan leader visited Beijing in 1954, warned of an imminent Chinese communist invasion as far back as the early 1940s and sought British military aid. Tharchin Babu and the office of *Tibet Mirror* became a confluence for exchange of ideas and action for effectively countering the challenges posed by a resurgent China.

Visualising Tibetan Worlds

Tarchin Babu captured the irony of Tibet losing its independence before realising the worth of a modern newspaper in the farewell issue of *Tibet Mirror* in which he wrote:

> When there was *rawang* (Tibetan Freedom),
> There was no *rawang*.
> When there is no *rawang*,
> There is *rawang*.

Tibetan Mirror gave way to *Tibetan Freedom* started by Gyalo Thondup (the fourteenth Dalai Lama's brother) in 1962. *Tibetan Freedom* was officially handed over to the government-in-exile at Dharamsala. The realisation that print media is an effective weapon in the propaganda war against China was acutely felt for the first time. Exile media institutions developed with *Sheja* coming into existence in 1968 and with the *Voice of Tibet* changing its name to *Tibetan Review* in 1968. The latter became the first official newspaper in exile. Through the media, Tibetan exiles have, to an extent, changed international public opinion in their favour and have succeeded in undermining the ability of the Chinese authorities to influence and shape the thinking of the people in Tibet. In this section, we examine the contents and effects of some of the representational strategies adopted by Tibetans and non-Tibetans (Western, Chinese and Indian) alike through the media and other fora centred around the idea of Tibet, Tibetanness, and the context of exile and resettlement.

An agonistic battle is being fought over representations of Tibet and Tibetanness in the media, particularly in the domain of human rights. The newly-arrived refugees, who from the late 1980s were crossing the mountains into Nepal, were called upon to present testimonies of their personal experience at international fora. Much of the force of Tibetan exile presentations and the media during this period derived from the idea that the authentic voice of ordinary Tibetans was being heard. Individuals, organisations and support movements sympathetic to the Tibetan cause took up the task, at times perilous, of collecting evidence of human rights violations in Tibet. The difference from earlier efforts was that this time, the main vehicle for propagating the information was the liberal media. Tibet had become a cross-party or centrist issue in western Europe and North America and was no longer confined to the conservative end of the political spectrum. Much of the evidence this time was coming from Westerners, many of them journalists, who had been allowed into Tibet when it was opened to tourism after 1979.

This led to the re-emergence, in some Tibet-related political discourse, of the term 'genocide' apparently on the assumption that the birth control policy was intended to wipe out Tibetans. Lhasang Tsering, a Tibetan writer and activist, voices similar concerns in *The Sun Behind the Cloud,* a documentary on the Tibetan struggle for freedom, by Ritu Sarin and Tenzin Sonam, two veteran filmmakers: 'I do not see we have that long before we reach the point of no return. I am not saying all Tibetans are going to disappear but by then there will be so many Chinese in Tibet, it will be no longer realistic for the Tibetan people to regain a Tibet for Tibetans. What has happened to the native Americans, to the native Australians, is happening in Tibet'.

On the whole, China's policies on ethnic minorities have provoked Tibetan resistance. In the months leading up to the Beijing Olympics in 2008, demonstrations spread from the capital, Lhasa, into eastern Tibetan regions that had previously been associated with unrest. These areas were at the epicentre of a series of self-immolations, primarily by Buddhist monks, but also by lay persons. The problem with the representation of Tibet as a site of human rights abuses was that it tended to become vulnerable because of what Barnett calls 'double orientalism'—the tendency to view the Chinese system of governance and society as deeply alien because it is Communist and totalitarian. Essentialist constructions of this kind rendered ineffective some of the evidence that was integral to the human rights case made about Tibet from 1980s onwards. In early 1994, the United States reversed its position on China's trading status and ended attempts to link that status to human rights conditions and essentially the role of human rights as a tool of leverage in international relations collapsed at least in relation to China.

Expressions of solidarity for the Tibetan cause is seen exhibited from lay Chinese who have shown a growing interest in Tibetan Buddhism and the Dalai Lama. This is evident from the ingenious use of the Internet for effecting a 'free dialogue' between the Dalai Lama and Chinese citizens, facilitated by the dissident writer, Wang Lixiong, best known for his work, 'Yellow Peril', published in 1991. Varied questions were posed to the Dalai Lama, such as independence and autonomy, relations between Tibetans and the Han people, and the future of Tibet (For more on this, see http://www.nybooks.com/daily/2010/05/24/talking-about-tibet/; downloaded on 25 September 2016).

The reception of the newly-arrived 'Sinicised' Tibetans hailing mainly from Kham and Amdo since the 1980s has taken on an ambivalent turn. The policy of voluntary repatriation instituted in the mid-1990s made it impossible for newly-arrived Tibetans to acquire the RC. The new arrivals (those who have recently come from Tibet due to continuing oppression), who are under the age of 30, receive education in the Tibetan Children's village, Suja, or in the Tibetan Transit school. They are left at a disadvantage vis-à-vis their counterparts who have lived in exile for long. Heidi Swank, in her recent work on Tibetan refugees in McLeod Ganj (2011), observes the practice of 'cham cham', or wandering about town, among new arrivals, an increasing duration and frequency of which is derided by other Tibetan youths. She notes that the literary activity among these new arrivals was based in and borrowed heavily from popular practices of poetry writing that have emerged in Tibet since the 1980s, notable among them is *Waterfall of Youth* penned by Dhondup Gyal and writings by Tibetan poet Woeser. In exile, Swank calls this genre of exile writing 'anti-language' (using Halliday 1976) in the way the new arrivals use their linguistic/poetic skills to convey otherness and feelings of sadness and longing in the midst of their own Tibetan co-ethnics in exile. Disillusioned, saddened and perplexed, some of the newly arrived have ultimately returned to China, taking with them both a sense and an experience of life in exile and English language skills (Vasantkumar 2013: 220). These cross-border movements prior to 2008 and Internet-based communication networks have made Tibetans acutely aware of how Tibetans in Tibet and those in the diaspora live.

The continuing traffic between Tibetans (both physical and Internet-based) on both sides of the Himalayas and dispersed in the diaspora has transformed practices of 'placemaking' in ways that imply an increased awareness among Tibetan refugees of the interconnectedness of places and people, centred on the idea of 'return' or 'myth of return' to their homeland. As Vasantkumar notes, 'a surprising consequence of the movements of exile, migration and return since 1959: a proliferation of modes of imagining what it means to be Tibetan. This proliferation has produced, in turn, not so much an augmented sense of Tibetan belonging but a generalised sense of unbelonging' (2013: 222). This requires us to rethink categories of territoriality, movement, national belonging as contingent and contextual rather than as pre-givens.

As Ralph and Staeheli note, 'The challenge ... is to conceptualise the simultaneity of home as sedentarist and mobile' (2011: 518). Decades of living in exile have also created divisive impressions between Tibetans and their hosts, between exiled refugees since 1959 and newly arrived refugees since 1980 and between Tibetans in exile and Tibetans back home, that threaten the very understanding of all Tibetans as co-ethnics on which the rhetoric of cultural preservation and ultimately the struggle for independence depends. This historical conjuncture militates against our received understandings of diaspora, nationalism, travel and homing. One of the implicit assumptions in diasporic theorising seen in Dibyesh Anand's writings is the fact that 'imagining Tibet as a nation is a "post-exilic phenomena"'. He asserts that 'while recognizing Tibetans as an "imagining community" problematizes simplistic interrogations of Tibetanness, it does not undermine the quest of a people for self-determination' (Anand 2009: 107)

This mode of thinking tends to privilege only those diasporic Tibetans who produce diasporic consciousness and reiterates the notion that nationalism is clearly the product of the process of forming the diaspora. It elides the question, what of those Tibetans who stay behind in China and maintain affective ties to the wider communities? How about those Tibetans who have multiple homes: in Tibet; in the 'country of first residence', such as in India; and in the 'country of second asylum', such as the United States? The spatial and economic marginalisation of Tibetans in Tibet as a result of Chinese state-led modernisation efforts, depicted in Emily Yeh's (2014) recent work, fills Tibetans with a profound sense of homelessness in their own homes, produced by consolidation of Chinese state power in the region. Thubten Samphel's novel, *Falling through the Roof* revolves around the life of a political-activist Tibetan student from Delhi University in the 1980s, who encounters a monk in Changistan, eventually to get absorbed in Buddhist belief. He takes up a new role of a preacher of Buddhism in Tibet under severe restrictions by the Chinese Communist Party. Tibet's past, its traumatic history and the strangeness of its exile present is brought out most forcefully.

Literary works from diaspora Tibetans like *The Mandala of Sherlock Holmes* (1999) by Jamyang Norbu and Tenzin Tsundue's *Kora* (2010) stands testimony to a distinct Tibetan identity. Chris Vasantkumar (2013) sees in this a 'somewhereelseness' consciousness of home for the Tibetans both in the diaspora and those at home in Tibet. The dynamics of exile in a mediatised context produces more than one version of nationalism, the strictly territorial model of the Herderian and Andersonian variety but also a 'portable' idea of nationalism allowing for multiple possibilities of belonging/unbelonging or homelessness in diasporic contexts. The notions of a homeland, spaces and time, as we have seen it evolve in the case of the Tibetans, themselves move spiritually, virtually and culturally, which produces among them different 'imaginings' about refugeeness, and what it means to be a Tibetan in the midst of others—at home and away.

Glossary

amala - mother
a mi ri ka - America
bal yul - Nepal
Bhot - Sanskrit name for Tibet
bod skad - language
bras ljongs - Sikkim
changa sa - marriage
chimie - camp leader
chos - religion
chos rgyal - religious kings
dngul - money
dorje den - Bodh-Gaya
gaon (Hindi) - village
go skabs - opportunity
grogs po - friend
gzhung - government
ka blon sbug - Kalimpong
kidu chu - Umbrella organisation of 10 Bhutia associations in Darjeeling town
lag shes - handicrafts
Lhamo - traditional folk operas
lo rgyus - history
Losar - Tibetan new year
mchod yon - priest-patron
mi sde - community
mnyam las - cooperative
nang - home
ngo tsha po - shame
Om Mani Peme Hung - Mantra of Chenrezig
rang tsho - Self-help

rangzen - independence
rdo rje gling - Darjeeling
rgya gar - India
rgyal gces - patriotic
rgya nag - China
rig gzung - culture
sa gnas - locals
sa thog - land
sgar - camp
shes yon slob sbyong - education
sku tsab - Settlement Officer
slob grwa - school
snying rje - compassion
tshong las byas - business
tshogs pa - associations
Zam ling Chisang - Universal Prayer Day

Bibliography

Adams, Vincanne. 'Karaoke as Modern Lhasa, Tibet: Western Encounters with Cultural Politics'. *Cultural Anthropology* 11, no. 4 (1996): pp. 510–46.

Anand, Dibyesh. '(Re)imagining Nationalism: Identity and Representation in the Tibetan Diaspora of South Asia'. *Contemporary South Asia* 9, no. 3 (2000): pp. 271–87.

———. 'A Guide to Little Lhasa in India: The Role of Symbolic Geography of Dharamsala in Constituting Tibetan Diasporic Identity'. In *Tibet, Self and the Tibetan Diaspora: Voices of Difference*, ed. Christiaan Klieger, pp. 11–36. Leiden: Brill Academic Publishers, 2002.

———. *Tibet: A Victim of Geopolitics*. New Delhi: Routledge, 2009.

Anderson, Benedict. *Imagined Communities: Reflections on the Origin and Spread of Nationalism*. London: Verso, 1991.

———. 'Exodus'. *Critical Enquiry* 20, no. 2 (1994): pp. 314–27.

Andrugtsang, Gompo. *Four Rivers, Six Ranges: Reminiscences of the Resistance Movement in Tibet*. Dharamsala: Information and Publicity Office of H.H. the Dalai Lama, 1973.

Anthias, Floya. 'Evaluating Diaspora: Beyond Ethnicity?' *Sociology* 32, no. 3 (1998): pp. 557–80.

Appadurai, A. 'Disjuncture and Difference in the Global Cultural Economy'. *Public Culture* 2, no. 2 (1990): pp. 1–24.

———. 'Global Ethnoscapes: Notes and Queries for a Transnational Anthropology'. In *Recapturing Anthropology: Working in the Present*, ed. R. Fox, Santa Fe: School of American Research Press, 1991.

———. *Modernity at Large: Cultural Dimensions of Globalization*. New Delhi: Oxford University Press, 1996.

Arakeri, A. V. *Tibetans in India: The Uprooted People and their Cultural Transplantation*. New Delhi: Reliance Publishing House, 1998.

Ardley, Jane. *The Tibetan Independence Movement: Political, Religious and Gandhian Perspectives*. London, New York: Routledge Curzon, 2002.

Aris, Michael, 'Preface', In *Tibetan Histories: A Bibliography of Tibetan Language Historical Works*, Dan Martin, London: Serindia Publications, 1997.

Armstrong, John A. 'Mobilized and Proletarian Diasporas'. *The American Political Science Review* 70, no. 2 (1976): pp. 393–408.

Asad, Talal, ed. *Anthropology and the Colonial Encounter.* Atlantic Highlands, NJ: Humanities Press, 1973.

Avedon, J. *In Exile from the Land of Snows: The Dalai Lama and Tibet since the Chinese Conquest.* New York: Harper Perennial, 1984.

Bagadi, S. B., and A. K. Danda. 'NE-BU-LA: A Movement for Regional Solidarity'. In *Tribal Movements in India, Vol. 1,* ed. K. S. Singh, pp. 339–48. New Delhi: Manohar, 1982.

Bammer, A., ed. 'The Question of Home'. *New Formations* 17 (1992): pp. 3–15.

Barber, Noel. *From the Land of Lost Content: The Dalai Lama's Fight for Tibet.* London: Collins, 1969.

Barnett, Robert, ed. *Resistance and Reform in Tibet.* London: Hurst, 1994.

———. Violated Specialness: Western Political Representations. In *Imagining Tibet: Perceptions, Projections, and Fantasies,* eds Thierry Dodin and Heinz Rather, pp. 269–316. Boston: Wisdom Publications, 2001.

Barth, Fredrik. *Ethnic Groups and Boundaries: The Social Organization of Cultural Difference.* Boston: Little Brown, 1969.

Bernstorff, Dagmar, and Hubertus Von Welck, eds. *Exile as Challenge: The Tibetan Diaspora.* Hyderabad: Orient BlackSwan, 2004.

Berry, J. W. 'Acculuration and Psychological Adaptation among Refugees'. In *Refugees—The Trauma of Exile,* ed. D. Miserez, pp. 97–110. Dordrecht: Martinus Nijhoff, 1988.

Bhabha, Homi. *Nation and Narration.* New York: Routledge, 1990.

Bishop, Peter. *The Myth of Shangri La: Travel Writing and the Western Creation of Sacred Landscape.* Berkeley: University of California Press, 1989.

———. *Dreams of Power: Tibetan Buddhism and the Western Imagination.* London: Athlone Press, 1993.

———. 'Not Only a Shangri La: Images of Tibet in Western Literature'. In *Imagining Tibet: Perceptions, Projections and Fantasies,* eds Thierry Dodin and Heinz Rather. Boston: Wisdom Publications, 2001.

Bose, Pradip, ed. *Refugees in West Bengal: Institutional Practices and Contested Identities.* Calcutta: CRG Publication, 2000.

Bourdieu, Pierre. *Outline of a Theory of Practice,* trans. Richard Nice. Cambridge, England: Cambridge University Press, 1977.

Boyarin, Daniel, and Jonathan Boyarin. 'Diaspora: Generational Ground of Jewish Identity'. *Critical Inquiry* 19, no. 4 (1993): pp. 693–725.

Bryman, Alan. *Social Research Methods.* Oxford: Oxford University Press, 2004.

Bulcha, M. *Flight and Integration: Causes of Mass Exodus from Ethiopia and Problems of Integration in the Sudan.* Uppsala: Scandinavian Institute of African Studies, 1988.

Bureau of Applied Economics and Statistics, Government of West Bengal. *District Statistical Handbook Darjeeling.* Kolkata, 2004.

Bureau of H.H. the Dalai Lama. *Tibetans in Exile, 1959–1969.* New Delhi, 1969.

Bushell, F. W. 'The Early History of Tibet from Chinese Sources'. *Journal of the Royal Asiatic Society* 12 (1880): pp. 435–535.

Calkowski, M. S. 'A Day at the Tibetan Opera: Actualized Performance and Spectacular Discourse'. *American Ethnologist* 18, no. 4 (1991): pp. 643–57.

Calkowski, Marcia S. 'The Tibetan Diaspora and the Politics of Performance'. In *Tibetan Culture in the Diaspora,* ed. Frank Korom. Papers presented at a Panel of the 7th Seminar of the International Association for Tibetan Studies, Graz, 1995, pp. 51–58.

———. 'The Tibetan Diaspora and the Politics of Performance'. In *Tibetan Culture in the Diaspora,* ed. Frank Korom. Vienna: Austrian Academy of Science Press, pp. 51–58, 1997.

Carter, Sean. 'The Geopolitics of Diaspora'. *Area* 37, no. 1 (2005): pp. 54–63.

Census of India. 'A-C Series'. New Delhi: Office of the Registrar General & Census Commissioner, Controller of Publications, 1991.

Census of India. 'Final Population Totals'. Series—1, 2001.

———. 'Provisional Population Totals'. Series—1, 2001.

Chattopadhyay, Alaka. *Atisa and Tibet.* New Delhi: Motilal Banarasidass, 1994.

Chimni, B. S. *International Refugee Law: A Reader.* New Delhi, London: Sage Publications, 2000.

Clifford, James. 'Diasporas'. *Cultural Anthropology* 9, no. 3 (1994): pp. 302–38.

———. *Routes: Travel and Translation in the Late Twentieth Century.* Cambridge: Harvard University Press, 1997.

———. *The Predicament of Culture: Twentieth Century Ethnography, Literature and Art.* Cambridge: Harvard University Press, 1998.

Clifford, James, and George Marcus, eds. *Writing Culture: The Poetics and Politics of Ethnography.* Berkeley and Los Angeles: University of California Press, 1986.

Clifton, Tony. 'Did an Obscure Tibetan Sect Murder Three Monks Close to the Dalai Lama?' *Newsweek.* (downloaded from www.myspace.com/dorjeshugden on 24 May 2015), April 1997.

Cohen, R. 'Citizens, Denizens and Helots: The Politics of International Migration Flows in the Post-War World'. *Journal of Social Studies* 21, no. 1 (1989): pp. 153–65.

Cohen, Robin. 'Diasporas and Nation States: From Victims to Challengers'. *International Affairs* 72, no. 3 (1996): pp. 507–20.

———. *Global Diasporas: An Introduction.* Seattle: University of Washington Press, 1997.

Cohon, Donald J. 'Psychological Adaptation and Dysfunction among Refugees'. *International Migration Review* 15, no. 1/2 (1981): pp. 255–75.

Cole, Carleton. *Spirit of Tibet.* In *World Tibet Network News,* Canada Tibet Committee, downloaded on 24 May 2007.

Connerton, Paul. *How Societies Remember.* Cambridge: Cambridge University Press, 1989.

Conway, John. 'The Tibetan Community in Exile'. *Pacific Affairs* 48, no. 1 (1975): pp. 74–86.

Corlin, Claes. *The Nation in your Mind: Continuity and Change among Tibetan Refugees in Nepal.* Unpublished Ph.D. Thesis, Institute of Anthopology, Goteborg University, Sweden, 1975.

Council for Religious and Cultural Affairs of H.H. the Dalai Lama. *Cho-Yang: Year of Tibet edition,* eds K. Yeshe and J. Russell, 1991.

Crapanzano, Vincent. 'Hermes' Dilemma: The Masking of Subversion in Ethnographic Description'. In *Writing Culture: The Poetics and Politics of Ethnography,* eds James Clifford and George Markus, pp. 51–76. California: University of California Press, 1986.

Dalai Lama. *My Land and My People.* New York: Warner Books, 1962.

Daniel, E. V., and C. K. Knudsen. *Mistrusting Refugees.* Berkeley: University of California Press, 1995.

Dasgupta, Atis. 'Ethnic Problems and the Movement for Autonomy in Darjeeling'. *Social Scientist* 27, no. 11/12 (1999): pp. 47–68.

Dash, Arthur Jules. *Bengal District Gazetteers: Darjeeling.* Alipore, Bengal: Bengal Government Press, 1947.

de Voe, Dorsh M. 'Framing Refugees as Clients'. *International Migration Review* 15, no. 1/2 (1981): pp. 88–94.

———. *Survival of a Refugee Culture; The Long-term Gift Exchange between Tibetan Refugees and Donors in India.* Ph.D. Thesis, University of California, Berkeley, 1983.

———. 'Keeping Refugee Status: A Tibetan Perspective'. In *People in Upheaval,* eds S. M. Morgan and E. Colson, pp. 54–65. New York: Centre for Migration Studies, 1987.

Department of Information and International Relations, Tibetan Government in Exile. *The Mongols and Tibet: A Historical Assessment of Relations between the Mongol Empire and Tibet.* Dharamsala, 1996.

Department of Information and International Relations, Central Tibetan Administration. *Tibet under Communist China.* Dharamsala, 2001.

Dharamsala: Information and Publicity Office of the Dalai Lama. *Tibet under Communist Rule: A Compilation of Refugee Statements 1958–1975*, 1976.

Dharlo, Rinchen. 'A Brief History of Tibetans in North America'. *Tibetan Review* 29, no. 10 (1994): pp. 12–17.

Dhavan, Rajeev. *Refugee Law and Policy in India.* New Delhi: PILSARC, 2004.

Dialogue with Tenzin Tsundue. In www.phayul.com, accessed on 12 April 2007.

Diehl, Keila. *Echoes from Dharamsala: Music in the Life of a Refugee Community.* California: California University Press, 2002.

Dodin, Thierry, and Heinz Rather, eds. *Imagining Tibet: Perceptions, Projections and Fantasies.* Boston: Wisdom Publications, 2001.

Dowty, A. *Closed Borders: The Contemporary Assault on Freedom of Movement.* New Haven, CT: Yale University Press, 1987.

Dozey, E. C. *A Concise History of Darjeeling District since 1835.* Calcutta: Jetsun Publishing House, 1989.

Dreyer, June. *China's Forty Millions.* Cambridge, Massachusetts: Harvard University Press, 1976.

Dreyfus, Georges. 'Are We Prisoners of Shangrila? Orientalism, Nationalism, and the Study of Tibet'. *Journal of the International Association of Tibetan Studies*, no. 1 (October 2005), pp. 1–21.

Dungkar, L. T. 'Development of the Monastic Education in Tibet'. *The Tibet Journal* 18, no. 4 (1993): pp. 3–48.

Durham, Peter. 'Exile, Nomadism and Diaspora: The Stakes of Mobility in the Western Canon'. In *Home, Exile and Homeland: Film, Media and the Politics of Place*, ed. Hamid Naficy, pp. 17–41. London: Routledge, 1999.

Durkheim, Emile. *The Rules of Sociological Method*, edited with an introduction by Steven Lukes, translated by W. D. Halls. New York: The Free Press, 1982 (first published in 1895).

Ekvall, Robert B. 'The Tibetan Self-Image'. *Pacific Affairs* 33, no. 4 (1960): pp. 375–82.

Epstein, Israel. *Tibet Transformed.* Beijing: New World Press, 1983.

Faist, T. *The Volume and Dynamics of International Immigration and Transnational Social Spaces.* Oxford: Clarendon Press, 2000.

Faraday, A., and K. Plummer. 'Doing Life Histories'. *Sociological Review* 27, no. 4 (1979): pp. 773–98.

Fischer, Andrew. *The Disempowered Development of Tibet in China: A Study in the Economics of Marginalization.* Lanham, MD: Lexington Books, 2014.

Fischer, Andrew M. 'The Great Transformation of Tibet? Rapid Labor Transitions in Times of Rapid Growth in the Tibet Autonomous Region'. *HIMALAYA, the Journal of the Association for Nepal and Himalayan Studies* 30, no. 1 (2011): pp. 63–77.

Fischer, Michael. 'Ethnicity and the Arts of Memory'. In *Writing Culture: The Poetics and Politics of Ethnography*, eds James Clifford and George Markus, pp. 194–233. California: University of California Press, 1986.

Forbes, Ann. *Settlements of Hope: An Account of Tibetan Refugees in Nepal.* Cambridge, MA: Cultural Survival Report, 1989.

Foster, R. 'Making National Cultures in the Global Ecumene'. *Annual Review of Anthropology* 20 (1991): pp. 235–60.

Gallagher, Dennis. 'The Evolution of the International Refugee System'. *International Migration Review* 23, no. 3 (1989): pp. 579–98.

Garratt, Kevin. 'Tibetan Refugees, Asylum Seekers, Returnees and the Refugee Convention: Predicaments, Problems and Prospects'. *Tibet Journal* 22, no. 3 (1997): pp. 18–56.

Gellner, Ernest. *Nations and Nationalism.* Oxford: Blackwell, 1983.

Ghosh, Suchitra. *Tibet in Sino-Indian Relations, 1897–1914.* New Delhi: Sterling Publications, 1977.

Gilroy, Paul. *There Ain't No Black in the Union Jack: The Cultural Politics of Race and Nation.* London: Taylor & Francis Books Ltd, 1987.

———. *The Black Atlantic: Modernity and Double Consciousness.* Cambridge, MA: Harvard University Press, 1993.

———. *Between Camps: Nations, Culture and the Allure of Race.* London: Allen Lane, 2000.

Goffman, E. *The Presentation of Self in Everyday Life.* New York: Anchor Books, Doubleday, 1959.

Golay, Bidhan. 'Rethinking Gorkha Identity: Outside the Imperium of Discourse, Hegemony and History'. *Peace and Democracy in South Asia* 2, no. 1&2 (2006): pp. 23–48.

Gold, Peter. *Tibetan Reflections: Life in a Tibetan Refugee Community.* London: Wisdom Publications, 1984.

Gold, R. L. 'Roles in Sociological Fieldwork'. *Social Forces* 36, no. 2 (1958): pp. 217–23.

Gold, S. *Refugee Communities: A Comparative Field Study*. Newbery Park, CA: Sage Publications, 1992.

———. 'Transnationalism and Vocabularies of Motive in International Migration: The Case of Israelis in the United States'. *Sociological Perspectives* 40, no. 3 (1997): pp. 409–27.

Goldstein, Melvyn C. *Anthropological Study of the Tibetan Political System*. Unpublished PhD Dissertation, University of Washington, 1968.

———. 'The Balance between Centralization and Decentralization in the Traditional Political System: An Essay on the Nature of Tibetan Political Macro-Structure'. *Central Asiatic Journal* 15, no. 3 (1971): pp. 170–82.

———. 'Ethnogenesis and Resource Competition among Tibetan Refugees in South India: A New Face to the Indo-Tibetan Interface'. In *Himalayan Anthropology: The Indo-Tibetan Interface*, ed. J. F. Fisher, pp. 395–420. Paris: Mouton, 1978.

———. *A History of Modern Tibet, 1913–1951: The Demise of the Lamaist State*. Berkeley: University of California Press, 1989.

———. *The Snow Lion and the Dragon: China, Tibet and the Dalai Lama*. California: University of California Press, 1997.

———. 'The Dalai Lama's Dilemma'. *Foreign Affairs* 77, no. 1 (1998): pp. 83–97.

Goldstein, Melvyn C., and Michael Kapstein, eds. *Buddhism in Contemporary Tibet: Religious Revival and Cultural Identity*. Berkeley: University of California Press, 1998.

Goldstein, Melvyn C., and Ngawangthondup Narkyid. *English-Tibetan Dictionary of Modern Tibetan*. Dharamsala: Library of Tibetan Works and Archives, 1999.

Goodwin-Gill, Guy. 'Refuge or Asylum: International Law and the Search for Solutions to the Refugee Problem'. In *Refuge or Asylum?—A Choice for Canada*, eds H. Adelman and C. M. Lanphier, pp. 27–40. Toronto: York Lanes Press, 1990.

Graham, Mark, and Shahram Khosravi. 'Home is Where You Make It: Repatriation and Diaspora Culture among Iranians in Sweden'. *Journal of Refugee Studies* 10, no. 2 (1997): pp. 115–33.

Grahl-Madsen, Atle. *The Status of Refugees in International Law (Volumes 1 and 2)*. Leiden: Sijthoff, 1966–72.

Grunfeld, Tom. *The Making of Modern Tibet*. Bombay: Oxford University Press, 1988.

Gupta, A. 'The Song of the Non-Aligned World: Transnational Identities and the Reinscription of Space in Late Capitalism'. *Cultural Anthropology* 7, no. 1 (1992): pp. 63–79.

Gupta, A., and James Ferguson. 'Beyond Culture: Space, Identity and the Politics of Difference'. *Cultural Anthropology* 7, no. 1 (1992): pp. 6–23.

Gurung, D. B. 'Darjeeling District: Struggle for Administrative Status'. *The Calcutta Journal of Politics* (Summer 1983).

Gyal, Dhondup. 'Waterfall of Youth'. *Manoa* 12, no. 2 (2000): pp. 9–13.

Gyatso, Sherab, 'The Crisis of Tibetan Language in Exile'. *Tibetan Review* 28, no. 9 (September 1993): pp. 15–19.

———. 'Of Monks and Monasteries'. In *Exile as Challenge: The Tibetan Diaspora*, eds Dagmar Bernstorff and Hubertus Von Welck. Hyderabad: Orient BlackSwan, 2003.

Gyatso, Tenzin Dalai Lama XIV. *My Land, My People*. New York: Potala Press, 1983.

Haddad, Emma. 'Who is (not) a Refugee'. *Working Paper SPS No. 2004/6*. European University Institute Florence, 2004.

Hall, Stuart. 'Cultural Identity and Diaspora'. In *Identity, Community, Culture and Difference*, ed. J. Rutherford, pp. 222–37. London: Lawrence and Wishart, 1990.

Halliday, M. A. K. 'Anti-Languages'. *American Anthropologist* 78, no. 3 (1976): pp. 570–84.

Handler. R. 'Authenticity'. *Anthropology Today* 2, no. 1 (1986): pp. 2–4.

Hannerz, Ulf. 'Cosmopolitans and Locals in World Culture'. In *Global Culture: Nationalism, Globalization and Modernity*, ed. Mike Featherstone, pp. 237–51. London: Sage Publications, 1990.

———. *Cultural Complexity: Studies in the Social Organization of Meaning*. New York: Columbia University Press, 1992.

Harrell-Bond, B. E. *Imposing Aid: Emergency Assistance to Refugees*. Oxford: Oxford University Press, 1986.

Harrell-Bond, B. E., and E. Voutira. 'Anthropology and the Study of Refugees'. *Anthropology Today* 8, no. 4 (1992): pp. 6–10.

Harrell-Bond, B. E., Eftihia Voutira and Mark Leopold. 'Counting the Refugees: Gifts, Givers, Patrons and Clients'. *Journal of Refugee Studies* 5, nos 3–4 (1992): pp. 205–25.

Harvey, David. 'Between Space and Time: Reflections on the Geographical Imagination'. *Annals of the Association of American Geographers* 80, no. 3 (1990): pp. 418–34.

Hathaway, James C. *The Law of Refugee Status.* Toronto: Butterworths, 1991.

Hein, J. 'Refugees, Immigrants and the State'. *Annual Review of Sociology* 19, no. 1 (1993): p. 45.

Herberer, Thomas. 'Old Tibet a Hell on Earth?' In *Imagining Tibet: Perceptions, Projections and Fantasies,* ed. Thierry Dodin and Heinz Rather, pp. 111–50. Somerville MA: Wisdom Publications, 2001.

Hess, Julia M. 'Statelessness and the State: Tibetans, Citizenship and Nationalist Activism in a Transnational World'. *International Migration* 44, no. 1 (2006): pp. 79–101.

Hobsbawm, E. *Nations and Nationalism since 1780.* Cambridge: Cambridge University Press, 1990.

Houston, Serin, and Richard Wright. 'Making and Remaking of Tibetan Diasporic Identities'. *Social & Cultural Geography* 4, no. 2 (2003): pp. 219–31.

Huber, T. 'Book Review of *Constructing Tibetan Culture: Contemporary Perspectives,* ed. F. J. Korom'. *Journal of Buddhist Studies* (1999). Accessed from http://jbe.gold.ac.uk/5/huber981.htm on 17 June 2007.

International Campaign for Tibet. 'Report on Dangerous Crossing Conditions Impacting the Flight of Tibetan Refugees in 2001'. 2002.

International Commission of Jurists. Tibet: Human Rights and the Rule of Law. Executive Summary, Geneva, ICJ, 1997.

Interview: Promoting Sports in the Tibetan Community. In www.phayul.com, accessed on 8 May 2007.

Jacobsen, Karen. 'Factors Influencing the Policy Responses of Host Governments to Mass Refugee Influxes'. *International Migration Review* 30, no. 3 (1996): pp. 655–78.

Jacobsen, Karen, and Loren Landau. 'The Dual Imperative in Refugee Research: Some Methodological and Ethical Considerations in Social Science Research on Forced Migration'. *Disasters* 27, no. 3 (2003): pp. 185–206.

Jacobson, Calla. *Spirituality, Harmony and Peace: Situating Contemporary Images of Tibet.* Unpublished paper, 1994.

Jaschke, H. A. *A Tibetan English Dictionary (first edition).* Motilal Banarsidass, 1981.

Joly, D. 'Odyssean and Rubicon Refugees: Towards a Typology of Refugees in the Land of Exile'. *International Migration* 40, no. 6 (2002), pp. 3–23.

Kaplan, Caren. 'Deterritorializations: The Rewriting of Home and Exile in Western Feminist Discourse'. *Cultural Critique* 6 (Spring 1987): pp. 187–98.

Kaviraj, Sudipta. 'On the Construction of Colonial Power, Structure, Discourse, Hegemony'. In *Politics in India,* ed. Sudipta Kaviraj, pp. 156–57. New Delhi: Oxford University Press, 1997.

Kellas, J. *The Politics of Nationalism and Ethnicity.* New York: St Martin's Press, 1991.

Keller, S. L. *Uprooting and Social Change: The Role of Refugees in Development.* New Delhi: Manohar Book Service, 1975.

Kibreab, G. 'Revisiting the Debate on People, Place, Identity and Displacement'. *Journal of Refugee Studies* 12, no. 4 (1999): pp. 384–410.

Kibreab, Gaim. *African Refugees: Reflections on the African Refugee Problem.* Trenton, NJ: Africa World Press of the Africa Research & Publications Project, 1985.

Klieger, Christiaan. *Accomplishing Tibetan Identity: The Constitution of a National Consciousness.* PhD dissertation, University of Hawaii, 1989.

———. *Tibetan Nationalism: The Role of Patronage in the Accomplishment of National Identity.* Berkeley, California: Folklore Institute, 1992.

———. 'Shangri-La and Hyperreality: A Collision in Tibetan Refugee Expression'. In *Tibetan Culture in the Diaspora,* ed. Frank Korom, pp. 59–68. Papers presented at a Panel of the 7th Seminar of the International Association for Tibetan Studies, Graz, 1995.

———, ed. *Tibet, Self and the Tibetan Diaspora: Voices of Difference.* Boston: Brill Publications, 2002.

Klieger, P. C. *Accomplishing Tibetan Identity: The Constitution of a National Consciousness.* Ph.D. dissertation, University of Hawaii, 1989.

Knight, David B. 'Identity and Territory: Geographical Perspectives on Nationalism and Regionalism'. *Annals of the Association for American Geographers* 72, no. 4 (1982): pp. 514–31.

Kok, W. 'Self-settled Refugees and the Socio-economic Impact of their Presence on Kassala, Eastern Sudan'. *Journal of Refugee Studies* 2, no. 4 (1989): pp. 419–40.

Kolas, Ashild. 'Tibetan Nationalism: The Politics of Religion'. *Journal of Peace Research* 33, no. 1 (1996): pp. 51–66.

Korom, Frank, ed. *Tibetan Culture in the Diaspora.* Papers presented at a Panel of the 7th Seminar of the International Association for Tibetan Studies, Graz, 1995.

Kuhlman, Tom. 'The Economic Integration of Refugees in Developing Countries: A Research Model'. *Journal of Refugee Studies* 4, no. 1 (1991): pp. 1–20.

Kunz, E. F. 'The Refugee in Flight: Kinetic Models and Forms of Displacement'. *International Migration Review* 7, no. 2 (1973): pp. 125–46.

Lammers, Ellen. *Refugees, Gender and Human Security: A Theoretical Introduction and Annotated Bibliography*. Netherlands: International Books, 1999.

Lixiong, Wang. *Yellow Peril.* Toronto: Mirror Books, 1991.

Loescher, G. *Refugee Movements and International Security*. Adelphi Paper 268, London: International Institute for Strategic Studies, 1992.

Lopez, Donald. 'Not Only a Shangri La'. In *Imagining Tibet: Perceptions, Projections and Fantasies*, eds Thierry Dodin and Heinz Rather, pp. 201–21. Boston: Wisdom Publications, 2001.

Lopez, Donald S. *Prisoners of Shangri La: Tibetan Buddhism and the West*. Chicago: University of Chicago Press, 1998.

Malkki, Liisa. 'National Geographic: The Rooting of Peoples and the Territorialization of National Identity among Scholars and Refugees'. *Cultural Anthropology* 7, no. 1 (1992): pp. 24–44.

———. *Purity and Exile: Violence, Memory and National Cosmology among Hutu Refugees in Tanzania*. Chicago: The University of Chicago Press, 1995a.

———. 'Refugees and Exile: From "Refugee Studies" to the National Order of Things'. *Annual Review of Anthropology* 24 (1995b): pp. 495–523.

———. 'Things to Come: Internationalism and Global Solidarities in the Late 1990s'. *Public Culture* 10, no. 2 (1998), pp. 431–42.

———. 'News from Nowhere: Mass Displacement and Globalized "Problems of Organization"'. *Ethnography* 3, no. 3 (2002), pp. 351–60.

Marcus, George E. 'Ethnography in/of the World System: The Emergence of Multi-Sited Ethnography'. *Annual Review of Anthropology* 24 (1995), pp. 95–117.

Marcus, George, and Michael Fischer. *Anthropology as a Cultural Critique: An Experimental Moment in the Human Sciences*. Chicago: University of Chicago Press, 1986.

Markham, C. R. 'Travels in Great Tibet and Trade between Tibet and Bengal'. *Journal of the Royal Geographical Society of London* 45 (1875): pp. 299–315.

Markus, George E., and Dick Cushman. 'Ethnographies as Texts'. *Annual Review of Anthropology* 11 (1982): pp. 25–69.

Marrus, M. *The Politics of Assimilation: The French Jewish Community at the Time of the Dreyfus Affair.* Oxford: Oxford University Press, 1980.

Martin, D. 'The Refugee Concept: On Definitions, Politics and the Careful Use of a Scarce Resource'. In *Refugee Policy: Canada and the United States*, ed. H. Adelman, pp. 30–51. Toronto: York Lanes Press, 1991.

Marx, Emanuel. 1990. 'The Social World of Refugee: A Conceptual Framework'. *Journal of Refugee Studies* 3, no. 3, pp. 189–203.

Massey, D. 'A Global Sense of Place'. *Marxism Today,* 38 (1991), pp. 24–29.

———. 'A Place Called Home?' *New Formations* 17 (1992): pp. 3–15.

McGranahan, Carole. 'Truth, Fear and Lies: Exile Politics and Arrested Histories of the Tibetan Resistance'. *Cultural Anthropology* 20, no. 4 (2005): pp. 570–600.

McLagen, Meg. 'Mystical Visions in Manhattan: Deploying Culture in the Year of Tibet'. In *Tibetan Culture in the Diaspora,* ed. Frank Korom, pp. 69–89. Proceedings of the 7th Seminar of the International Association for Tibetan Studies, Graz, 1995.

———. *Mobilizing for Tibet: Transnational Politics and Diaspora Culture in the Post-Cold War Era.* Doctoral dissertation, Department of Anthropology, New York University, 1996.

McMillin, L. H. *English in Tibet, Tibet in English: Self-Presentation in Tibet and the Diaspora.* New York: Palgrave, 2001.

Mehra, Purshottam. *The North-Eastern Frontier: A Documentary Study of Internecine Rivalry between India, Tibet and China—Vol. 1, 1906–14; Vol. 2, 1914–54.* New Delhi: Oxford University Press, 1979.

Mercer, Kobena. 'Diaspora Culture and the Dialogic Imagination: The Aesthetics of Black Independent Film in Britain'. In *Blackframes: Critical Perspectives on Black Independent Cinema,* eds M. Cham and C. Watkins, pp. 50–61. Cambridge: MIT Press, 1988.

Methfessel, Thomas. 'Socioeconomic Adaptation of Tibetan Refugees in South Asia over 35 Years in Exile'. In *Tibetan Culture in the Diaspora,* ed. Frank Korom, pp. 13–24. Proceedings of the 7th Seminar of the International Association for Tibetan Studies, Graz, 1995.

Michael, Franz. *Rule by Incarnation: Tibetan Buddhism and its Role in Society and State.* Boulder: Westview Press, 1982.

———. 'Survival of a Culture: Tibetan Refugees in India'. *Asian Survey* 25, no. 7 (1985): pp. 737–44.

Miles, William F. S., and Gabriel Sheffer, 1998. 'Francophonie and Zionism: A Comparative Study in Transnationalism and Trans-statism'. *Diaspora: A Journal of Transnational Studies* 7, no. 2 (1998), pp. 119–48.

Morgan, Scott, and Elizabeth Colson, eds. *People in Upheaval.* New York: Center for Migration Studies, 1987.

Naficy, Hamid. 'Exile Discourse and Televisual Fetishization'. *Quarterly Review of Film and Video* 13, no. 1–3 (1991), pp. 85–116.

———. *The Making of Exile Cultures: Iranian Television in Los Angeles.* Minneapolis: University of Minnesota Press, 1993.

Nora, Pierre. 'Between Memory and History'. *Representations* 26 (Spring 1989): pp. 7–24.

Norbu, Dawa. 'The 1959 Tibetan Rebellion'. China Quarterly, no. 77 (1979), pp. 74–93.

———. 'The Europeanization of Sino-Tibetans, 1775–1907: The Genesis of Chinese Suzerainty and Tibetan Autonomy'. *Tibet Journal* 15, no. 4 (1990), pp. 28–74.

———. *Culture and Politics of Third World Nationalism*. London: Routledge, 1992.

———. *Tibetan refugees in South Asia: Implications for Security*. Paper presented at the International Seminar on Refugees and Internal Security in South Asia, organised by Regional Centre for Strategic Studies (RCSS), Colombo, 1994, pp. 1–17.

———. 'Han Hegemony and Tibetan Ethnicity'. *International Studies* 32, no. 3 (1995): pp. 297–314.

———. 'Tibetan Refugees in South Asia: A Case of Peaceful Adjustment'. In *Refugees and Regional Security in South Asia*, eds S. D. Muni and Lok Raj Baral, pp. 78–98. New Delhi: Konark, 1996.

———. 'Tibet in Sino-Indian Relations: The Centrality of Marginality'. *Asian Survey* 37, no. 11 (1997): pp. 1078–95.

———. 'Is Tibetan Culture Congruent with Modernity? Some Clues from Asian experience'. *Tibetan Review* 34, no. 2 (1999): pp. 8–14.

———. *China's Tibet Policy*. Richmond, Surrey: Curzon Press, 2001.

———. 'The Settlements: Participation and Integration'. In *Exile as Challenge: The Tibetan Diaspora*, eds Dagmar Bernstorff and Hubertus Von Welck, pp. 186–212. Hyderabad: Orient BlackSwan, 2004.

Norbu, Jamyang. 'The Tibetan Resistance Movement and the Role of the CIA'. In *Resistance and Reform in Tibet*, eds Robert Barnett and Shirin Akiner, pp. 186–96. London: Hurst and Co., 1994.

———. *The Mandala of Sherlock Holmes*. New Delhi: Harper Collins, 1999.

———. *Shadow Tibet: Selected Writings 1989 to 2004*. New Delhi: Bluejay Books, 2006.

Nowak, Margaret. *Tibetan Refugees: Youth and the New Generation of Meaning*. New Brunswick, New Jersey: Rutgers University Press, 1984.

O'Malley, L. S. S. *Bengal District Gazetteers Darjeeling*. Government of West Bengal: Basumati Corporation Limited, 2001 [1907].

Ortner, Sherry B. 'On Key Symbols'. *American Anthropologist* 75, no. 5 (1973): pp. 1338–46.

Palakshappa, T. C. *Tibetans in India: A Case Study of Mundgod Tibetans.* New Delhi: Sterling Publications, 1978.

Peck, J. M. 'Refugees as Foreigners: The Problem of Becoming German and Finding Home'. In *Mistrusting Refugees,* eds E. Valentine Daniel and John Kundsen. Berkeley: University of California Press, pp. 102–25, 1995.

Penny-Dimri, Sandra. 'Conflict amongst the Tibetans and Indians of North India: Communal Violence and Welfare Dollars'. *Australian Journal of Anthropology* 5, no. 3 (1994): pp. 280–93.

Phuntso, Tsewang. 'Government in Exile'. In *Exile as Challenge: The Tibetan Diaspora,* eds Dagmar Bernstorff and Hubertus Von Welck, pp. 125–35. Hyderabad: Orient BlackSwan, 2004.

Pinn, Fred. *The Road of Destiny: Darjeeling Letters 1839.* New Delhi: Oxford University Press, 1986.

Planning Council, Central Tibetan Administration. *Tibetan Demographic Survey 1998, Volume 1–2.* Dharamsala, 2000.

Powell, Andrew. *Heirs to Tibet: Travels among the Exiles in India.* London: Heinemann, 1992.

Powers, John. *History as Propaganda: Tibetan Exiles versus the People's Republic of China.* Oxford: Oxford University Press, 2004.

Pratt, Mary Louise. 'Fieldwork in Common Places'. In *Writing Culture: The Poetics and Politics of Ethnography,* eds James Clifford and George Markus, pp. 27–50. Berkeley: University of California Press, 1986.

Prost, Audrey. 'The Problem with "Rich refugees" Sponsorship, Capital and the Informal Economy of Tibetan Refugees'. *Modern Asian Studies* 40, no. I (2006): pp. 233–53.

Rabgey, Losang C. *Rethinking Tibetan Identity.* TibetWrites.org, July 2002.

Radhakrishnan, R. 'Ethnicity in the Age of Diaspora'. *Transition* 54 (1991): pp. 104–15.

Ralph, D., and L. A. Staeheli. 'Home and Migration: Mobilities, Belongings and Identities'. *Geography Compass* 5, no. 7 (2011): pp. 517–30.

Tibetan Refugee Self-Help Centre. 'Report of Tibetan Refugee Self Help Centre' (1999). See http://www.tibetancentredarjeeling.com/index.html, accessed on 26 May 2016.

Rhodes, Nicholas, and Deki Rhodes. *A Man of the Frontier: S. W. Laden La His Life and Times in Darjeeling and Tibet.* Calcutta: Mira Bose Library of Numismatic Studies, 2006.

Richardson, H. E. *Tibet and its History.* London: Oxford University Press, 1962.

Richardson, Hugh. *Tibet and its History.* Boston: Shambhala Publications, 1984.

———. *High Peaks, Pure Earth: Collected Writings on Tibetan History and Culture.* London: Serindia Publications, 1998.

Rinpoche, Samdhong. *Tibet: A Future Vision.* New Delhi: Tibetan Parliamentary and Policy Research Centre, 1996.

Roemer, Stephanie. *The Tibetan Government-in-Exile, Politics at Large,* New York: Routledge, 2008.

Rogowski, R. 'Causes and Varieties of Nationalism: A Rationalist Account'. In *New Nationalisms of the Developed West: Toward Explanation,* eds E. Tiryakin and R. Rogowski, pp. 87–108. Boston: Allen & Unwin, 1985.

Rosaldo, Renato. 'Ideology, Place and People Without Culture'. *Cultural Anthropology* 3, no. 1 (1988): pp. 77–87.

Rossabi, Morris. *China and Inner Asia: From 1368 to the Present Day.* London: Thames and Hudson, 1975.

Rouse, Roger. 'Mexican Migration and the Social Space of Postmodernism'. *Diaspora: A Journal of Transnational Studies* 1, no. 1 (1991): pp. 8–23.

Sack, Robert D. 'Human Territoriality: A Theory'. *Annals of the Association of American Geographers* 73, no. 1 (1983): pp. 55–74.

Safran, William. 'Diasporas in Modern Societies: Myths of Homeland and Return'. *Diaspora* 1, no. 1 (Spring 1991): pp. 83–97.

———. 'Comparing Diasporas: A Review Essay'. *Diaspora* 8, no. 3 (1999): pp. 255–92.

Said, Edward. *The Question of Palestine.* New York: Times Books, 1979.

———. 'Mind of Winter: Reflections on Life in Exile'. *Harper's Magazine,* 1984.

———. *After the Last Sky.* New York: Pantheon Books, 1986.

———. 'Representing the Colonized: Anthropology's Interlocutors'. *Critical Inquiry* 15, no. 2 (1989), pp. 205–25.

Saklani, Girija. *The Uprooted Tibetans in India: A Sociological Study of Continuity and Change.* New Delhi: Cosmo Publications, 1984.

Samaddar, Ranabir. 'The Cruelty of Inside/Outside'. In *Refugees in West Bengal,* ed. Pradip Bose, pp. 203–04. Calcutta: Calcutta Research Group, 2000.

Samphel, Thubten. 'Virtual Tibet: The Media'. In *Exile as Challenge: The Tibetan Diaspora,* eds Dagmar Bernstorff and Hubertus Von Welck, pp. 167–85. Hyderabad: Orient BlackSwan, 2004.

———. *Falling Through the Roof.* New Delhi: Rupa, 2008.

Samuel, G. 'Tibet as a Stateless Society and Some Islamic Parallels'. *Journal of Asian Studies* 4, no. 2 (1982): pp. 215–29.

———. *Civilized Shamans: Buddhism in Tibetan Societies.* Washington: Smithsonian Institution Press, 1993.

Sandler, R. H., and T. C. Jones, eds. *Medical Care of Refugees.* Oxford: Oxford University Press, 1987.

Sarkar, D. K., and D. J. Bhaumik. *Empowering Darjeeling Hills: An Experience with Darjeeling Gorkha Hill Council.* New Delhi: Indian Publishers Distributors, 2000.

Schram, Stuart. *The Political Thought of Mao Tse-tung.* New York: Praeger, 1969.

Schrempf, Mona. 'From "Devil Dance" to "World Healing": Some Representations, Perspectives and Innovations of Contemporary Tibetan Ritual Dances'. In *Tibetan Culture in the Diaspora,* ed. Frank Korom, pp. 33–50. Papers presented at a Panel of the 7th Seminar of the International Association for Tibetan Studies, Graz, 1995.

Schwartz, Ronald D. *Circle of Protest: Political Ritual in Tibetan Uprising.* London: Hurst and Co., 1994.

Seidel, Michael. *Exile and the Narrative Imagination.* New Haven and London: Yale University Press, 1986.

Sen, Chanakya. *Tibet Disappears.* Bombay: Asia Publishing House, 1960.

Shacknove, Andrew E. 'Who is a Refugee?' *Ethics* 95, no. 2 (1985): pp. 274–84.

Shain, Yossi. *The Frontier of Loyalty: Political Exiles in the Age of the Nation-State.* Middletown, Conn.: Wesleyan University Press, 1989.

Shakabpa, T. *Tibet: A Political History.* New York: Potala Publications, 1984 [1967].

Shakya, Tsering. *Dragon in the Land of Snows: History of Modern Tibet since 1947.* New York: Columbia University Press, 1999.

Sheffer, G. 'Jewry, Jews and Israeli Foreign Policy: A Critical Perspective'. In *Diasporas in World Politics: The Greeks in Comparative Perspective,* eds D. Constas and A. Platias, pp. 203–29. London: Macmillan, 1993.

———. 'Ethno-national Diasporas and Security'. *Survival* 36, no. I (1994), pp. 60–79.

———. 'A Nation and its Diaspora: A Re-examination of Israeli–Jewish Diaspora Relations'. *Diaspora: A Journal of Transnational Studies* 11, no. 3 (Winter 2002), pp. 331–58.

Sheffer, Gabriel. *Diaspora Politics: At Home Abroad.* Cambridge: Cambridge University Press, 2003.

Shiromany, A. A. *The Political Philosophy of His Holiness the XIV Dalai Lama—Selected Speeches and Writings.* New Delhi: Tibetan Parliamentary and Policy Research Centre, 1998.

Skran, Claudena. *Refugees in Inter-War Europe: The Emergence of a Regime.* Oxford: Clarendon Press, 1995.

Smith, A. *The Ethnic Revival in the Modern World.* Cambridge: Cambridge University Press, 1981.

Smith, Anthony. *The Ethnic Origins of Nations*. New York: Blackwell Publishers, 1986.

Smith, Warren. *Tibetan Nation: A History of Tibetan Nationalism and Sino-Tibetan Relations*. Boulder: Westview Press, 1996.

Snellgrove, Hugh, and David Richardson. *A Cultural History of Tibet*. New York: Frederick A Praeger, 1968.

Soguk, Nevzat. *States and Strangers: Refugees and Displacements of Statecraft*. Minneapolis: University of Minnesota Press, 1999.

Sonam, Bhuchung D. *New York! New York!* In tibetwrites.org, 2007. Accessed on http://tibetwrites.in/index.html%3FA-Song-from-a-Distance.html, on 26 April 2012.

———. *Song from a Distance*, 24thNovember, 2008. In tibetwrites.org, 2007. Accessed from http://tibetwrites.in/index.html%3FA-Song-from-a-Distance.html on 26 April 2012.

'Statement of the Dalai Lama on the 38th Anniversary of Tibetan National Uprising Day on 10 March, 1997, Dharamsala' downloaded from http://tibet.net/1997/03/statement-of-his-holiness-the-dalai-lama-on-the-thirty-eighth-anniversary-of-the-tibetan-national-uprising-day-10-march-1997/ on 5 July 2012.

Stein, Barry N. 'The Refugee Experience: Defining the Parameters of a Field of Study'. *International Migration Review* 15, no. 1 (1981): pp. 320–30.

Stein, R. A. *Tibetan Civilization*. Stanford: Stanford University Press, 1972.

Strom, Axel K. 'Between Tibet and the West: On Traditionality, Modernity and the Development of Monastic Institutions in the Tibetan Diaspora'. In *Tibetan Culture in the Diaspora*, ed. Frank Korom, pp. 33–50. Papers presented at a Panel of the 7th Seminar of the International Association for Tibetan Studies, Graz, 1995.

Subba, T. B. *Flight and Adaptation: Tibetan Refugees in the Darjeeling-Sikkim Himalaya*. Dharamsala: Library of Tibetan Works and Archives, 1990.

———. *Ethnicity, State and Development: A Case Study of the Gorkhaland Movement in Darjeeling*. New Delhi: Har-Anand Publications, 1992.

Subba, Tanka. 'Peace in the Angry Hills?' *Sunday*, 24–30 July 1988, pp. 13–15.

Swank, Heidi. 'A Wanderer in a Distant Place: Tibetan Exile Youth, Literacy and Emotion'. *International Migration*, 49, no. 6 (2011): pp. 50–73.

Sztucki, Jerzyv. 'Who is a Refugee? The Convention Definition: Universal or Obsolete?' In *Refugee Rights and Realities: Evolving International Concepts and Regimes*, eds Francis Nicholson and Patrick M. Twomey, pp. 55–80. Cambridge University Press, 1999.

Tabori, Paul. *The Anatomy of Exile: A Semantic and Historical Study*. London: Harrap and Co. Ltd, 1972.

Takla, T. N. 'Notes on Some Early Tibetan Communists'. *Tibetan Review* 2, nos 6–7 (June–July 1969): pp. 6–7.

Tambiah, Stanley J. *World Conqueror and World Renouncer: A Study of Buddhism and Polity in Thailand against a Historical Background.* Cambridge: Cambridge University Press, 1976.

The Office of H. H. the Dalai Lama. *Tibetans in Exile: 1959–69. A Report on Ten Years of Rehabilitation in India.* Dharamsala, 1969.

The Telegraph. Dashain Strikes Harmony Note. Calcutta, 21 October 2004.

Tololyan, Kachig. 'The Nation-State and its Others: In Lieu of a Preface'. *Diaspora* 1, no. 1 (1991): pp. 3–7.

———. 'Rethinking Diaspora(s): Stateless Power in the Transnational Moment'. *Diaspora* 5, no. 1 (1996): pp. 3–36.

Topgyal, Tsering. 'The Birth of Nationalism and the Death of National Government: The Tragic Irony of the 1959 Tibetan Uprising against Chinese Occupation'. *Tibetan Review* 38, no. 3 (March 2003): pp. 14–20.

———. 'The Birth of Nationalism and the Death of National Government: The Tragic Irony of the 1959 Tibetan Uprising against Chinese Occupation'. *Tibetan Review* 38, no. 4 (April 2003): pp. 19–23.

Tse-Tung, Mao. *Selected Works Vol. V.* Beijing: People's Publishing, 1977.

Tsering, Gellek. 'The Role of Buddhist Institutions in the Tibetan Diaspora', Feinstein International Famine Center, Working Paper no. 4, 2001. Accessed from www.famine.tufts.edu on 12 September 2014.

Tsering, Topden. *Indian Cinema and Tibetan Refugees.* In www.timesoftibet.com, 2004; accessed on 14 October 2012.

———. *Identity Interrupted: The Story of Exile Tibetan Youth.* In www.*The Times of Tibet.*com, 2007. Accessed from http://tibetwrites.in/index.html%3FIdentity-Interrupted.html on 14 April 2011.

Tsundue, Tenzin. *Kora: Stories and Poems, Sixth edition.* Dharamsala: Imperial Press, 2010. Accessed from http://tibetwrites.in/IMG/pdf/kora.pdf TibetWrites on 18 November 2014.

———. *My Kind of Exile.* Accessed from http://www.friendsoftibet.org/tenzin/essays/my_kind_of_exile.html on 17 May 2012.Tucci, Guiseppe. *The Religions of Tibet.* London: London: Routledge & Kegan Paul, 1980.

Turner, T. Anthropology and Multiculturalism: What is Anthropology that Multiculturalists Should be Mindful of? *Cultural Anthropology* 8, no. 4 (1993), pp. 411–29.

Turner, Victor. 'Betwixt and Between: The Liminal Period in Rites of Passage'. In *The Forests of Symbols: Aspects of Ndembu Ritual*, ed. Victor Turner, pp. 93–110. Ithaca, NY: Cornell University Press, 1967.

———. 'A Journey Made Them: Territorial Segmentation and Ethnic Identity among the Mursi'. In *Segmentary Lineage Systems Reconsidered*, ed. Ladislav Holy, pp. 119–43. Belfast: Queen's University Papers in Social Anthropology, 1979.

Turton, David. 'Migrants and Refugees'. In *In Search of Cool Ground: War, Flight and Homecoming in Northeast Africa*, ed. Tim Allen, pp. 96–110. Trenton: Africa World Press, 1996.

United Nations, Office of the United Nations High Commissioner for Refugees. *The State of the World's Refugees (1995): In Search of Solutions*. Oxford: Oxford University Press, 1995.

United Nations High Commissioner for Refugees. *Basic International Legal Documents on Refugees*. New Delhi: UNHCR, 2004 (Fifth edition).

Van Hear, N. *New Diasporas*. London: UCL Press, 1998.

———. 'Refugees in Diaspora: From Durable Solutions to Transnational Relations'. *Refuge* 23, no. 1 (2006): pp. 9–15.

Van Walt Van Praag, Michael C. *The Status of Tibet: History, Rights and Prospects in International Law*. Boulder: Westview Press, 1987.

Vasantkumar, Chris. 'Tibetan Peregri-nations: Mobility, Incommensurable Nationalisms and (Un)belonging Athwart the Himalayas'. *Journal of Ethnic and Migration Studies* 39, no. 2 (2013): pp. 219–35.

Venturino, Steven. 'Reading Negotiations in the Tibetan Diaspora'. In *Constructing Tibetan Culture: Contemporary Perspectives*, ed. Frank Korom, pp. 98–121. Quebec: World Heritage Press, 1997.

Vertovec, Steven. 'Three Meanings of "Diaspora", Exemplified among South Asian Religions'. *Diaspora* 6, no. 3 (1999): pp. 277–300.

Von-Furer Haimendorf, Christoph. *The Renaissance of Tibetan Civilization*. Oxford: Oxford University Press, 1990.

Waddell, L. A. *Among the Himalayas*. Kathmandu: Ratna Pustak Bhandar, 1978.

Wang Furen, and Suo Wenqing. *Highlights of Tibetan History*. Beijing: New World Press, 1984.

Wangyal, Tsering. 'Tibetans in Kalimpong, Darjeeling and Gangtok'. *Tibetan Review* 13, no. 4 (1978): pp. 3–19.

Weiner, M. 'Labour Migrations as Incipient Diasporas'. In *Modern Diasporas in International Politics*, ed. G. Sheffer, pp. 47–75. London: Croom Helm, 1986.

———. *The Impact of Nationalism, Ethnicity and Religion on International Conflict.* Boston, MA: MIT Centre for International Studies, 1991.

Werbner, P. 'The Place which is Diaspora: Citizenship, Religion and Gender in the Making of Chaordic Transnationalism'. *Journal of Ethnic and Migration Studies* 28, no. 1 (2002): pp. 119–33.

Werbner, Pnina. 'Introduction: The Materiality of Diaspora—Between Aesthetic and "Real" Politics'. *Diaspora* 9, no. 1 (2000): pp. 5–20.

Whyte, William Foote. *The Street Corner Society: The Social Structure of an Italian Slum.* Chicago: University of Chicago Press, 1955.

Wilson, Dick. *The Long March 1935: The Epic of Chinese Communism's Survival.* New York: Viking Press, 1971.

Woeser. *Tibet does not Exist, Tibet does Exist.* In TibetWrites.org. Accessed from http://www.phayul.com/news/article.aspx?id=19142&article=TIBET+DOES+NOT+EXIST%2c+TIBET+DOES+EXIST%3a+Woeser on 24 March 2012. 2008.

Wood, William B. 'Forced Migration: Local Conflicts and International Dilemmas'. *Annals of the Association for International Geographers* 84, no. 4 (1994): pp. 607–34.

Xenos, Nicholas. 'Refugees: The Modern Political Condition'. *Alternatives* 18, no. 4 (1993): pp. 419–30.

Yeh, Emily. 'Will the Real Tibetan Please Stand Up! Identity Politics in the Tibetan Diaspora'. In *Tibet, Self and the Tibetan Diaspora: Voices of Difference,* ed. Christiaan Klieger, pp. 231–54. Boston: Brill Publications, 2002.

———. *Taming Tibet: Landscape Transformation and the Gift of Chinese Devleopment.* Ithaca, NY: Cornell University Press, 2014.

Zetter, Roger. 'Labelling Refugees: Forming and Transforming a Bureaucratic Identity'. *Journal of Refugee Studies* 4, no. 1 (1991): pp. 39–62.

———. 'The Greek-Cypriot Refugees: Perceptions of Return under Conditions of Protracted Exile'. *International Migration Review* 28, no. 2 (1994): pp. 307–22.Zhou, Min. 'Segmented Assimilation: Issues, Controversies and Recent Research on the New Second Generation'. *International Migration Review* 31, no. 4 (1997): pp. 975–1008.

Zolberg, Aristide, Astri Suhrke and Sergio Aguayo. *Escape from Violence: Conflict and the Refugee Crisis in the Developing World.* Oxford: Oxford University Press, 1989.

Zolberg, A. 'The Formation of New States as a Refugee-Generating Process'. *Annals of the American Academy of Political and Social Science* 467 (May 1983): pp. 24–38.

Index